# International Student Engagement in Higher Education

Full details of all our publications can be found on http://www.multilingual-matters.com, or by writing to Multilingual Matters, St Nicholas House, 31–34 High Street, Bristol BS1 2AW, UK.

# International Student Engagement in Higher Education

Transforming Practices, Pedagogies and Participation

**Margaret Kettle**

**MULTILINGUAL MATTERS**
Bristol • Blue Ridge Summit

DOI https://doi.org/10.21832/KETTLE8194

**Library of Congress Cataloging in Publication Data**
A catalog record for this book is available from the Library of Congress.
Names: Kettle, Margaret, author.
Title: International Student Engagement in Higher Education:
    Transforming Practices, Pedagogies and Participation/Margaret Kettle.
Description: Bristol, UK; Blue Ridge Summit, PA: Multilingual Matters,
    2017. | Includes bibliographical references and index.
Identifiers: LCCN 2017000271| ISBN 9781783098194 (hbk: alk. paper) | ISBN
    9781783098217 (epub) | ISBN 9781783098224 (kindle)
Subjects: LCSH: Students, Foreign–Services for–Western countries. | College
    students–Services for–Western countries. | College student development
    programs–Western countries. | College environment–Western countries. |
    Student adjustment–Western countries. | Universities and
    colleges–Western countries–Administration.
Classification: LCC LB2375 .K47 2017 | DDC 378.1/98091821–dc23 LC record available
at https://lccn.loc.gov/2017000271


**British Library Cataloguing in Publication Data**
A catalogue entry for this book is available from the British Library.

ISBN-13: 978-1-78309-819-4 (hbk)
ISBN-13: 978-1-78892-001-8 (pbk)

**Multilingual Matters**
UK: St Nicholas House, 31-34 High Street, Bristol BS1 2AW, UK.
USA: NBN, Blue Ridge Summit, PA, USA.

Website: www.multilingual-matters.com
Twitter: Multi_Ling_Mat
Facebook: https://www.facebook.com/multilingualmatters
Blog: www.channelviewpublications.wordpress.com

The policy of Multilingual Matters/Channel View Publications is to use papers that
are natural, renewable and recyclable products, made from wood grown in sustainable
forests. In the manufacturing process of our books, and to further support our policy,
preference is given to printers that have FSC and PEFC Chain of Custody certification.
The FSC and/or PEFC logos will appear on those books where full certification has been
granted to the printer concerned.

Typeset by Deanta Global Publishing Services Limited.
Printed and bound in the UK by the CPI Books Group Ltd.
Printed and bound in the US by Edwards Brothers Malloy, Inc.

# Contents

# Preface

*International Student Engagement in Higher Education: Transforming Practices, Pedagogies and Participation* is about international student engagement and its relationship to transformation in higher education. Engagement is currently a highly valued and much vaunted concept in university mission statements and teaching and learning policies. This book explicates the complex institutional, social and psychological factors that coalesce in the engagement of international students with academic practices in a foreign university. At a time when student mobility is growing and participation in overseas study programmes is increasing (Organisation for Economic Co-operation and Development [OECD], 2014), diversity and change are the norm in higher education. Indeed, diversity is considered to be one of the defining features of the 21st century (Green *et al.*, 2011). Development in global capitalist societies has been marked by increases in diversity, pluralism and differences in communities, as well as increased interrelations between communities (Reich, 2011). The ensuing issue for policy designers, decision makers and citizens is the paradox of addressing sameness and difference in ways that ensure democratic participation, equity of opportunity and recognition within community.

In higher education, the prevailing conditions require university policymakers, administrators and teachers to have an understanding of diversity and to know how to respond ethically and educationally to the diversifying cultures, languages, ethnicities and races characterising the student population. A persistent conundrum permeating university policy and research, especially in Anglophone contexts, is how to reconcile sameness and difference, or put another way, majority culture with minority culture. That is, how to move from a focus on interactions between cultures, with one dominant and more powerful, to the embracing of possibilities that arise from a new transculture which is generated through mutual dialogue and respect (Ryan, 2011). New nationalisms are putting this question under pressure: Brexit in the UK; anti-migrant protests in Germany; unyielding border control measures and the rise of Islamophobia in Australia. Yet, economic pressures mean that universities and higher education systems continue to pursue greater enrolments of overseas students. In Australia, international education has its own federal government portfolio with the minister celebrating a significant increase in 2015 student numbers and a promise to 'facilitate further growth' in the sector (Colbeck, 2016).

In the face of this growing diversity in university classrooms, the questions remain about valued knowledge, relevance of learning and responsive teaching approaches. For example, should dominant Western forms of scientific knowledge, understandings and skills be valued over other forms in the academy? Is it the role of all students to comply with academically mandated expectations? If so, to what end? What, if any, are the benefits? How can university teachers reconcile universally mandated, standardised curricula and assessment with diverse student capabilities and experiences?

These questions align with many of the debates in the higher education literature. In the Australian context – the most internationalised higher education system in the world (OECD, 2013a) – internationalisation has been highly marketised with the use of vigorous recruitment strategies for over four decades. It is an approach that is mirrored in other English-speaking countries and is increasingly being adopted by universities in non-native English-speaking environments such as Denmark. Despite the longevity of the internationalisation project, questions continue to be asked across the world about teaching for diversity and inclusion in universities, especially for students from different cultural backgrounds and using English as a second/additional language (ESL/EAL) (e.g. Bailey, 2013; Brew, 2007; Foster, 2012; Kettle & Luke, 2013; Lee & Rice, 2007; Marginson et al., 2010).

Ryan (e.g. 2000, 2005, 2011, 2013) has worked extensively in the area of teaching and learning for international students in higher education. She notes that the increasing mobility and enrolment of overseas students mean that they are no longer a minority group in some courses. Yet, debates persist about internationalisation and whether teaching approaches have moved on given that many of the complaints of teachers continue to echo those from past decades (e.g. Singh, 2009, in Ryan, 2013). Ryan applauds these debates and argues that more work needs to be done in developing creative approaches to teaching, learning and assessment that address ethical issues such as the role of English and the dominance of Western knowledge systems and intellectual traditions. She maintains that much still needs to be done to convince many university lecturers to change their teaching approaches to the new imperatives around international students. Instead, many academics adopt a type of academic imperialism that casts their role as educating students simply in 'our ways' (Ryan, 2011). Initiatives in the field must bring these academics on board and assist them to teach in ways that enrich the learning and cross-cultural experiences of both local and international students. This book responds to the call of researchers such as Ryan and presents exemplars of teaching that were deemed by international students to be highly beneficial to their learning, scholarship and participation in the new academic culture.

## The Field

The international student literature emerges in three discernible themes that resonate with other fields such as migrant ESL education (Kettle & Luke, 2013). Initial Australian research on overseas students in universities during the 1980s and early 1990s adopted a classic diagnosis/remediation approach to non-native English-speaking students entering the Australian tertiary model, particularly in relation to English language proficiency and approaches to learning. This approach was rejected in the 1990s and superseded by 'culturalised' understandings that highlighted culturally differentiated learning approaches and transitions. Later in the 2000s, influenced by ascendant critical and post-structural perspectives in sociology, research shifted away from the deficiencies and adaptations of international students to power and the power structures of the university. Researchers were interested in how particular practices came to dominate in the institution and how they co-opted students implicitly and explicitly into ways of knowing, doing and being.

A recent example of this approach is the book by Chowdhury and Phan (2014), *Desiring TESOL and International Education: Market Abuse and Exploitation*. In the book, the authors argue that English and teaching English to speakers of other languages (TESOL) have exercised power to create certain identities for international TESOL students that serve the interests of hyper-marketised higher education systems especially in English-speaking countries such as Australia. The focus of the book is the institutional and larger global mechanisms that have commodified TESOL into a desirable and taken-for-granted good, and the ways that international TESOL students resist or acquiesce to these discourses. The book offers a critique of the neo-liberal forces that have exploited TESOL in the highly competitive global market for international students. Indeed, the authors claim that the language of the market is so prevalent in talking about international students that they have become an economic object in the discourse of higher education.

The successive 'waves' of literature on international students canvassed above represent a historical continuum of research perspectives; each identifiable body of work represents a reaction to its predecessor with the deployment of a different set of theoretical tools to explain similar phenomena. This process is not surprising given the understanding that new knowledge is generated through problematising and critiquing existing knowledge (for more on the production of scientific knowledge, see the debate between Popper and Kuhn, e.g. Rowbottom, 2011). *International Student Engagement in Higher Education: Transforming Practices, Pedagogies and Participation* aims to build on the critique of Chowdhury and Phan and other insights from previous research to move the field towards engagement as an explanation of the international student experience. Engagement as it is proposed here involves the dynamic, ongoing, reflexive efforts of international students to mediate institutional expectations in their everyday experiences.

International student engagement, then, is practice. By focusing on engagement, the focus is the student as she/he negotiates the practices of the new academic context. The student is positioned as the expert on engagement. This centring of the student and her/his practice of engagement is an important new direction in understanding the international student experience of teaching and learning in a foreign university. Interestingly, it aligns with Ryan's (2011) point that international students are often neglected in discourses of internationalisation in higher education. She argues that this position is illogical given that international students are one of the most effective sources of intercultural knowledge and understanding. In the same way, the argument in this book is that the best place to investigate the conditions, actions and achievements of international student engagement is the students themselves. While critical positions might decry the economic objectification of the international student, this book foregrounds lived experience and the students as the embodiment of engagement. The orientation asserts the primacy of the international student who within higher education practices and literature as well as the popular media has been variously marginalised and maligned. If the Chowdhury and Phan work focuses on international student objectification, this book foregrounds student action.

The conceptual framework proposed here is critical in that it investigates power relations but is innovative in its priority to explicate positive practices, that is, exemplars of higher education teaching practices that international students appraised as helpful and affirming. The theoretical orientation is to productive power and the ways that institutional power structures can be exploited by both students and teachers to achieve personal and pedagogical ends. Rather than positioning the students as dupes in need of a preordained programme of 'Truth' (Freebody, 2003), this book privileges their voices, experiences and actions. The argument is that at a time when interest in engagement is escalating, the best way for institutions to learn about international student engagement is by listening to the students themselves.

The student accounts of engagement are explained through a theory of social practice in conjunction with work on engagement. The objective is to present a comprehensive theorisation that encapsulates and explicates all aspects of what is a complex construct. A necessary condition of explaining complexity is a repertoire of theoretical resources that can be pragmatically gathered together for explanatory purposes. A feature of this book is a re-examination of debates that have traditionally isolated different research approaches from each other, for example, psychological approaches to learning from sociocultural ones. The focus is synthesis and commensurability between perspectives that can be productively combined to explain international student engagement, especially given the elusiveness of engagement as a concept in the current literature.

## The Genesis

The genesis of the book lies in my personal experience as an international student in Germany and an academic English teacher in Australia. As an English teacher in academic preparation programmes at an Australian university, my job was to teach literacy and oracy skills to undergraduate and postgraduate international students, both before commencement of their studies and during their first semester. I was privy to troubling accounts from the students about their experiences in mainstream programmes. In one instance, a group of Master of Business Administration (MBA) students told me about a group case-study project in which they were pointedly excluded from decision-making roles by their Australian peers. The latter distributed the tasks and commandeered the key roles for themselves. A pattern began emerging when an international student enrolled in an undergraduate media studies course recounted a similar experience on a survey I conducted with the class:

> I found that a group project was a bit hard for us, because Ausee students want to do everything perfect and they wouldn't let us do things, except very easy works like typing.

During my seven years as an English language teacher in Australia, it was not uncommon to hear comments from teachers and academics essentialising the behaviours of 'Asian' students. As I read more, I realised these utterances, while appearing in disparate contexts, formed a theme that was pervasive and coherent; it was a discourse characterising 'Asian' students as quiet and non-participatory. And it was not benign – this discourse had material effects in shaping teachers' views and influencing their teaching practices. Not that the students were unaware of what was happening. The MBA students in my academic English class recognised their marginalisation and actively sought to redress their situation. The students seemed to draw strength and validation from our class discussions, which resembled what Canagarajah (1997: 7) called a 'safe house', that is, 'a parallel but safe site' where the students could 'respond to, reflect on, and comment about classroom concerns'. I was struck by the tension between the agency of the students and the disempowering discourses at work in other parts of their university experience. Equally, I was aware of my mediatory role and the affordances it provided for collective reflection and action. It was this tension between structure, agency and mediation that set the grounds for the case study of international student engagement and, ultimately, this book.

The students' stories of marginalisation resonated with aspects of my own experience as a foreign student in Germany. My studies were conducted at the Üniversität München, Ludwig-Maximilians Universität during the 1980s and 1990s, and were mainly language focused. While my German host family was generous and welcoming, it was difficult to establish contact with local students, an experience that I attributed to my non-native, intermediate-level German. My friends were the other international students with whom I used German as a lingua franca. Back in Australia, the MBA students also blamed their difficulties on language. Language is our major semiotic resource for self-representation. Operating in a moderately proficient second language (L2) leaves the user exposed to misrepresentation and misunderstanding. This is a highly visceral experience for many international students and is an important consideration in this book.

## The Book

*International Student Engagement in Higher Education: Transforming Practices, Pedagogies and Participation* draws on a research project conducted with six international students enrolled in a Master of Education programme at a large metropolitan university in Australia. Most of the students were in their first semester and using English as their second or third language. The research investigated the new ways of knowing, doing and being that the students recognised as valued in the Western academy and their strategic actions to engage with these institutional expectations. For the students, these actions were the grounded in their personal and academic goals for achievement and personal accomplishment. In addition, the book utilises the students' views on excellence in teaching to highlight classroom practices that facilitated their learning and participation. The students' accounts are triangulated with university policy documents and microethnographic analyses of videoed classroom interactions to build a comprehensive evidence-based explanation of international student engagement as it is lived and negotiated across a period of study. That the students were postgraduates links to the growing interest in postgraduate and doctoral levels of study by international students and the increasing number of international enrolments in Australian postgraduate courses

(Australian Government, 2015a). The students in the case study were from Argentina, China, Mozambique, Singapore, Thailand and Vietnam, while the lecturer was a senior academic with a reputation for excellence in teaching and reform in minority education.

Engagement, like practice, is a concept that is used in multiple ways and has what Fairclough (2001b) calls 'felicitous ambiguity'; that is, it has multiple meanings that refer to both action and entity. Engagement then is doing something as well as a thing in its own right – either achieved or aspirational. It can also reference the antecedents for engagement, that is, the conditions that make student engagement possible. These might be institutional or personal. The argument proposed here is that engagement is a productive way of investigating international students' efforts to mediate institutional expectations through their immediate actions and interactions, driven by goals of appropriation and enactment and larger professional and personal motivations. The mediation of structure and agency inherent in this understanding of engagement invites the invocation of theories of social life, particularly those prioritising social practice (e.g. Chouliaraki & Fairclough, 1999; Foucault, 1996d). The position of this book is that engagement and social practice can be usefully drawn together to provide an explanatory model of international student engagement in higher education.

Social practices involve particular configurations of elements such as actions, interactions, objects, values, expectations and language that are dialectically related and responsive to change. By recognising student engagement as academically situated social practice, new understandings are created about the elements that students recognise as salient in the practices of the foreign academy and the actions that they take in response. Furthermore, the outcomes of their actions are made visible in the analysis. By focusing on practices, students are positioned as the arbiters of the international experience with the authoritative voice on what matters. This approach affords insights not only into the students' actions but also their interpretations of what works in the university to assist academic transitions. Of particular interest are the pedagogies that the students find effective in promoting their learning and participation in course practices.

For the students in this book, international higher education is an investment in professional development, cultural and linguistic know-how, and improved credentialing; it is also an opportunity to imagine and pursue a new life. There is an aesthetic dimension to the overseas study experience whereby austerity and sacrifice are embraced as part of a larger programme of personal transformation. International study is not only the path to improved financial and professional prospects; it is also a significant personal undertaking absorbing extensive energy and resources.

The detail provided through the research in this book will be of interest to institutional policymakers and researchers attempting to understand the international student experience. Of note will be the conditions, processes and outcomes of engagement, in particular what is working institutionally to assist students and what is not. Equally, the comprehensive analysis of teaching, classroom interaction and assessment will be useful for higher education teachers interested in expanding their pedagogical repertoires to accommodate student diversity and change. The contribution of the book is threefold: (i) it presents a model of international student engagement; (ii) it extends existing research to practice-orientated understandings of engagement as a means of capturing the complexity of the international student experience; and (iii) it highlights in micro-analytic detail the features of classroom teaching interactions that international students found exemplary. The insights afforded by the research have benefits for university personnel as well as researchers at a time of increasing cultural and linguistic diversity within the student population.

The book has nine chapters including this Preface. Chapter 1 provides contextualisation and the global and national trends associated with international higher education. Chapter 2 examines the myriad representations of international students reflecting the changing zeitgeist on difference and diversity in higher education from the 1980s. Chapter 3 presents a theory of engagement drawing together existing work on engagement and understandings of social practice and student agency. Chapter 4 'pictures' the university and the ways that internationalisation is being realised in university spaces and places. It also introduces the international students in the study and the lives they craft for themselves in the overseas context. Chapters 5 through 7 present the salient features of engagement as identified by the students themselves: what counts as English in the English-speaking Western academy; what is effective university teaching and how does it facilitate learning and participation; how do international students resource their academic, social and linguistic transitions; in what ways are students transforming their lives and impacting institutional practices? Chapter 8 concludes the book with a synthesis of the issues raised about international student engagement and the implications for student rights, institutional responsibilities and the transformation of higher education.

# 1 The Globalisation and Internationalisation of Higher Education

## Introduction

This chapter builds on the Preface in which the rationale for the book and its focus on international student engagement were introduced. The point was made that diversity and change are the norm in contemporary higher education as increasing numbers of students leave their home countries to enrol in study programmes abroad (Organisation for Economic Co-operation and Development [OECD], 2014). This chapter explicates the student mobility patterns, government policy initiatives and debates that are contextualising international higher education around the world.

More than 4.5 million students were enrolled in universities outside of their country of citizenship in 2012 (OECD, 2014). This number represents more than double the number of internationally mobile students enrolled at overseas institutions in 2000, with an almost 7% annual increase for the years from 2000 to 2012. The dramatic change reflects the interest of sending countries and students themselves in moving beyond national borders to pursue different languages, cultures and knowledge systems. One way to gain this valued knowledge, together with qualifications, is to undertake study at universities in overseas countries.

For governments, mobility helps foster economic and social interconnectedness with other countries, while for students, overseas tertiary experience is a means of credentialing for participation in the international labour market. The historical data on international student mobility and higher education enrolments indicate a dynamic and volatile environment, highly responsive to global and national forces. Currently, national priorities and individual aspirations in Asia are driving mass interest in overseas education. Students from Asian countries represent 53% of all international students, with China, India and Korea leading as the top source countries (OECD, 2014). The main destinations are Anglophone, dominated by the US, the UK and Australia, pointing to the desirability of English language capacity in national and international job markets. In response, the landscape is diversifying with more and more universities in non-Anglophone countries such as Denmark and the Philippines offering courses in English and playing to the preferences of European and Asian students to study beyond their national borders but within their region (McGeown, 2012; OECD, 2013a).

At present, the country sending most students to external study destinations is China. Within the 34 member states of the OECD,[1] students from China accounted for 22% of all international higher education enrolments in 2012 (OECD, 2014). Of the Chinese students studying overseas, 28% chose the US, 11% studied in Australia, 6% were in Korea, 13% in Japan and 11% studied in the UK. The second-largest group of international students in OECD countries in 2012 was from India (5.8%) with approximately 45% enrolled in the US, 17% in the UK, 6% in Canada and 5% in Australia.

The main destination for international students is the US, with 16.5% of the total population of international students (Australian Education International [AEI], 2013). The next preferred destination is the UK, followed by Germany, France and Australia. These five countries, together with Canada, receive more than 50% of all foreign students worldwide (OECD, 2014). Interestingly, Germany and France are large sending as well as receiving countries. Japan receives a high number of Chinese enrolments through its educational aid programme which it uses to facilitate internationalisation of universities and society more broadly (Marginson et al., 2010). China is the recipient of 65% of Japan's educational aid.

Despite these consistent trends, patterns of student mobility are highly susceptible to influences such as marketing and recruitment approaches. For example, the share of international students choosing the US as their country of destination for tertiary education fell from 23% in 2000 to 16% in 2012 (OECD, 2014). In the same period, Germany's share dropped by three percentage points. In contrast, Korea's and New Zealand's proportions grew by 1% and the UK and the Russian Federation grew by 2% (OECD, 2014). Furthermore, universities in Africa, Latin America and the Caribbean attracted increasing numbers of international students. The changes reflect differences in countries' approaches to internationalisation ranging from marketing campaigns in the Asia-Pacific region and elsewhere to more local and university-driven approaches in the US.

In addition, the deterioration of the US market might be attributed to high tuition fees for international students compared with lower fees in other English-speaking destinations offering similar courses. The attraction of New Zealand can be partly explained by the reduction in tuition fees of advanced research programmes for international students to the same level as that paid by domestic students (OECD, 2014). Lee (2015) maintains that despite the fall in international enrolments in US institutions in 2011–2012, their financial contributions were still significant. In 2012, international students and their families injected US$25 billion into the US economy, with over 70% coming from sources outside the country (Institute of International Education [IIE], 2013).

Student mobility as captured in the statistics above shows mass movement across regional, national, cultural, educational and linguistic lines into new and unfamiliar spaces. Yet, the wandering scholar is not a new phenomenon. Indeed, Teichler (2004) finds surprising claims that universities are internationalising or should internationalise given that universities have always been regarded as the most international of a society's institutions. Gathering information and innovations from all over the world has always been highly valued by academics (Teichler, 2004). What has changed is the scale, momentum and directions of student flows – a fivefold increase since 1975 (OECD, 2013a).

Across all the statistics, Australian higher education is an obvious presence. Indeed, Australia's percentage of international students within its tertiary cohort is the highest in the world – 19.8% or almost one-fifth (OECD, 2013a). The countries with the next highest proportions of international students at universities are, in descending order, the UK, Switzerland, New Zealand and Austria, as ranked in relation to other OECD and Group of 20 (G20) nations (OECD, 2013a). Not surprisingly, the trend in student mobility is leading to more culturally and linguistically diverse student populations in universities around the world. In response, the OECD (2008) has called for educational institutions to turn their attention to curricula and teaching methods.

The challenge for universities is that they have been national institutions growing up alongside and under the protection of nation states. In Australia, universities have been understood as internationally linked but nationally aligned, principally to nation-building and local priorities. Internationalising raises questions about a consciousness and commitment beyond national concerns. Initial calls in Australia for an internationalised curriculum that focuses on educational, cultural and linguistic difference through new approaches to curriculum planning, design and delivery (Rizvi & Walsh, 1998) continue to be works in progress. The peak body representing Australia's 39 established universities, Universities Australia (UA, 2013), has produced a statement on global engagement and called for institutions to develop a more global curriculum.

In Europe, similar calls have been made. For example, a report titled *Internationalisation of Higher Education* produced for the European Parliament found that internationalisation initiatives have largely remained focused on student and staff mobility and transnational course offerings rather than developing internationalised curricula 'at home' (Havergal, 2015). The report makes the argument that an internationalised curriculum develops intercultural programmes which provide education for all students about citizenship in an interconnected global world.

## Why students are going global

The overall increase in international student mobility around the world is attributable to phenomena at both global and local levels. Worldwide there is an 'exploding demand for higher education' and the pervasive perception that studying abroad at a prestigious post-secondary institution is a highly valuable experience (OECD, 2013a: 304). At the local level, governments are initiating policies to promote mobility within certain geographic areas as well as targeting support at students interested in studying abroad in fields important to the country's development.

Additional factors accounting for the increased momentum in student mobility are concerted efforts by some countries to recruit beyond their national boundaries. Australia is one country that has adopted such an approach and assiduously marketed its education programmes overseas, particularly in the Asian region. For recruiting countries such as Australia, higher education becomes an export industry and a highly lucrative revenue source. In addition, it becomes an avenue for immigration, especially for high-achieving graduates with qualifications in priority occupations and skill categories. Indeed, several OECD countries have changed their immigration policies to facilitate temporary or permanent residency for international students (OECD, 2014). For smaller and less-developed countries, boosting support for students to study overseas is one way to alleviate local costs. Funding students to travel ensures an educated workforce but is more cost-effective than expanding the local tertiary system. Notably, international students' choices of study programmes tend to be different to those of their local counterparts (OECD, 2013a). Following the priorities of their sending countries and the nature of scholarships, international students may choose courses that are not available in their home countries or are highly specialised and well regarded in the host institution. Equally, the students' choices may be linked to their own employment prospects and gaining a competitive edge in the field.

Individual aspirations and agendas are potent forces in decisions about overseas study, particularly as the financial capacity of families in sending countries increases. For most students, the selection of a study destination is based on four criteria: the language of instruction, the quality of the programme, the tuition fees and, to a lesser degree, the immigration policy of the host country (OECD, 2013a). The dominance of English-speaking countries in the list of top international student destinations attests to the importance of English for many students – both the opportunity to develop English proficiency in an immersion setting as well as the value of English language qualifications and expertise.

The accentuated role of English in the destination choices of international students has been recognised since the beginning of the 21st century when scholars were attempting to account for new globalised interactions and transactions and their links to increases in student movement across national borders. Luke (2001) argued that the increased mobility was largely to do with students seeking to gain access to English and skills that could promote greater workplace flexibility and geographical mobility. She noted that the student flows were not bidirectional; rather they were primarily from south to north and east to west. Central to the search for English was the pursuit of Western credentials and knowledge (Luke, 2001; Rizvi, 2000).

Bruch and Barty (1998) were also interested in the phenomenon of increased international student mobility and pointed to globalisation and growing affluence in sending countries as factors. They argued that globalised commerce and communication were creating networks that affected education systems and made isolation almost impossible. These factors together with the growing affluence of middle-class families in sending countries were leading to higher numbers of students travelling overseas to study (Bruch & Barty, 1998). More students could afford the costs of international study and more institutional places were being offered. With the improved ease and speed of international travel, students could match their resources and expectations with the educational opportunities abroad.

The conditions have not receded and more latterly, an overseas education continues to be a major investment for students and their families as they seek upward social mobility and financial and job security either at home or in a migration-oriented English-speaking country (Marginson *et al.*, 2010). The direction of international student flows continues to be largely from developing countries to developed, English-speaking countries although this is changing (Ryan, 2013). As discussed in Chapter 5, many non-Anglophone countries in Europe and Asia are now tapping into the desire for English and actively entering the international education market with offerings of courses in English. Countries such as Japan and increasingly China are attracting students without an emphasis on English but rather on knowledge sharing and mutual exchange – interests which are more acute at a time of increased diplomacy, trade and security (IIE, 2011). Despite the ongoing power of English and teaching English to speakers of other languages (TESOL) in the international student market (Chowdhury & Phan, 2014), the patterns and drivers of mobility are beginning to become more variegated and multidirectional.

Possibly because of the increased provision of programmes around the world, quality has become a key factor in students' decisions about where to study (OECD, 2013a). Perceptions of quality are growing in importance and are part of the escalating regime of university ranking underway nationally and internationally. Well-known ranking scales include the Academic Ranking of World Universities (ARWU) Shanghai Jiao Tong and the Times Higher Education World University Rankings. The ARWU Shanghai Jiao Tong scale prioritises research indicators such as Nobel Prize winners and citations in journals such as *Nature* and *Science* (Shanghai Ranking, 2015) while the Times Higher Education World University Rankings scale combines research with teaching, knowledge transfer and international outlook which includes student diversity and international collaborations (TES Global, 2016). Students have ready online and print access to the rankings and information about top-ranked higher education institutions and are using these data to inform their decisions. Marginson *et al.* (2010) note that reputation and course quality are key factors in many postgraduate students' decision to study in the US, despite the perception that it is not entirely safe as a destination. US institutions dominate the world university rankings; in 2014–2015 the ARWU Shanghai Jiao Tong listed 8 American universities in its top 10; the Times Higher Education World University Rankings featured 7 in its top 10.

In addition to language of instruction and programme quality, tuition fee structures are fundamental considerations for students when deciding on a study destination (OECD, 2013a). Since the beginning of the 21st century, education systems have diversified and marketised. Patterns of tuition fees and funding arrangements have reflected national policies and also the political, cultural and economic relationships between countries including those across the OECD. For example, some OECD countries such as Finland, Iceland and Norway have combined low or no tuition fee structures with the increased availability of English-medium programmes. These initiatives have contributed to a growth in international students numbers (OECD, 2013a). However, in other countries, the absence of fees means that international enrolments have created a financial burden on the countries of destination. In response, countries such as Denmark and Sweden have introduced some fees and similar changes are being discussed in Finland (OECD, 2014).

In other contexts such as Australia and New Zealand, patterns of fees that have dictated higher tuition costs for international students over domestic students have not hampered growth in international enrolments. In Australia, foreign students are ineligible for government-subsidised places and are required to pay full costs; at postgraduate level this can mean fees four times higher than those of their domestic counterparts. The close political relationship between Australia and New Zealand means that New Zealanders are exempted from the international fee structure and pay the same fees as Australian students. New Zealand has a similar model with reciprocal rights for Australian students. The success of the two countries in attracting international students lends itself to the conclusion that tuition costs may not discourage students, especially if they perceive the quality of the education to be high and the return on investment worthwhile (OECD, 2013a).

The increasing capacity and discernment of students in their choices of programmes and study destinations across the world together with the increased availability and multiplicity of study options provided by universities highlight the complex supply and demand relationships characterising global higher education. Indeed, commercially driven higher education in countries such as Australia has long been characterised as operating along market logics, co-opting principles and practices from business models and redeploying them in education contexts (Fairclough, 1993; Marginson, 2006; Marginson *et al.*, 2010; Sidhu, 2006; Tootell, 1999). For Marginson *et al.* (2010: 36), 'globalisation, policy and market forces' are at the root of escalating cross-border mobility by tertiary-level students.

A market cannot operate without goods and the globalised higher education market has a hierarchy of educational 'goods' that are highly valued and sought after by students willing to pay for them (Marginson, 2006). As noted above, choices of international study destinations are determined nationally and individually and are driven by the social, economic and occupational advantage to be gained from English, quality instruction and programme design, optimal tuition fees and, to a lesser degree, immigration possibilities. These priorities exist in a reflexive relationship with the higher education market: they are responses to prevailing offerings as well as agents of differentiation and segmentation. Within the global context of higher education, market differentiation operates between categories of nations, categories of institutions and categories of students and student places (Marginson *et al.*, 2010).

Within the category of nations, the US is the major market for international students, as borne out in the statistics on student mobility above. The US tends to focus on student quality rather than quantity with about a third of all international students enrolled in doctoral research degrees. These students often immigrate to the US after their studies, thus contributing to the country's knowledge economy. Lee (2015) argues that many international students, especially graduate students and postdoctoral fellows, are vital to the US maintaining its competitive edge in the areas of science, technology, engineering and mathematics (STEM). The domestic shortage in these areas means that universities increasingly rely on international students for the production of STEM knowledge. In addition to providing extensive expertise and assistance in laboratories and on research grants, these students are contributing to the prestige of many elite US universities (Lee, 2015).

In the categorisation of higher education institutions, the market differentiates on quality and recognises research universities in the US, and to a lesser extent, the UK as the prestige institutions. This point is borne out in university rankings such as the ARWU Shanghai Jiao Tong and the Times Higher Education World University Rankings which also include medium-prestige research institutions in Australia, Japan, parts of Europe and the UK. Categorisation also occurs in types of student enrolments and the economic support they attract. As noted above, public subsidisation of international student places is undertaken by both sending and receiving nations, although in most English-speaking countries, study subsidies are mainly reserved for doctoral students. Overwhelmingly, Anglophone countries outside North America adopt a commercial approach to international students.

## Internationalisation or Globalisation

Is this globalisation or internationalisation of higher education? What is the difference? Considerable confusion exists between the terms and indeed they are often used interchangeably (Altbach, 2004; Al-Youssef, 2013). While related, they are not the same and refer to different levels of response to the changes in higher education during the past three decades. The increased interest in the field along with the exploding plurality of programme options has led to a plethora of terms, with meanings that have hardened over time. Commonly used terms are *globalisation, internationalisation* and *cross-border education.*

*Globalisation* has been defined extensively in the literature across multiple fields. Definitions take into consideration the flows of social, cultural, economic, technological and knowledge-based concepts and artefacts across borders with the effect of greater interconnectedness and interdependence (Knight, 2006). Implicated in the discussions of globalisation are power relations and the distribution of resources and opportunities. Higher education is highly susceptible to globalised forces because of the economic, social and knowledge-related possibilities for nations and institutions. *Internationalisation* on the other hand, orientates nationally and is particularly relevant to institutions. In one well-known definition, it is 'the process of integrating an international, intercultural, and global dimension into the purpose, functions (teaching, research, service) and delivery of Higher Education' (Knight, 2006: 18). Sidhu (2006) argues that differences also exist between the terms *internationalisation* and *international education*. *Internationalisation* is used more in institutional mission statements and policies while *international education* is most commonly associated with the recruitment and enrolment of international students. The debates around these terms and their realisations in practice are discussed in more detail below.

Linked to internationalisation is *cross-border education* which is an attempt to capture the range of providers operating in post-secondary education and the plurality of services they offer (Knight, 2006; OECD, 2006). Cross-border education is defined as the movement of people, programmes and institutions across national jurisdictions. People mobility focuses on the movement of students, academics, researchers and consultants between countries and is the most researched dimension of cross-border internationalisation. Programme mobility is the transfer of curricula and other programmes via mechanisms such as e-learning, partnerships and joint planning and design. Finally, institutional mobility encapsulates the phenomenon of institutions setting up campuses offshore with curriculum delivery by either local and/or host country staff (OECD, 2006).

A key variant of cross-border education is *transnational education* which involves the offshore provision of courses by universities and other higher education providers. Through a variety of arrangements such as overseas campuses, distant education and twinnings with partner organisations, students can remain in their own countries and receive degrees from awarding institutions in major education-exporting countries. The two biggest operators are Australia and the UK with most of their students undertaking their studies in Asian countries (Clark, 2012). Another dimension of cross-border education is the so-called *internationalisation at home* (IaH) option which was conceived in Sweden in the late 1990s (e.g. Malmö University, n.d.). At its inception, IaH involved building intercultural and international competence particularly with ethnic groups without students leaving home (Beelen, 2011). However, in subsequent elaborations largely proposed by Knight (2008) it has been conceptualised to include teaching and learning processes, research and internationalisation of the curriculum, options that Australian higher education institutions have espoused although the extent of implementation has been debated.

Two core similarities and differences exist between the terms *internationalisation* and *globalisation* as they have come to be used in higher education since the 1990s (Teichler, 2004). The similarities are: (i) they both indicate a policy direction away from a more or less closed national system of higher education to a more long-distance transfer of knowledge and a more complex environment of actors; and (ii) they both refer to a context of change that challenges and leads to change within higher education itself. The differences, on the other hand, are: (i) internationalisation tends to refer to an increase in cross-border activities while recognising the persistence of national higher education systems; and (ii) globalisation has little regard for nations and transcends national boundaries and systems. Moreover, internationalisation is associated with physical mobility, academic cooperation and academic knowledge transfer while globalisation has come to refer more to competition and the market, transnational education and, finally, the commercial transfer of knowledge (Teichler, 2004).

The relationship between the two has been posited as a push effect with globalisation defined as 'the economic, political, and societal forces pushing 21st century higher education toward greater international involvement' (Altbach & Knight, 2007: 290). While these forces are highly relevant, internationalisation needs to be seen as more than simply an economic, political and societal impulse (Kettle & Luke, 2013). Rather, the rationale for internationalising higher education also incorporates educational, cultural, linguistic and transformative objectives (Al-Youssef, 2013). Indeed, the objectives of this book are to explicate the complexity of international engagement and to show that the outcomes accrued by students go well beyond economics. This is timely as concerns are growing about the state of internationalisation as it is being implemented by governments and institutions. Sidhu (2006) cautioned that globalisation does not exist as an entity in itself but rather is spoken and enacted into being through particular policies and regulatory apparatuses. It becomes the logic and justification for the recruitment of fee-paying international students and other competition- and market-related agendas.

Questions are now being asked about whether internationalisation has become a catch-all term and is losing its way; indeed, is internationalisation having a mid-life crisis (Knight, 2011)? The argument is that internationalisation has not only changed higher education; it has also undergone dramatic changes itself. Referring to recent surveys of internationalisation policies in universities around the world, Knight (2011) found that greater priority is being given to the establishment of global standing than to the achievement of international standards of excellence. Furthermore, focus on status-building initiatives is replacing capacity building and international cooperation projects. Brandenburg and de Wit (2012) issue the provocation that higher education institutions have become fixated with form over substance and need to stop 'bragging' about inputs and outputs such as numbers of fee-paying students. Rather, they argue, universities need to focus on learning outcomes and preparing students for an increasingly intercultural and interconnected world.

Further debates about internationalisation and international education point to the preoccupation of universities and governments with the economics and revenue potential of fee-paying international students. Indeed, Chowdhury and Phan (2014) charge that international education is most commonly perceived as a global business with explicit links to revenue and the market; a university's international status is determined in part by its capacity to generate income from international sources such as student fees. These critiques are certainly borne out in the statements of government ministers such as the Australian International Education minister referred to in the Preface. The minister, Richard Colbeck (2016), celebrated rising international numbers in terms of benefits to the economy and a demonstration of Australia's strong global competitiveness in education. In the US, Lee (2015) argues that 'internationalisation' is a hot buzzword among American colleges and universities seeking prestige by recruiting international students and, at times, staff. For her, the problem is that the focus on numbers is a ploy to attract full fee-paying international students and neglects the opportunity to internationalise perspectives and cultures both inside and outside of the classroom.

Other debates relate to policy and critique of dominant Western models of internationalisation. Despite decades of rhetoric about internationalising the curriculum, much of the discussion about internationalisation continues to reside in policy, often directed at marketing and partnership initiatives. As indicated in the Preface, many of the concerns of teachers about curriculum, teaching and assessment for diverse student cohorts remain unresolved. Singh (2009) and others maintain that the current concerns of teachers appear to be the same as those of decades ago. Ryan (2011) argues that extensive internationalisation activity in British universities has been mainly directed at student recruitment and partnership development, with only relatively modest moves towards the internationalisation of teaching and learning practices. More could be done to take advantage of international students as resources and to put into practice universities' rhetoric of internationalisation.

The literature points to the need for internationalisation initiatives and international education to be less preoccupied with economic gains and more oriented to the values of cross-cultural learning and mutual exchange. New practice-informed exemplars can operate reflexively with policy to expand understandings of the benefits of internationalisation for both domestic and international students. Notwithstanding the debates, Knight (2011: 1) maintains that positive examples of international cooperation, exchange and partnership are occurring in educational institutions and as such, are contributing to the 'development of individuals, institutions, nations, and the world at large'.

Thus far, this chapter has presented the historical, political, social and economic factors that contextualise global student mobility and the networked systems of higher education around the world. Halliday and Hasan (1985) in their development of a socio-semiotic model of language stress the importance of the relationship between text and context. They argue that understanding a text is always dependent on understanding the other text that accompanies and influences it, namely the *con*-text, where the prefix *con* foregrounds *with*. Context is not merely the detached background to people's language choices. Rather, context is the total environment in which a text emerges: 'it serves to make a bridge between the text and the situation in which texts actually occur' (Halliday & Hasan, 1985: 5). This chapter presents the dynamic conditions of higher education and the Australian university in particular as the context necessary for understanding international students' accounts about what matters and what makes a difference when studying in a foreign university.

The focus on Australian higher education is not to suggest that it is indicative of all tertiary internationalisation programmes. The relevance of the Australian context is that it is the most internationalised in terms of student enrolments and has much in common with other large-scale, commercially driven education-as-export countries such as the UK and New Zealand (Marginson *et al.*, 2010). It also bears similarities to other English-speaking higher education contexts such as the US and Canada where English prevails and the curriculum is often locally orientated (Bailey, 2013; Lee & Rice, 2007; Marginson *et al.*, 2010). Furthermore, Australian postgraduate education adopts a largely critical, dialogic approach to knowledge and classroom interactions that is evident in many Western universities enrolling international students (Kettle & Luke, 2013). The scale, longevity and commercial success of the Australian international higher education programme make it a worthy case to investigate. In the remainder of the chapter, I outline the particularities of Australian higher education: its historical trajectory, relationship to Australian society, internal and external agendas and programme of internationalisation.

## Australian Higher Education

The Australian higher education system is characterised by change, from student profiles and teaching technologies to the profiles and numbers of providers. The official figures from the Australian national regulator Tertiary Education Quality and Standards Agency (TEQSA, 2015a) indicate that the sector comprises 171 providers. These providers are differentiated according to university and non-university status: 43 universities and 128 non-university higher education providers (NUHEP). Flux within the NUHEP sector is evident in the statistics: in June 2015, the number of providers was 130 (TEQSA, 2015b); by September 2015 it was 128 (TEQSA, 2015a). These changes can be caused by a number of factors including amalgamation, expiry of registration and, in more extreme cases, deregistration. The non-university providers are divided into those who are accredited to offer students government-sponsored fee assistance and those who are not, effectively meaning that the latter are full-fee charging institutions. The orientations of the NUHEPs are varied; examples include those affiliated with professional organisations such as the Australian Institute of Business and Management while others have affiliations with religious organisations, for example, the Christian Heritage College (TEQSA, 2015b).

Within the university sector, a four-way categorisation occurs with public universities overwhelming the biggest group, as evident in Table 1.1.

The peak university body UA has 39 members: 37 public universities and 2 private universities (UA, 2015a). Of the 1,332,687 students enrolled in Australian higher education in 2013, 93% were in universities (TEQSA, 2015b).

**Table 1.1** Profiles of universities in Australia

| Australian public university | 37 | Australian Catholic University |
|---|---|---|
| | | Australian National University |
| | | Central Queensland University |
| | | Charles Darwin University |
| | | Charles Sturt University |
| | | Curtin University of Technology |
| | | Deakin University |
| | | Edith Cowan University |
| | | Federation University |
| | | Griffith University |
| | | James Cook University |
| | | La Trobe University |
| | | Macquarie University |
| | | Monash University |
| | | Murdoch University |
| | | Queensland University of Technology |
| | | Royal Melbourne Institute of Technology |
| | | Southern Cross University |
| | | Swinburne University of Technology |
| | | Flinders University |
| | | University of Adelaide |
| | | University of Melbourne |
| | | University of Queensland |
| | | University of Sydney |
| | | University of Western Australia |
| | | University of Canberra |
| | | University of New England |
| | | University of New South Wales |
| | | University of Newcastle |
| | | University of South Australia |
| | | University of Southern Queensland |
| | | University of Tasmania |
| | | University of Technology Sydney |
| | | University of Sunshine Coast |
| | | University of Western Sydney |
| | | University of Wollongong |
| | | Victoria University |
| Australian private university | 3 | Bond University |
| | | University of Notre Dame Australia |
| | | Torrens University Australia |
| Australian university of specialisation | 1 | Melbourne College of Divinity |
| Overseas university | 2 | Carnegie Mellon University |
| | | University College London |

Source: TEQSA (2015a) and UA (2015a).

Another view of Australian universities is proposed by Marginson (2006) who differentiates according to histories. The five-way segmentation operates as follows:

(1) The Sandstones: The so-called Group of Eight (Go8) universities – Queensland, Sydney, New South Wales, Monash, Melbourne, Western Australia, Adelaide and the Australian National University. These are largely Australia's older universities and fashioned originally on British models including the construction of sandstone buildings.
(2) The Gumtrees: Second or newer universities built prior to 1987.
(3) The Unitechs: Five universities known as the Australian Technology Network (ATN). They were large vocationally focused institutes of technology that became universities from 1987.
(4) The New Universities: Other institutions that achieved university status after 1987. Many of these specialise in rural and distance education.
(5) The private universities: For example, Bond University bearing the name of former businessman Alan Bond whose company was one of the initial developers of the university.

A sixth category might now be added with the arrival of two overseas universities and their accreditation in 2014.

As is evident in Table 1.1, Australian universities are overwhelmingly public institutions that since the 1990s have evolved with uniformity of mission and form. The uniformity has been realised in the large, comprehensive public university catering for the bulk of higher education in degrees from undergraduate to doctoral level (Coaldrake & Stedman, 2013). Total student enrolments were approximately 719,000 in 2001; a decade later they had risen to 929,000 (Australian Bureau of Statistics [ABS], 2013b). As noted above, they were 1,332,687 by 2013 (TEQSA, 2015b). Universities in Australia have been particularly successful in promoting mass tertiary education with Australian degree attainment some of the highest in the world. They incorporate academic, vocational and professional courses: business and management, and teacher education followed by nursing, accounting and law were the most popular choices for undergraduate students in 2012 (ABS, 2013b).

Through their course structures and on campuses universities accommodate students from diverse backgrounds including those who are part-time, older and located outside a metropolitan centre. More recent efforts have been directed at increasing the participation of students from low socio-economic and indigenous groups that have traditionally had low representation in the tertiary sector (Gale & Tranter, 2011). New online teaching methodologies are taken up enthusiastically with some regional universities graduating the majority of their students online. In terms of international education, as noted above, Australian universities have been highly effective at attracting overseas students with enrolment levels in universities from the beginning of the 21st century consistently around 20% or one-fifth of the total student population.

Universities are traditionally national institutions that have grown up alongside and under the protection of nation states (Scott, 1998). In the Australian context, they were initially aligned with nation-building although also acknowledged as internationally linked. Their responsibilities included the provision of a class of professional and business people, as resources and also mass producers and consumers. The university mandate was also to foster the social sciences for administrative and social purposes, and to sustain the arts and humanities. Post-Hiroshima, their ultimate function was to power the sciences and technologies in pursuit of industrial development, social progress and economic competitiveness (Marginson, 2002).

Since the beginning of the 21st century, the Australian higher education system has had to confront questions about its role and capability as an instrument of nation-building. These questions have been wrought by changes in public funding, the 'stand-off' between corporate and academic practices in universities and the need to engage globally while continuing to support national agendas (Marginson, 2002). Attempts to reconcile national and global concerns as well as corporate and academic practices are dominant themes in contemporary Australian higher education: localisation, rationalisation, marketisation and internationalisation play out constantly in political and institutional rhetoric.

The university sector is being increasingly subjected to local and global forces. Concerns about the effects of the global financial crisis (GFC) in the years 2007–2008 saw governments around the world implement fiscal stimulus packages. In the Asia Pacific region, the sizes of the fiscal packages were considerable: (in US dollars) Australia (26 billion); China (795 billion); Indonesia (6.1 billion); Japan (125 billion); Singapore (13.7 billion); Vietnam (1 billion) (United Nations Educational, Scientific and Cultural Organization [UNESCO], 2012). The financial interventions and lessons learned during the Asian crisis of 1997 meant that most higher education sectors in the region were less harshly impacted than those in Europe and the US. For example, Indonesia incurred more financial costs from natural disasters than the GFC, thanks to government spending on education (UNESCO, 2012). Similarly, Australia escaped the worst of the GFC through massive injections of government spending into the economy, a measure which is now attracting much discussion about how to balance the national budget.

Consensus is growing that the political imperatives to reduce government funding and the heightened exposure to competition mean Australian higher education is at a critical juncture. Within universities, increased student numbers, greater technology demands and developing specialisations together with staffing and infrastructure needs have come at a cost. These costs have occurred at a time when governments are demanding greater accountability and productivity, and are reducing subsidisation of student places and research. The reduction in government spending is apparent in the 2012–2013 figures: despite an increase of 88% in domestic student load, total funding outlay to Australian higher education in 2012–2013 was lower than the early 1990s (Coaldrake & Stedman, 2013). International comparisons highlight the government underfunding of higher education in Australia. In 2011, Australia ranked 30th out of 31 OECD countries for public investment in tertiary education as a percentage of gross domestic product (GDP) (UA, 2015b). Annual public expenditure on Australian tertiary institutions per student was US$7475 which was 17.5% below the expenditure level in the US (US$9057) and almost 19% below the OECD average of US$9221 (UA, 2015b). In response to growing competition, UA (2013) has argued the need for universities to become more globally engaged and has called for a facilitative policy from government to ensure growth in the sector.

The UA call comes as the sector is beset by concerns about so-called reforms being proposed by the current conservative Liberal-National government. The changes in the 'Higher Education and Research Reform Bill 2014' include a 20% reduction in government funding per student; the introduction of student contributions for research degrees; and the deregulation of fee structures (Commonwealth of Australia, n.d.). Concerns have been raised that the changes will place higher education beyond the financial reach of equity groups and burden many others with long-term debt (Jericho, 2014). As well, there are charges that the reform package is ideologically driven and not evidence based and that it will produce a two-tiered system with elite, selective universities on the one hand and for-profit private colleges with no obligations to support teaching with research on the other (Marginson, 2014; Rice, 2014).

The protests against the changes have been loud and consistent. The Federal Opposition Australian Labor Party (ALP) launched a campaign warning of '$100 000 degrees' and students all over the country have been protesting the threatened fee hikes. In contrast, universities have largely supported the move to deregulated student fees but have a number of remaining concerns including the 20% reduction in funding rates and the introduction of fees for research students (UA, 2015b). To add weight to their concerns, UA (2014) has launched a petition to politicians called *Keep it Clever: Let's Not Get Left Behind Australia*. Given the amount of protest, the proposed changes to higher education have not passed into law. Rather their passage has been blocked twice by the senate, despite some amendments by the government. The controversy around the issue and the level to which it has been exploited by the Opposition have seen the government shelve plans for deregulation until 2018 and instead launch a consultation paper titled 'Driving Innovation, Fairness and Excellence in Australian Higher Education' (Australian Government, 2016). It remains to be seen what the future will hold for student fees and government funding of universities.

## The historical development of internationalisation

One of universities' major entrepreneurial responses to counteract financial pressures has been to target fee-paying international students. Indeed from the 1980s onwards, international education has been increasingly conceptualised as a market rather than a teaching and learning site (Marginson, 2002). International students have become an important income stream for many Australian universities; almost half have onshore student populations comprising around one-quarter international students (AEI, 2015d). In the nationally and internationally competitive education environment, position in the segmented hierarchy of Australian universities has largely determined university resources and status. The prestige of The Sandstones has prevailed and has been reinforced by their access to student markets and research funding. The case study presented here was conducted at a Sandstone.

A discussion of internationalisation in Australian higher education cannot proceed without reference to the broader historical relationship between the Asia region and Australia. In 2003, the proportion of students from Asian countries enrolled in Australian tertiary courses was 84%; in 2011 it was 80.7% (AEI, 2013). In the period from 2004 to 2014, students from the Asia region accounted for two-thirds (67.3%) of all students across education sectors in Australia (AEI, 2015c). The source countries have changed slightly but not the region. Writing at the time of accelerated marketisation of Australian higher education in the 1990s and 2000s, McNamara and Coughlan (1997) maintained that the increased visibility of 'Asian' faces in the community were in fact largely overseas students.

The term *Asian* is highly contested in Australian social and historical discourses with arguments that the predominant definition of Asianness involves lumping all of Asia together as a homogeneous monolithic entity (Ang, 2000; Nichols, 2003). Indeed, the high number of students from Asian countries in Australian universities means that the term *international* has come almost to mean *Asian*. However, the contested nature of the term means that it is avoided in favour of the more neutral and inclusive *international* (Nichols, 2003). The term *international student* has also been the focus of disagreements. In earlier work, I refer to the debate among academics about the term and its failure to differentiate student groups (Kettle & Luke, 2013). Rather, the term is seen as homogenising students' diverse backgrounds and obfuscating their varied needs and resources. Within the Australian education policy domain, *international student* has become a panacea, replacing *fee-paying overseas student* in the early 1990s as a response to the criticisms of excessive commercialisation (Back *et al.*, 1996). *International* is primarily an administrative term, related to status and fee-paying profile. *Domestic* in Australia is the equivalent of *home* in the UK: local and government subsidised.

The increased numbers of Asian students on university campuses have coincided with the growing numbers of Asian migrants arriving in Australia. The two phenomena have commonalities but were generated by different histories. In 1973, Australia abolished its highly controversial 'Immigration Restriction Act of 1901', more commonly known as the White Australia policy. The policy was introduced at the turn of the 20th century as Australia was acquiring sovereignty and jurisdictional power from its colonial master, Britain. The policy was designed to prevent non-Europeans from migrating to Australia by giving immigration officials the power to exclude applicants who failed a dictation test of 50 words in any European language.

With the abolition of the policy and its discourses of 'yellow peril' and the introduction of a so-called 'non-discriminatory' immigration policy, the number of migrants from diverse Asian backgrounds began to increase steadily. By the mid-1990s, about 5% of the Australian population was from Asian backgrounds, helped by numbers of Vietnamese refugees who were permitted to settle permanently after fleeing the Vietnamese-American War in which Australia sided with the US.

Australia's policy of multiculturalism implemented in the 1970s was devised to recognise non-British ethnic groups who had migrated to Australia during the post-World War II period of nation-building, many from southern European countries such as Greece and Italy. Critique of the policy in its original incarnation was that it was a primarily European affair. Ang (2000) maintains Australia's vision of homogeneity that centred on 'essential Europeanness' was only really ruptured with the arrival of Vietnamese refugees and later with the large-scale settlement of business migrants from East and South-East Asia in the 1980s. These arrivals were followed by Chinese students fleeing China in the wake of the Tiananmen Square massacre in 1989. The cultural difference that these Asian migrants represented in relation to European migrants was 'arguably far more challenging to mainstream Australia traditionally so insistent on its espousal of racial and cultural whiteness as the core of national identity' (Ang, 2000: xvii).

In such an environment, it comes as no surprise that the spectre of 'Asianisation' has been conjured up at times in Australian political discourses to rally nationalist support. One highly publicised and divisive attempt was by rookie politician Pauline Hanson[2] in her maiden speech to the Australian Parliament on 10 September 1996 in which she spoke of Australia being 'in danger of being swamped by Asians (who) have their own culture and religion, form ghettoes and do not assimilate'

(Hanson, 1996). For Hanson and her supporters, as with so many of Australia's past and present policymakers, ethnicity, race and nationality were conflated. While many migrants have done much to blunt the harshly racist attitudes towards Asia and things 'Asian' in Australian public discourse (Mackie, 1997), racism remains at work. Hanson has now thrown her lot in with an anti-Islamic group called Reclaim Australia (Rao, 2015). Reclaim Australia (2015) claims to be concerned about threats from Islam to Australia and Australian values including sharia law and halal food certification. The group's profile is growing and has attracted violent clashes with anti-racism protestors (Rao, 2015).

In the 2016 federal election, Pauline Hanson was returned to the Australian senate with three other members of her One Nation Party. Her speech to the senate – delivered almost 20 years to the day after her 1996 speech – provocatively repeated the words about Australia being 'swamped' – this time by 'Muslims'. She claimed that Muslims 'bear a culture and ideology that is incompatible with our own' and insisted that Australians would be forced to live under sharia law if something did not change (Norman, 2016). During her right-wing, anti-immigration speech, Greens senators staged a walkout in protest. The party later tweeted that racism has no place in Australia.

In the post-September 11 era, a major theme exercising Australian politicians and the public imagination is the so-called 'war on terror' and border protection with its various representations of refugees arriving by boat as security threats and queue-jumpers. One infamous incident was in 2001 with the 'children overboard' affair when the conservative Australian government refused to grant asylum to a group of Iraqi and Afghani refugees. The refugees were accused of throwing their children into the sea in order to be rescued by the Australian navy and gain entry to the country. The affair greatly influenced public discourses and contributed to the re-election of Prime Minister John Howard's conservative government (Macken-Horarik, 2005). Fears about security and fundamentalist Islam were exacerbated in October 2002, when bombs in two popular bars in Bali, Indonesia, killed 202 people, including 88 Australians. Public discourse appeared to shift from panic about an Asian contagion in the 1990s to one about Islam that conflated Muslims, terrorists and 'queue-jumping' asylum seekers.

More recently in 2009–2010, repeated attacks on Indian students including murder, particularly in Sydney and Melbourne, have raised concerns about the role of racism in the experiences of international students. While some of the attacks were attributed to 'opportunistic urban crime', the hurling of racist abuse indicated that racism was also involved (The Age, 2010). In a study of international student security with 200 students across three states, Marginson et al. (2010) found that over 50% had experienced hostility or prejudice. For many, the negativity sprang from their appearance or limited English and a non-English accent. Accent is a strong trigger for racism and has been investigated in the US (Lippi-Green, 2012) and in the Australian context with international students (Kettle, 2013).

Social history does not operate in isolation; rather it implicates other histories including that of higher education. The first major initiative involving overseas student recruitment to Australia was the Colombo Plan in 1950 (Tootell, 1999). The plan originated in discussions between foreign ministers from Commonwealth countries in Colombo, Sri Lanka, and was designed to provide financial, technical and educational aid to foster the economic development of countries in South and South-East Asia (Bassett, 1994). Education aid was seen as a way of developing a technologically literate and administratively competent elite which would ensure the development of their respective countries. Even during the days of the White Australia policy, students were coming to Australia. It has been argued that educational aid was only a secondary aim to the primary motivation of ensuring political stability in the Asian region (Alexander & Rizvi, 1993). While the 'yellow peril' represented a traditional fear in Australia, the new threat in the 1950s and 1960s was red. The world was in the grip of a Cold War and communism was taking hold throughout Asia. The Domino Theory dominated thinking at the time. Part of the logic associated with the Colombo Plan was that Australian-educated graduates in strategically important positions in Asia would be predisposed to Western democratic values and act as buffers against the spread of communism. The motivations were mixed: on the one hand, altruism and a desire to ameliorate regional inequities, and on the other, racist and xenophobic views which were held by many Australians about Asia.

In the 1970s, changes started to occur. The Eurocentric curriculum was not meeting the needs of Asian students and there were concerns that an elite group of individuals was benefiting from the programme rather than the country at large. Also, the economies of various Asian countries were accelerating to the point where it was inappropriate to classify them as 'developing'. In 1979, the Australian government introduced the overseas student charge (OSC) and removed the limit on overseas students. The OSC was less than full cost and was progressively increased until 1988 when it was 55% of the average cost of a place at an Australian university (Harris & Jarrett, 1990). In other words, private overseas students were being 'subsidised' by the government and education was still part of Australia's aid programme (Tootell, 1999).

In 1984, two reports were published which shifted Australia's approach to overseas students definitively from 'aid' to 'trade'. In a political climate increasingly dominated by rationalist ideas and concern about the balance of payments, the Jackson report (Joint Committee on Foreign Affairs and Defence, 1985) recommended that full-cost fees be introduced and scholarship funds from overseas aid be established to promote development and equity. The report was enthusiastic about the potential of education to be a major source of income, not just for cash-strapped universities but for the nation as a whole (Alexander & Rizvi, 1993). Conversely, the Goldring report (Committee of Review of Private Overseas Student Policy, 1984) rejected 'user pay' ideas about education and recommended that the OSC be set at 30%–40% with postgraduate students exempt from the charge. In 1985, the Jackson position prevailed and a new 'Policy on Overseas Students' was launched for Australian higher education.

According to Tootell (1999: 3), what ensued was a marked change in how academic institutions perceived overseas students: 'from an altruistic perspective of students in developing countries to the financial perspective of prospective customers contributing to the financial situation of the institution'. The conditions were that institutions could offer an unlimited number of places to full-fee paying overseas students as long as they met the entry requirements and did not displace an Australian student. In 1992, in part because of the criticism of excessive commercialisation, the federal government signalled a shift from *trade* to *internationalisation of education* (Smart & Ang, 1996). A number of strategies were deployed to pursue internationalisation including acknowledgement of the need to internationalise the curriculum and as noted above, avoidance of the term *fee-paying overseas student* and other overtly marketing and commercial terms in the student recruitment process (Back *et al.*, 1996).

A more recent report is the 2008 Australian Labor Government commissioned *Review of Australian Higher Education*, chaired by former Vice-Chancellor Professor Denise Bradley. The review was tasked with examining the state of higher education as a major contributor to Australia's economic and social well-being at a time of global economic crisis and change. Its recommendations focused on the ongoing viability, sustainability and quality of higher education and its capacity to address domestic and global agendas. Domestic priorities included social inclusion and widening participation on equity grounds; the development of a highly skilled workforce; the provision of a just and civil society; and the capacity to produce new knowledge and applications through research and innovation. The review acknowledged the significance of international education in Australia's higher education sector and its evolution into a so-called third phase, where phases one and two were as outlined above: the eras of educational aid and educational trade (Bradley *et al.*, 2008).

The third phase takes in the present conditions in which Australia cannot take for granted its traditional base of students from the Asia-Pacific region and its attractiveness as a safe, English-speaking destination not far from home. Many of these countries are now developing their own higher education systems and are also seeking to attract international students. The recommendations of the Bradley *et al.* (2008: 95) review were more than aid or trade; rather, they advocated for a more 'holistic and sustainable long-term sustainable strategy for global engagement in education'. To this end, the review called for greater student diversity to ensure sustainability; more research students with potential to build Australia's academic and research workforce; improved quality of the educational experience and preparation of students to work in Australia if desired; more work on inter-governmental coordination including support for skilled migration; and increased international collaboration and building of international networks (Bradley *et al.*, 2008).

Direct responses to the Bradley report's recommendations have been the 2010 *International Students Strategy for Australia: 2010–2014* (Council of Australian Governments [COAG], 2010) and the 2011 *Internationalising the Student Experience in Australian Tertiary Education: Developing Criteria and Indicators* (Arkoudis *et al.*, 2012). The *Students Strategy* was a concerted effort by national and state governments to ensure a high-quality experience for international students framed around initiatives to address concerns in four areas: (i) well-being and safety; (ii) consumer protection; (iii) quality education; and (iv) provision of up-to-date and accurate information (COAG, 2010). The *Internationalising the Student Experience* project was commissioned by the Australia Education International (AEI) branch of the Australian government to develop criteria and indicators for universities to monitor, evaluate and improve the internationalisation of students' experience. The project focused on internationalisation in the contexts of teaching and learning and in the relationships between domestic and international students, arguing that students often remained isolated from each other both inside and outside the classroom (Arkoudis *et al.*, 2012).

The 2015 initiative in international education is the Australian Government (2015a) 'Draft National Strategy for International Education (For Consultation) April 2015' which will form the foundation of the government's long-term development strategy 'Australian International Education 2025'. The draft strategy presents international education as a core element of Australia's economic prosperity, social advancement and international standing. It is built around three pillars: getting the fundamentals right; reaching out to the world; and staying competitive. The document outlines a number of measures by which success for the international education strategy will be measured. One of the measures is the retention of Australia's position within the top five study destinations in the world. Another is elevation of Australia's reputation as a world leader in international education through improvements in the global connectedness of Australians, for example, through more research publications and partnerships especially with emerging markets in Africa, the Middle East and Latin America. Another indicator of success will be the expansion of Australian education and training overseas. A final measure of success prioritises the experiences of international students in Australia and is directed at increased English language proficiency and greater interaction with Australian students and communities, a point that was highly relevant to the international students introduced in this book.

## Key international education statistics

Australian higher education is represented as punching above its weight in the global education market. Numbers are often juxtaposed that highlight small population but large outcomes. For example, the Australian government website titled 'Study in Australia: Future Unlimited' lists 10 reasons for prospective students to study in Australia, all attractively presented and pitched competitively against other international education providers around the world:

> Did you know Australia has the third highest number of international students behind only the United Kingdom and the United States despite having a population of only 23 million; ... Australia has seven of the top 100 universities in the world; ... Australia sits above the likes of Germany, the Netherlands and Japan ranking eighth in the Universitas 2012 U21 Ranking of National Higher Education Systems. ... Australia has five of the 30 best cities in the world for students ... There is every chance that Australia has (your specific study area of interest) covered, with at least one Australian university in the top 50 worldwide across the study areas of Natural Sciences & Mathematics, Life & Agricultural Sciences, Clinical Medicine & Pharmacy, and Physics ... Australia has produced 15 Nobel prize laureates and every day over 1 billion people around the world rely on Australian discoveries and innovations ... Why wouldn't you want to study with some of the best minds in the world? (Commonwealth of Australia, 2013b)

Australian international education since the 1980s has been commercially oriented and designed primarily to generate export revenues (Marginson, 2006). This makes education providers and governments highly sensitive to market forces, especially significant economic downturns such as those experienced since the GFC. International education operates across five main sectors in Australia: higher education, English language intensive courses for overseas students (ELICOS), vocational education and training (VET), schools and non-award courses. Higher education is consistently the best performing sector. Between 1990 and 2003, Australian universities experienced a rapid increase in overseas enrolments, with the total of onshore and offshore students going from 24,998 to 210,397 (Department of Education, Science and Training [DEST], 2005). The overall value of Australia's education exports in 2003–2004 was $5.6 billion.

A decade later, the top source countries for Australian international education remain in Asia, as outlined in Table 1.2 (AEI, 2014b, 2015c; DEST, 2005). The numbers and export earnings have manifestly increased but are characterised by fluctuation. In 2009, international education activity peaked as Australia's third largest export industry, generating $16.1 billion from international students living and studying in Australia (AEI, 2014a). By 2012, export income had dropped to $14.5 billion, representing a decline of 6.9% in overall enrolments (AEI, 2013). Most of the decline was in the VET sector which has high enrolments of Indian students. These enrolments were badly affected by negative images of Australia in India following racially motivated attacks on Indian students in 2009–2010 (The Age, 2010). Two years later in 2014, export income from international students living and studying in Australia rose 17.3% on 2012 figures to $17 billion (AEI, 2015a). Higher education contributed $11.7 billion (68.5%) of the total export income. In 2014, international education was Australia's fourth largest export industry, after iron ore, coal and natural gas (AEI, 2015a).

International enrolments at Australian universities increased to 230,280 in 2014; up 6.5% on the 2013 figures of 216,298 (AEI, 2015d). In 2014, international students represented 19.2% of the total university student population although some universities had much higher percentages, for example, Federation University Australia (42.3%) and Bond University (37.1%). Overall, undergraduate commencements increased significantly in 2014–2015 while postgraduate commencements were varied: research declined but other postgraduate commencements increased (Australian Government, 2015b).

For many international students the preferred field of study is commerce. This has been the case in Australian higher education for over a decade. In 2003, management and commerce programmes attracted the highest number of international enrolments (37%), followed by information technology (IT) (16%) (Australian Vice Chancellors Committee [AVCC],

**Table 1.2** Changing demographics: Top 10 source countries for Australian universities

| Ranking | 2003 (DEST, 2005) | 2013 (AEI, 2014b) | 2014 (AEI, 2015c) |
|---------|-------------------|-------------------|-------------------|
| 1 | Singapore | China | China |
| 2 | Hong Kong | India | India |
| 3 | Malaysia | Republic of Korea | Vietnam |
| 4 | China | Vietnam | Republic of Korea |
| 5 | Indonesia | Malaysia | Malaysia |
| 6 | India | Thailand | Thailand |
| 7 | USA | Indonesia | Brazil |
| 8 | Thailand | Brazil | Indonesia |
| 9 | Taiwan | Nepal | Nepal |
| 10 | Norway | Pakistan | Pakistan |

2005). In 2014, 'management and commerce' continued to be the most popular field for international students in both higher education and VET (AEI, 2015b). Across the two sectors, management and commerce accounted for over half (56.3%) of all enrolments while courses related to STEM attracted 20% of students from the top sending nations (AEI, 2015b).

Within national groups, students tend to orient towards particular education sectors. For example, in Australia, Chinese students are more likely to enrol in higher education, notably at undergraduate level, while Indian students are studying more in the VET sector (AEI, 2015b). Around the world, New Zealand is the country with the highest proportion of international students in vocationally oriented courses while Australia has the highest proportion in theory-based tertiary courses – 21% of all students (OECD, 2013a). At least one-quarter of students undertaking advanced research programmes in Australia, Belgium, Ireland, Sweden and the US are international.

## Looking to Engagement

This chapter has provided the context of international higher education – its drivers and conditions. The following chapters explicate the experiences of a group of international students negotiating these conditions at an Australian university. As noted above, the Australian example is not intended to be representative but is illustrative given the pervasive and prolonged programme of internationalisation in Australian policy settings. The global drive for greater recruitment of international students and the accelerating mobilisation of students mean it is beneficial to make visible positive examples of international study experiences. It is necessary to ask what an exemplary international experience looks like and, from an institutional point of view, what can be done in teaching to facilitate learning, participation and personal growth among students whose profiles are marked by diversity.

These questions exercise many university teachers and policymakers; in this book, these attributes of the international experience combine in the concept of engagement. The aim of the book is to define engagement in a way that incorporates all the elements in the lived experience of the student. The students introduced are from some of Australia's top source countries: China, Republic of Korea, Singapore, Thailand, Vietnam, as well as Mozambique and Argentina. Three of the students are studying on Australian government AusAid scholarships (China, Thailand, Mozambique)[3]; one is on a privately sponsored philanthropic scholarship (Vietnam)[4]; and two are self-funded (Singapore and Argentina).

This book provides a picture of international student engagement as appraised and articulated by the students themselves. The students' voices indicate what works in international higher education, that is, what affords them new ways of knowing, doing and being at an overseas university.

Explicit in many students' accounts, especially at the outset, are difficulties related to negotiating language and culture in their everyday and academic lives. Affordances are not to be confused with affordability. For the students profiled in the book, the experience of studying abroad in an unfamiliar culture and language, away from home and family, was at times lonely, frustrating and financially difficult. Nonetheless, it offered opportunities that they accepted and managed to their own advantage. Through the conditions of possibility, the students were able to turn adversity into advantage and to act as agents of their own change.

This is not to suggest that the research findings presented in this book are self-congratulatory justifications for higher education as it operates in Australia. Indeed, as noted above, Australian higher education is currently beset by rancorous debates about how best to implement reforms that ensure high-quality, sustainable higher education. Furthermore, despite 40 years of actively recruiting fee-paying international students into their academic programmes, Australian universities continue to ask questions about the best ways to teach students from diverse cultural, educational and linguistic backgrounds. There is no doubt that infrastructure has been introduced to support students' transitions to English language tertiary study. Academic language and literacy services are offered and academics are being encouraged to embrace diversity and inclusion in their teaching (Brew, 2007; Devlin & Samarawickrema, 2010). University mission statements highlight the importance of intercultural competence and inclusive teaching.

Despite these initiatives, many academics continue to be concerned about student English language levels and academic integrity especially as universities escalate international enrolments in the face of falling government funding. In the early 2000s, a government survey of academics at three major universities in the state of Victoria (Auditor-General, 2002) found that two-thirds believed underdeveloped English was the major cause of international students' academic problems including poor student writing. They wanted English language entry scores raised and increased assistance with marking written work. A decade later, a more controversial study used international student data in the business faculties of two Australian universities to claim low English language levels and cultural barriers were impeding student progress (Foster, 2012). The study also claimed that despite these barriers, international students were benefitting from grade inflation, particularly in courses with high concentrations of international enrolments. Over the past decade, media reports and online blogs have continuously presented stories on low student English language levels and so-called 'soft marking' (Frijters, 2011; Hare, 2013; Livingstone, 2004a, 2004b; Trounson, 2011). More recently, reports have highlighted 'ghost writing' and illicit essay writing services that provide assignments for a fee (e.g. Visentin, 2014).

This book problematises the concerns of academics and their taken-for-granted assumptions about international student language levels and academic achievement. Blaming academic problems on English language levels is highly seductive. While language thresholds are undoubtedly important and universities have a responsibility to enrol only those students whose thresholds are appropriate, it is crucial to recognise that language, culture and pedagogy are entwined in participation and entry into an academic community. Academic literacy practices and ways of presenting knowledge in written texts are culturally situated and reproduced across centuries of social and educational practices. Students from different educational backgrounds bring the writing traditions of their scholarly systems with them to the overseas study experience. It becomes the overseas institution's responsibility to help these students transition to its valued academic practices. This position encapsulates the principles of access, equity and participation. The role of the university academic as teacher and mentor is pivotal in the process of transforming student knowledge, skills and understandings. Through the students' accounts, this book examines good teaching and its relationship to student engagement and success.

## Notes

(1)   The OECD has 35 member states: Australia, Austria, Belgium, Canada, Chile, Czech Republic, Denmark, Estonia, Finland, France, Germany, Greece, Hungary, Iceland, Ireland, Israel, Italy, Japan, Korea, Latvia, Luxembourg, Mexico, Netherlands, New Zealand, Norway, Poland, Portugal, Slovak Republic, Slovenia, Spain, Sweden, Switzerland, Turkey, United Kingdom, and United States. The European Commission is a special, additional member, although with restricted rights (OECD, 2016). The G20 is comprised of 20 major economies oriented towards economic cooperation and trade (Commonwealth of Australia, 2016). Its current members are: Argentina, Australia, Brazil, Canada, China, France, Germany, India, Indonesia, Italy, Japan, Republic of Korea, Mexico, Russia, Saudi Arabia, South Africa, Turkey, United Kingdom, United States, and the European Union.

(2)   Pauline Hanson is a controversial politician who was elected to the Australian Parliament in 1996 as an independent member but went on to lead the One Nation party, which reached its peak in 1997–1998. Hanson's polices included more gun control, less welfare assistance to indigenous Australians and the reduction of Asian migration. Australian opinion was divided on whether she was speaking up for the concerns of 'ordinary Australians' or if she was uninformed and a racist. Her public appearances sparked heated confrontations between her supporters and protestors. Hanson lost her seat in the 1998 federal election. In 2003, she was jailed briefly for electoral fraud but had the conviction quashed on appeal. After years of attempting to re-enter Parliament at state and federal levels, she and three other members of her party were elected to the federal senate in 2016. The group campaigned on a right-wing, anti-immigration platform and wields considerable power as a voting bloc.

(3)   AusAid scholarships link to the Australian government's assessment of a country's economic situation and are increasingly shifting from Asian to African countries.

(4)   Hanh from Vietnam was sponsored by an American philanthropic organisation called Atlantic Philanthropies. The organisation sponsored 15 students per year from three of Vietnam's universities to travel to Australia for master's level study. The sponsorship programme ran for five years.

# 2 International Students in the Western Academy: Representations Across Time

## Introduction

This chapter presents the changing representations of international students in the research literature on teaching and learning in the Western academy. The time span begins with the targeted recruitment programmes of the 1980s–1990s when significant numbers of overseas students began impacting the profiles of student cohorts in university courses. The goal of the chapter is to provide a historical account of the shifting perspectives that have characterised four decades of international student involvement in higher education, notably in Australia. These insights are important for highlighting the historically situated and one-sided institutional representations of international students in the literature. They contextualise the intransigence of negative views and strengthen the argument in this book for new understandings about the discernment and dynamism of international student engagement.

This new orientation is highly warranted in pastoral and equity terms; it is also necessary as a means of identifying the ingredients for international student academic success. Data from the OECD (2013b) indicate that international students using English as their second language (ESL) are highly achieving in their overseas studies and contributing significantly to tertiary graduation rates, particularly in Australia. This book is about showing how that success is achieved; it utilises engagement to conceptualise the students' mediation of the institutional conditions through actions and thinking in order to shape their academic outcomes. Within this context, teaching can be transformed. The case study presented here offers an exemplar of higher education pedagogy that was adapted to provide the conditions of academic possibility for students from diverse cultural, educational and linguistic backgrounds.

# Historical Views of International Students in Higher Education

The historical passage of higher education has generated different images of international students in the research literature. The changing representations reflect not only shifts in the conditions of higher education but also changes in educational research itself. Like work in other areas of education across the same time frame, the changing characterisations align with the prevailing zeitgeist (Kettle & Luke, 2013). Where the 1980s were dominated by orientations to psychological factors and individualised remediation, the 1990s were marked by the foregrounding of culture and psychosocial cultural adaptation. This work was in turn succeeded by a heightened interest in power relations and sociopolitical critiques of institutional power in the 2000s. The metaphor of 'waves' is useful here as a means of conceptualising the nature of these research orientations – and their declines and residual influences. Like a wave forming to a peak and then rolling into shore, the metaphor encapsulates the rise to prominence of a particular research orientation and its subsequent collapse into the field, to be superseded by the next wave. The following section summarises the respective waves that have peaked in Australian higher education literature. These waves form the point of departure for the argument in this book that engagement is the best approach to explain the international student experience in higher education.

## The first wave of literature: International student as deficient

The first 'wave' of research literature coincided with the initial phase of the programme to internationalise Australian higher education in the mid to late 1980s. As discussed in Chapter 1, the adoption of the Jackson report in the mid-1980s saw a change in how academic institutions perceived overseas students: 'from an altruistic perspective of students in developing countries to the financial perspective of prospective customers contributing to the financial situation of the institution' (Tootell, 1999: 3). Institutions were able to offer an unlimited number of places to full-fee-paying overseas students as long as they met the entry requirements and did not displace an Australian student. What followed was a marked increase in the number of students from Asian countries which led to a raft of research studies.

The studies were often conducted by student counsellors such as Ballard (1987), Ballard and Clanchy (1984, 1991), Gassin (1982) and Samuelowicz (1987) who were at the coalface of providing support services to overseas students and to the lecturers presented with increased numbers of non-native English-speaking students (NNES) from non-Australian backgrounds. Ballard and Clanchy (1991) state in their manual for Australian academics on teaching students from overseas that students bring a new and strange dimension to the classroom. They argue that problems can be resolved through efforts on the part of both the students and academics to change attitudes and behaviours.

The research studies at the time were concerned primarily with the 'problems' experienced by the staff and students. Some concentrated on the nature of the students' educational 'problems' and attempted to provide solutions to these problems for staff and students alike (Ballard, 1987; Ballard & Clanchy, 1984, 1991; Burns, 1991; Gassin, 1982). Others such as Samuelowicz (1987) compared the perceptions of student learning problems between the academics and students themselves. Other researchers emphasised English and its role in the academic performances of overseas students (Bradley & Bradley, 1984; Neumann, 1985; Wicks, 1996). Overwhelmingly, the perceived problems can be distilled into language and learning issues, with the students posited as embodying approaches derived from their cultural, social, political, economic and educational backgrounds that were valid at home but inappropriate in the Australian context (Ninnes, 1999). The dominant view in the literature was that study in Australian universities was significantly different to the educational experiences of students, particularly those from Asian and Pacific backgrounds. The key preoccupations of 'first wave' researchers with student language and learning approaches are summarised below.

## Language issues

For first wave researchers, a lack of English language proficiency was seen as a major impediment to academic and social adjustment in Australian universities (e.g. Ballard & Clanchy, 1984, 1991; Barker et al., 1991; Bradley & Bradley, 1984; Burns, 1991; Gassin, 1982; Neumann, 1985; Nixon, 1993; Robertson et al., 2000; Samuelowicz, 1987). Ballard and Clanchy (1984) in their manual for Asian students studying abroad stated that nearly all foreign students who came to Australia at the time had problems with English.

In other work in the 1980s, Bradley and Bradley (1984) found that students from non-English-speaking countries often ranked language as their primary problem. A number of authors and student counsellors at the time (Ballard, 1987; Barker et al., 1991; Samuelowicz, 1987) made the point that if Asian students were having problems with their studies, both they and their university teachers automatically assumed that the fault lay with the students' English language levels.

## Learning issues

First wave researchers were also focused on overseas students' learning approaches. These approaches were indexes of the culturally inscribed education systems of home countries that were seen as indelible and immutable, and at odds with the requirements of the host system. Researchers such as Ballard and Clanchy (1991) proposed differences between Eastern and Western cultural systems as explanations for the problems experienced by students. They wanted academics to move beyond what they saw as the clichés about inappropriate student thinking and poor English. These researchers and others (e.g. Barker *et al.*, 1991; Bradley & Bradley, 1984; Burns, 1991; Felix, 1993; Samuelowicz, 1987) argued that the problems could be ameliorated by strategies and intervention programmes, especially during the pre-study phase.

Different cultural attitudes to knowledge were one of the features of teaching and learning proposed to explain the misalignments between overseas students and the Western academy. Ballard and Clanchy (1991) argued that attitudes to knowledge can be conserving or extending, and are on a continuum in all cultures but often prioritised at different stages in the education system. In Australian education, conserving attitudes dominate the classroom in primary and secondary schools. Teachers present the information, attitudes and skills. The students reproduce what has been taught, learning largely through imitation and memorisation.

There is a shift in late secondary school from reproductive to more analytical and critical approaches to learning. By the end of tertiary education, particularly for research degrees, the emphasis has moved again to a more speculative approach in which students are expected to hypothesise and create new understandings. Ballard and Clanchy (1991) maintained that the other side of the binary in this model is the Eastern system. For them:

> Many Asian cultures place much greater emphasis than ours does on the conserving attitude to knowledge: scholarship is traditionally manifested by an extensive and accurate knowledge of the wisdom contained in authoritative texts or the sayings of earlier scholars and sages. (Ballard & Clanchy, 1991: 15)

They acknowledged that while 20th-century education systems in China, Japan and South-East Asian countries are no longer characterised by explicit reliance on ancient texts or early scholars, there remains the legacy of earlier educational traditions in all societies and their classrooms. In societies where respect for the past predominates and the authority of the teacher is supreme, the classroom will reflect this. The classroom will not be a place where it is appropriate to question the teacher or to argue a different point of view. Yet, questioning and probing is precisely what lecturers in Western universities are expecting of students (Ballard & Clanchy, 1991). These culturally shaped differences are often not recognised but cause many of the problems encountered by academics teaching overseas students.

The concerns of academics working with international students were another focus of first wave research. For example, Samuelowicz's much-cited 1987 study found that academics overwhelmingly believed that overseas students presented learning approaches that were incompatible with Australian Western-orientated traditions. For academics, the problems posed by overseas students included language difficulties, inappropriate study skills, reproductive and surface-level approaches to learning, little experience in participating in group discussions and a lack of ability to think critically and speculatively. Overall, the finding was that many Asian students adopt a 'reproducing orientation' and surface approach to learning, characterised by a reliance on memorisation, excessive attention to isolated facts, details and parts of arguments. The view was that this approach was in stark contrast to the Australian system that encouraged students to guess, estimate, try out possible solutions and make judgements (Samuelowicz, 1987). In relation to classroom behaviour, overseas students were seen as passive and accustomed to being recipients of knowledge rather than active participants in the critical construction of new knowledge. Moreover, overseas students were seen as having excessive regard for authority and were not questioning of the teacher. In other words, the teacher was expected to be the constant authority on what was 'correct'. Samuelowicz (1987: 124) attributed this behaviour to the 'educational practices in many Asian countries' where one point is presented and arguments about different points of view or a personal point of view are not developed.

Samuelowicz (1987) also investigated the concerns of students and found that postgraduate students were more aware than undergraduates of the need to think critically and independently. The students' awareness was explained as the capacity to compare several different tertiary education systems and to recognise the greater emphasis on critical and speculative thinking in postgraduate courses. Felix (1993) also researched the experiences of international postgraduate students and found they were in a delicate situation because they were mature-age people from educated and professional backgrounds who in their own countries were respected and functioning successfully at high levels of expertise. However, as overseas students in Australia they often needed help with basic tasks such as writing an essay but found it difficult to ask for help.

## What is the literature saying?

The wave metaphor is useful in capturing the ongoing salience of some elements of this approach in current international higher education. The models of intervention proposed by first wave researchers continue to be mainstays in university responses to international students' academic needs. Most interventions are offered as preparation programmes that are designed to have a hypodermic effect on students' academic capabilities (Kettle & Luke, 2013): treating problems through short, sharp injections of academic literacy and English language skills. English language centres are a feature of university campuses, progressing students through general English and academic English programmes in preparation for entry into award courses.

A key discourse running through first wave literature was difference and deficiency in terms of most overseas students' English language levels and approaches to learning and classroom participation. The view was that while students' approaches were appropriate in their home contexts, they were incommensurate with Australian expectations. Students' skills, resources and approaches were considered deficient and best addressed through intensive 'top-up' in intervention programmes. These understandings were well-meaning; indeed, as already noted, many of the researchers were student counsellors interested in the well-being of both students and academics. Their descriptions of the reproduction of culturally based knowledge systems through different levels of education continue to be useful reference points. For example, in Australia, school-based curricula are often developmental, progressing knowledge from reproduction to more critical and speculative approaches.

Despite the insights provided by the initial body of research, a number of limitations exist which can be summarised into four points, as argued by Ninnes (1999): (i) the focus on shortcomings in students' approaches to learning; (ii) exaggeration of the extent to which analytical and critical approaches are adopted by students in Australian universities; (iii) assumptions that international students' approaches to learning are static and require external intervention to change; and (iv) misrepresentations of learning in students' home countries. These critiques highlight the defining assumption in first wave literature that culturally derived knowledge systems are static and immutable – in both the institution and the student. Cultures are essentialised and there is little recognition of change. Essentialisation invites power relations that assert 'us' and 'them', and the marginalisation of Others. Chowdhury and Phan (2014) argue that in the literature such as summarised above, Western styles of learning are taken for granted and 'other' ways of learning are constructed as deficiencies. They maintain that stereotyping and generalisations largely hide the dynamic of international student engagement in learning – a point that this book actively addresses.

## The second wave of literature: International students as different but adaptive

The second wave of research on international students in higher education emphasised development and adaptation; it recognised difference but also the adaptive strategies that students used to adjust their learning to the new academic context. Research with this orientation was most evident during the 1990s in the work of Renshaw and Volet (1995), Chalmers and Volet (1997) and Volet et al. (1994).

Renshaw and Volet (1995) in their study of first-year university students at an Australian university compared the tutorial participation of local and South-East Asian students. An aim of the study was to rebut what the researchers saw as the essentialising claims of previous research that South-East Asian students were 'quiet, compliant and reproductive learners' (Renshaw & Volet, 1995: 89). The researchers' position was that:

> If a more positive and differentiated perception of overseas students is to emerge among Australian academics, there needs to be sustained research on the needs of these students (academic, social, financial, and cultural needs) and an examination of their approaches to study that is sensitive to differences within and between groups. (Renshaw & Volet, 1995: 87)

Key findings from the study centred on tutorial participation and help-seeking initiatives (Renshaw & Volet, 1995). Observations in tutorials indicated that both local and South-East Asian students participated in tutorial discussions of their own accord and at the instigation of the tutor. Local students featured at the extreme high and low levels of participation while the South-East Asian students participated in a more uniform way. In terms of self-perceptions about tutorial participation, South-East Asian students rated themselves as significantly lower than the local students. When seeking help, it was found that both local and South-East Asian students preferred to check a textbook as a way of clarifying a misunderstanding. The Asian students gave higher ratings to the help-seeking strategies of asking a friend and consulting the tutor after the tutorial.

Renshaw and Volet (1995) concluded their report with the statement that their study was intended as a provocation to university staff to reassess their perceptions of South-East Asian students. They argued that the findings indicated adjustment to academic life was not predictable on the basis on a student's designation as 'South-East Asian'. Indeed, many self-perceptions about participation were similar between the local and overseas students. The researchers acknowledged that students from South-East Asian countries often had to deal with English language proficiency issues and make adjustments to their new academic, social and cultural environment. The emphasis, however, was on 'socially and culturally constituted strategies and resources that students will draw on as they move forward through their programs of study' (Renshaw & Volet, 1995: 104). For these researchers, advocacy was about altering deficit views and recognising the resourcefulness of students to progress their skills development and adjustment.

Chalmers and Volet (1997) adopted a similar position and canvassed first wave literature for what they claimed to be the misconceptions held by university teachers and administrators about South-East Asian students studying in Australia. They rejected what they saw as the homogenising tendency in Australian universities to refer to students from the Asian region as a group with similar cultural backgrounds and educational experiences. The misconceptions that they examined pertained to claims in earlier research about rote learning, passivity in class, a failure to mix socially, the inability to analyse and think critically and failure to adjust to Australian academic standards. The findings from the Chalmers and Volet (1997) study were:

(1) Rote learning: The researchers found that considerable confusion existed among academics about the difference between rote learning and memorisation, with the latter often associated erroneously with surface learning.
(2) Participation: A lack of class participation was not based on students being passive; rather, the researchers found that students were sensitive to issues of language competence and to feelings of insecurity if they were a minority group in a class.
(3) Not mixing with local students: Chalmers and Volet found that contrary to this claim, students wanted greater interaction with local students.
(4) South-East Asian students lack the skills for analysis and critical thinking: The researchers found that all the South-East Asian students in their study were aware of the need to critically analyse information and were prepared to adjust their learning styles accordingly.
(5) South-East Asian students do not easily adjust their learning to the Australian context: The researchers introduced the notion of adapting strategically over time as a means of explaining the long-term achievements of many overseas students.

## What is the literature saying?

The representation of international students constructed in the literature was motivated by the explicit objective to promote better understanding of the strategic efforts made by overseas students to adjust to a new academic context. The work was particularly directed at repudiating what it considered to be the stereotyping views of South-East Asian students reported in the first wave literature. The researchers argued for sensitivity to individual and group differences and highlighted the students' skills in adapting culturally and academically to the new context – similar, indeed, to their Australian counterparts.

The strength of this work was its empirical base. Many of its arguments continue to have relevance, for example, the focus on academic development in the form of skills and strategies and the emphasis on improving social cohesion. The desire of overseas students to have greater contact with local students has been borne out in a number of later studies, for example, Smart *et al.* (2000) and Smith *et al.* (2002), and is a priority in the Australian Government (2015a) 'Draft National Strategy for International Education'.

## The third wave of literature: The institution and its power relations

The third wave of literature on international students in the Western academy drew heavily on postcolonial and poststructuralist explanations that grew to prominence in the 2000s. The theories went beyond isolated skills and strategy development and endeavoured to provide a more comprehensive consideration of the social world incorporating power, discourse, identity and agency. In the Australian higher education context, Ninnes (1999) used Foucault's (1977) framework of disciplinary power to interrogate the mechanisms by which knowledge structures are established and maintained in universities. His study examined the responses and acculturation processes of a group of Indian students to the knowledge structures in a Master of Business Administration (MBA) course. The research objective was to identify the range of techniques deployed by the university to coerce students into adopting its forms of knowledge and the students' processes of acquiescence and resistance as they interacted with these demands.

In another Australian study, Doherty and Singh (2003) utilised the concept of 'Othering' from postcolonial theory to investigate the knowledge presented in academic preparation programmes for international students. The researchers found that the programmes provided an imagined version of Western knowledge and were designed to reassert the purity of 'how the West is done' in Australian universities (Doherty & Singh, 2003). They maintained that a stark contrast existed between the culture-boundness that academic English teachers associated with Asian international students and the transculturality the students ascribed to themselves.

Another study adopting a postcolonial perspective was conducted by Bullen and Kenway (2003) to compare the imagined views of international postgraduate women students held by academics and those held by the women themselves. The researchers maintained that the construction of so-called Oriental or Asian learning styles in much of the Australian literature set up a binary relation of us/them and west/east oppositions and that this opposition enabled Western educational superiority to be asserted. The researchers found mismatches existed with the academics persisting with colonialist representations of the women despite empirical evidence to the contrary. The academics in the study considered the women's learning styles to be irrational, as opposed to the Western rational; uncritical as opposed to critical; and static and regressive as opposed to flexible and progressive (Bullen & Kenway, 2003).

In the US, similar work was being done using notions of discursive practices and power to examine how people with different social profiles were marginalised in high-stakes educational practices. Like the Australian work, the American studies had overt normative agendas to achieve social change through revelation and critique. One much-cited example is Kubota's (2001) study on language and culture in the US classroom with particular focus on the experiences of Asian-American students. Kubota used theories of colonialism and postcolonialism to build a theory about the ways that the white, English-speaking American Self assumes the status of the norm while different cultures become the Other. This binary was made possible by the processes of essentialisation and homogenisation: the language and culture of the Other were reduced to elements of difference while the characteristics of the Self were posited as unproblematic and normal.

Kubota (2001: 23) identified three discursive practices 'that regulate the formation and interpretation of certain cultural images about learning and teaching'. The first discursive practice was Othering, that is, the practice whereby cultural differences are highlighted in order to distance the Other. Otherness becomes a problem only when it interferes with or presents a challenge to the Self. The second was the polarisation of the Self and the Other. This is achieved through comparisons where images of Self are often positive and contrasted with negative images of the Other. The third discursive practice assumes the culture of the Self as the norm, and by implication the Other as outside the norm. These practices operate to produce and maintain unequal relations of power between two cultures (Kubota, 2001). Kubota's work advanced the argument that culture can never be neutral and objective. Rather, it becomes the site of a struggle in which various power positions (ideological and political) compete with each other to promote representations of what is 'normal' and 'truth'. Through certain discursive practices, particular relations of power are reinforced in culturally and linguistically diverse classrooms that by virtue of exposure in critical work such as Kubota's, can be resisted and changed.

In another study directly related to international students in American universities, Leki (2001) focused on language and the social/academic interactions between native English-speaking (NES)[1] and NNES during group work projects. Her rationale was that despite the fact that many English learners in English-dominant countries are surrounded by NES students, not a lot was known about the social/academic relationships between the two groups. Leki found in her naturalistic case studies of six NNES/bilingual students over five years that the students' experiences of group interactions in the US context were not positive. This was despite reporting positive group work experiences in their home countries. She found that most of the problems were related to the social aspects of group work such as task allocation, individual contributions to the project and native speaker expectations of the capacities of non-native English speakers. The main concern for the international students was the lack of opportunity to contribute to the group; the domestic students made it clear that the NNES/bilingual international students were considered incapable of making significant contributions to the project. Four of the international students expressed dissatisfaction with the way that their domestic counterparts ignored and overruled their contributions. The experiences of the students in Leki's study were not dissimilar to those of the students in my classes, introduced in the Preface.

Leki (2001) utilised theories of power to conclude that the NNES students were constructed as less capable and as apprentices/novices while the domestic students positioned themselves as masters and experts. The NNES students did not see themselves as apprentices; rather, their assumptions were that they would be on an equal footing with their domestic counterparts. By refusing to allocate activities equitably, the domestic students used their power to deny the international students access to full participation in the project. Leki (2001) drew attention to the operation of power within group work tasks:

> Certainly group work evokes issues of power – the power to define others and to force them to behave in ways consonant with that construction. The voices of the least powerful, the NNES students, tended to be muted or ignored in the unsatisfactory group work experiences. Their own presumption of equality with the domestic students collided with the domestic students' construction of the NNES students as variously handicapped. (Leki, 2001: 61)

By 'variously handicapped', she is referring to the linguistic 'less than proficient' profiles of some NNES students and the bias on the part of some NES students that 'linguistic difficulty suggests intellectual incapacity' (Leki, 2001: 59). In response to her findings, Leki insisted that university teachers have a role to play in ensuring that there is equality of roles among students working as a group on a project task.

## Arguing the Need for Engagement as a New Approach

The changing representations of the international student are discernible in three chronological 'waves' of literature that have different points of prominence and continue to exist residually in the literature and practices of higher education. The first wave was motivated by concerns about difference in the academy and took a psychological/remediation approach. These orientations were superseded by a second wave grounded in social psychology that acknowledged the presence of difference but highlighted the efforts of students to adapt to the new academic requirements through skill and strategy development. The third wave moved beyond student difference to institutional power and the material effects of power and politics in the academic experiences of international students, especially those from different cultural and linguistic backgrounds.

Politics here is not in the sense of parliaments and politicians, but rather in what Pennycook (2001) calls understandings of power, to be found in all domains of life. While well-meaningness is evident in the work of all researchers across the decades, third wave researchers explicitly articulated power as an area of interest in the experience of the international student. The researchers' rationale is that critical examination of institutional practices can make visible inequities and the means by which they achieve naturalness and permanence. This approach is deconstructive in that it 'unpacks' the hegemonic nature of inequitable power relations for the purposes of awareness-raising and social change. To this end, some research highlights the ways that institutional power is resisted and selectively appropriated (e.g. Chowdhury & Phan, 2014; Ninnes, 1999).

Reconceptualising international student engagement as social practice necessitates drawing on behavioural, cognitive and sociopolitical understandings that were dominant in previous waves of literature. Following the wave metaphor, resonances of past work can contribute to new perspectives on international students and their relationship with the Western university, especially in relation to teaching and learning. Engagement foregrounds student discernment, actions and achievements in learning. It recognises agency while also acknowledging the power relations operating in high-stakes institutional practices. The students' efforts and authority on 'what counts' in the new setting take centre stage rather than the institution. The orientation in this incipient fourth wave of research pushes the research trajectory beyond the discourses of difference, dominance and disenfranchisement, not to dismiss or diminish them but to examine micro-ethnographically how the students respond to the confluence of new academic demands. To continue the alliteration, the approach dispenses with past preoccupations: the students as deficient, or different, or dupes subjected to the dictates of the university. Critical work that casts the students as unwitting subjects in their own subjugation misses the point about discernment, agency and the complex negotiation of social conditions that all social interactants participate in.

This 'critique of the critical' is evident in various fields. For example, House (2003) argues vehemently against critical positions in the field of English as a lingua franca (ELF) that decry the spread of English for communication as linguistic imperialism (e.g. Phillipson, 1992). She maintains that the position is patronising and implies that EFL users do not know what is in their interest; ELF users are posited as pawns in a new form of imperialism. House argues that in contrast, languages for communication (such as ELF) should not be confused with languages for identification, and she cites examples from Europe of how English was the preferred language in post-World War II Germany and in Eastern European struggles against the Soviet empire and Russian.

In the field of international higher education, critical research on the subjection of international students within discourses of marketisation and difference is a crucial first step in explaining how dominant power structures are assembled and maintained. The work makes visible the marginalisation and exploitation of certain social groups – often minorities within the majority but not always. The proposition in this book is that social change benefits not only from negative criticism but also positive critique, that is, a step beyond exploitation and marginalisation to new knowledge about democratic participation and engagement. The need for this work is evident in commentary from the international education field. Ryan (2011) argues that despite critical efforts to explicate the 'rules of the game' to international students, concerns are still voiced by students about aspects of higher education teaching and learning, and academics continue to complain about the students' lack of skills. In addition, critical scholars such as Chowdhury and Phan (2014) maintain that the dynamic of international student engagement in learning is yet to be addressed.

The implication for research is investigations that are reconstructive, that is, they identify practices, discourses and texts that are positive and transformative in promoting student equity and opportunity. Luke (2004) argues that positive research can offer exemplars of equitable practice. The argument here is that exemplars provide insights into areas that are working and those that are not, and can inform decisions in the field. The approach prioritises students' experiences of 'what works' in the university, or more specifically 'which bits work' and 'how'. This is a productive starting point for universities needing to address teaching and learning concerns that have remained unresolved for decades and will be made more acute by ratcheting up recruitment imperatives.

This book presents a case study of exemplary teaching as judged by a group of postgraduate international students. The objective of the study was to identify in micro-ethnographic detail the practices that afforded the students participation, legitimation and academic success. It accords with calls for greater practice-based research in higher education as a means of understanding the impact of institutional initiatives on the lived experiences of students and academics (e.g. Clegg, 2009). The approach required a practice-based approach to uncover the complexity of engagement. As such, it demanded 'thinking through the middle' and enlisting different epistemological perspectives, including those dominating previous waves of research.

This work holds the promise of new insights into the complexity of student engagement and the factors that generate transition towards academic competence and confidence. The emphasis is on 'becoming' and the facilitators of new academic 'becomings' including institutional practices such as teaching where transgressive spaces can be found to do things differently, albeit within the sanctions of the university. This is an account of power at the everyday level; it is about people managing themselves and the conditions tentatively and with growing levels of success across time, aided by 'supportive others' such as teachers.

The following chapter draws these points into an explanatory framework that provides deeper understandings of international student engagement in tertiary study. Moreover, it shows how the institution can embrace diversity while also retaining valued standards. This is not a triumphalist account but an attempt to throw into relief the complexity of engaging in the everyday academic practices that constitute the international study experience.

## Note

(1)  The terms *native-English-speaking* (NES) and *nonnative-English-speaking* (NNES) are Leki's (2001).

# 3 Conceptualising International Student Engagement

## Introduction

### The ubiquity of engagement

*Engagement* is a word that is currently everywhere. It is pervasive in the school, teacher development and university literature. School policies and teacher standards by organisations such as the Australian Institute for Teaching and School Leadership (AITSL, 2013) link engagement to improved student learning outcomes, although they concede that engagement is an ambiguous term and is often poorly defined. In the higher education literature, the word is ubiquitous but used in a multitude of ways. A scan of online mission and vision statements from a sample of universities in Australia, New Zealand, the UK and the US points to the extensive use of the word. Examples can be clustered according to meaning: engagement as multiple entities (*practical engagement, student engagement, community engagement, real-world engagement, lifelong engagement, institutional engagement, critical engagement*); engagement as part of a dyadic or triadic relationship, often related to learning (*learning, discovery and engagement; focus, engagement and experience; engagement and participation; engagement and collaboration; institutional engagement, academic empowerment and their sense of belonging*); engagement as partnership (*engagement with the broader community; engagement with our alumni*); engagement as attribute (*engagement of practitioners; engagement of researchers*); and engagement as process (*connect, engage and creatively support; engagement plans; engagement strategies*). At my university, the current mission statement, known as the Blueprint, contains 9 references to *engagement* and 2 to *engage*: a total of 11 references across a 9-page document (Queensland University of Technology, 2016). *Engagement* is posited overwhelmingly as positive and aspirational but the references, like in other policy documents, are multifarious.

In the Preface, the point was made that engagement has felicitous ambiguity, that is, it can be an action and a thing. This functionality means that the term can be utilised in multiple ways by policy writers and others as shown in the text analysis above. The concept is clearly popular but its almost cavalier use raises questions about whether it has become a catch-all term in danger of losing its potency. For example, what is being referenced in *student engagement* and *real-world engagement*? Their syntactic structures are the same (noun as adjective+noun) but their references are different: the first refers to the student and her/his actions while the second refers (silently) to the university and its aspirations towards partnerships with the 'real world'. These statements might appear benign in policy; in practice, however, they are difficult to identify and quantify. Indeed, AITSL (2013) maintains that much of the school literature has focused on disengagement rather than understanding and promoting engagement. The organisation acknowledges that engagement is complex and urges more work in defining it and explaining its links to learning outcomes.

## Engagement in schooling and higher education literature

In an attempt to address the ambiguity around engagement in the school sector, AITSL (2013) has prepared a paper providing definitions and indicators for the measurement of engagement. The paper drew on the work of Fredricks *et al.* (2004) to conceptualise engagement as a multilevelled construct comprising cognitive, behavioural and emotional engagement. The work of Fredricks *et al.* is well-cited in the academic literature and often forms the foundation of discussions on engagement, particularly in relation to schooling. Subsequent work by Fredricks and McCloskey (2012) also relates to school student engagement (and disengagement) and presents methods for assessing engagement.

The Fredricks *et al.* (2004) and Fredricks and McCloskey (2012) literature defines cognitive engagement as a student's psychological investment in her/his own learning. It refers to the student's use of learning strategies and self-regulation to promote learning. Behavioural engagement is the student's participation in class and extracurricular activities; in the school setting, behavioural engagement might include whether a student attends class on time (AITSL, 2013). It links to cognitive engagement in that it ensures that students are physically ready to learn. The third construct is emotional and foregrounds the student's relationships. It highlights the interest and values that students attribute to teachers, classmates and the school. Emotional engagement can include whether the student feels a sense of belonging and being important in the school. In school and learning practices, this type of engagement is also called 'identification' (AITSL, 2013).

The higher education literature on engagement mirrors the school literature in that it references the work of Fredricks *et al.* (2004) and Fredricks and Closkey (2012) and is concerned primarily with disengagement. With the rise of mass high education, the question is being asked about how to prevent disengagement and promote engagement for greater student retention and improved academic performance (e.g. Baron & Corbin, 2012; Kahn, 2014). In the Australian context, academics are increasingly concerned about poor attendance, a lack of preparation for tutorials and disinterest in active learning (Baron & Corbin, 2012). The concerns are with the general student population and are not focused on international students. The Australian government has linked student engagement with quality and funding. One of the markers of engagement is attrition, leading to concerted efforts by universities to retain students, particularly those in first year. Based in the UK, Kahn (2014) also highlights the growing problem of student engagement with reference to the general student cohort. He identifies weak theorisation of engagement as a construct and notes that while some research has identified certain practices that are deemed effective in engaging students, little has been done to foreground the role of the student in shaping her/his own engagement. He invokes Fredricks *et al.*'s (2004) call for a richer view of students' behaviours, feelings and thoughts and utilises realist social theory to propose student engagement as a mode of reflexivity and co-reflexivity. While Kahn's work is an attempt to include social relations and tasks in the definition of student engagement, it does not reference the particular conditions encountered by international students. Nonetheless, his work is helpful in highlighting the role of reflexivity and social relations, and in reinforcing the need for students to be at the centre of efforts to explain their engagement in learning.

In American colleges and universities, Harper and Quaye (2015) maintain that engagement, connectivity and belongingness continue to be problematic for students from diverse backgrounds. With a focus on undergraduate study, they argue that groups such as students of colour, veterans and gay, lesbian and bisexual people buy into the rhetoric of inclusiveness and equity but are disappointed by the carelessness with which their engagement is treated in practice. Rather, institutions have a responsibility to engage all students; the diversity of contemporary student cohorts means that universities and colleagues cannot depend on sameness. Faculty need to listen to students and gain nuanced understanding of their needs. The questions remain about the nature of engagement; how it is achieved; and its impact on outcomes (Harper & Quaye, 2015).

One body of work focused exclusively on engaging international students is by Lee (2015) in the American higher education context. She orientates to the discrimination suffered by international students based on the colour of their skin and negative assumptions about their home country and proposes neo-racism as an explanatory framework. The strategies that she proposes are designed to improve conditions for students and are directed at institutions and staff. They include the development of 'international consciousness' in educators and the provision of services such as financial support and student affairs officers. By engaging students, Lee (2015) means the initiatives that colleges and universities can take to prevent discriminatory acts against international students.

## Proposing engagement as practice

This chapter proposes a model of international student engagement as practice. It places social practices at the centre of student engagement in the academic life of an overseas university. The benefits of focusing on practice are threefold: (i) practice foregrounds human action, that is, how social life gets *done* within the prevailing social conditions; (ii) practice prioritises the *doers* as the authorities on the experience, in this case, the students and their processes of engagement; and (iii) practice as socially contextualised action has been usefully theorised (e.g. Fairclough, 2003; Foucault, 1982) in ways that illuminate the complex antecedents, actions and achievements that I argue constitute international student engagement.

The insights garnered from a practice perspective provide a powerful reflection back to university administrators and teachers of the institutional conditions and efforts of international students. The approach has the potential to 'make strange' institutional orthodoxies and contribute new understandings of 'what works and what doesn't work' in the institution for culturally and linguistically diverse students. By orienting engagement to social practice, the negotiation of structure and agency in the student experience is foregrounded, thus emphasising the student's efforts to mediate the external order of university practices through her/his internal resources and actions. In play as well is institutional support, most crucially social 'others' such as teachers.

The research focus on practice aligns with the calls for clearer understandings of what international students actually do to support their success at an overseas university (e.g. Clegg, 2009; Ryan, 2011). The chapter presents one theorisation of engagement in higher education (Kahu, 2013) and extends it by incorporating social theories of the human subject (Foucault, 1982) and practice (Chouliaraki & Fairclough, 1999; Fairclough, 2003; Kettle, 2011). Social practice is the point at which the institutional order of the university takes effect in people's lives. It is here that the human subject is subjected to the social conditions and responds using her/his available resources and individual actions. Social practice is the driver of social activity in institutional settings and at the heart of student engagement.

# Towards a Conceptual Model of International Student Engagement

## Promising new directions

As noted above, the concept of student engagement in higher education research literature is plagued by poor definitions. In work from New Zealand, Kahu (2013) argues that a lack of distinction exists between three key dimensions of engagement: (i) the state of engagement and being engaged; (ii) the factors or antecedents that influence engagement; and (iii) the consequences of engagement. Like much of the literature presented above, Kahu's approach to engagement relates to the dominant majority of university students rather than international students. It is of interest here because it goes beyond some of that above to include sociocultural and holistic considerations.

Kahu (2013) identifies four relatively discrete approaches to engagement: (i) the behavioural; (ii) the psychological; (iii) the sociocultural; and (iv) the holistic. As noted above, the behavioural perspective links student behaviour and teaching; it aligns student engagement with high-quality learning outcomes (Australian Council for Educational Research [ACER], 2010). Attempts to measure student engagement have been conducted in the US with the National Survey of Student Engagement (NSSE) (Kuh, 2001) and in Australia and New Zealand with the Australasian Survey of Student Engagement (AUSSE). The NSSE has canvassed approximately four million undergraduates since 2000 and comprises 10 engagement indicators and a set of high-impact practices; categories include academic challenge, learning with peers, experiences with faculty, campus environment undergraduates and high-impact practices (Harper & Quaye, 2015).

The AUSSE is conducted in universities with staff and students at undergraduate and postgraduate levels (ACER, 2010). The student questionnaires on engagement have six scales: active learning, academic challenge, student and staff interactions, enriching educational experiences, supportive learning environment and work-integrated learning. In addition, there are measures of seven outcomes: higher-order thinking, general learning outcomes, general development outcomes, career readiness, average overall grade, departure intention and overall satisfaction (ACER, 2010). Concerns have been raised that surveys such as AUSSE are not defining engagement comprehensively enough (e.g. Kahu, 2013). By focusing on the factors that institutions can control, this version of engagement is excluding student issues such as motivation and emotion, and blurring the distinctions between three key dimensions of engagement: (i) the state of being engaged; (ii) the factors that influence it; and (iii) its consequences.

The psychological approach as defined by Kahu (2013) is most evident in school literature and views engagement as an internal social-psychological process that operates across time at varying levels of intensity. It includes behavioural considerations such as positive conduct and rule-following as well as involvement in learning through time-on-task and asking questions. Additional considerations are cognition and affect. Cognition refers to students' investment in learning and their strategies for self-regulation and deep learning, while affect refers to the emotions associated with learning. The affective dimension is considered a strength of the psychological approach because it acknowledges the intensity of learning and the importance of feelings such as belonging and the role of motivation (Kahu, 2013). In second language acquisition (SLA) theory, motivation is a wellspring of research. Much of the work seeks to establish motivation as a prerequisite for effective second language learning. For example, one second language theory of motivation foregrounds the importance of success in achieving success; in other words, success and self-efficacy in SLA drive effort and generate further success (e.g. Macaro, 2003).

As in many other fields, the exclusive 'in the head' focus of the psychological approach has given rise to questions about the influence of factors beyond the individual. The sociocultural approach examines the impact of contextual factors on engagement, or more often, on alienation and the lack of engagement (Kahu, 2013; Mann, 2001). This literature is often orientated to power and marginalisation, such as disciplinary power and the pressure of performativity within disciplines (Mann, 2001). Questions of identity and market-driven changes in universities such as increased fee structures are investigated as reasons for engagement or, conversely, a lack of engagement or alienation.

Finally, Kahu identifies a fourth approach to student engagement that is holistic and attempts to draw together the other perspectives. She cites work from the UK (Bryson *et al.*, 2009) which conceives of student engagement as the amalgam of perceptions, expectations and experiences as a student. Engagement is a continuum that is dynamic across different tasks, classrooms, courses and institutions. This approach highlights teachers and the importance of the teacher's disposition and capacity to generate respect and a sense of belonging in the classroom. In New Zealand, Zepke and Leach (2010) found that teachers play a major role in promoting student engagement through strategies such as enriching the educational experience and raising students' expectations. Kahu (2013) regards the holistic position as useful because it foregrounds emotion but critiques it for failing to distinguish between engagement and its antecedents. She maintains that student attributes such as heightened expectations are antecedents to engagement; engagement itself is the individual psychological state comprising affect, cognition and behaviour. A conceptual framework for engagement needs to distinguish between the three dimensions of (i) the antecedents of engagement, (ii) the moment of engagement and (iii) the consequences of engagement. It needs to ensure the connections between sociocultural and sociopolitical factors and the psychological (Kahu, 2013).

## Putting the student in engagement

Kahu's framework represents an attempt to broaden the concept of engagement, incorporating dimensions that have been historically disaggregated. The different approaches to engagement identified in her work mirror the literature on international students and the waves of research orientations discussed in Chapter 2. The benefits of complementarity are highlighted in Kahu's holistic approach and in the practice-based model proposed in this book. Bringing together traditionally separated behavioural, psychological and sociocultural perspectives embraces complexity and makes available a suite of conceptual tools that can be deployed as needed.

Practice is the means adopted here to conceptualise international student engagement in ways that are informative and productive for research and teaching. Practice offers a perspective that is located in experience; its focus is the range of elements that combine in particular relationships to form the lived actions, knowledges, and identities associated with engagement. Kahu (2013) makes an important contribution to the literature on engagement. The work, however, does not prioritise student actions and experiences. Nor does it focus on international students as a significant minority group within the student population; rather, the assumed student is a member of the dominant majority at the university.

This book extends Kahu's work by examining the particularities of international student engagement. Three considerations are in play:

(1) antecedents (the contextual conditions including disciplinary practices in the institution; student variables such as English language proficiency, academic skills and expectations; and institutional support for students including teaching);
(2) actions (the students' behaviours; cognition and emotions, including learning strategies);
(3) achievements (the student outcomes including the attainment of academic and personal goals).

These three 'As' constitute the dimensions of engagement that are proposed in this book; they foreground context, interrelationships between social and psychological factors, and time. Social practice provides an effective means of explaining engagement in students' lives; that is, how the students do engagement as a mediated response to the contextual conditions, through available resources and actions, for the purpose of achieving certain ends. Associated with doing are knowing and being; practice incorporates the students' doing, knowing and being as they 'practise' their way into the academic expectations of the foreign university. Social practice is the foundation of academically contextualised social life and is elaborated below.

## International Student Engagement as Social Practice

Social practice is defined here using theories of the human subject in social life (Foucault, 1982) and social practice as the centre of life, including institutional life (Chouliaraki & Fairclough, 1999; Fairclough, 2003; Kettle, 2011). While Foucault's theory of social life is often associated with poststructuralism (although he never referred to himself as a poststructuralist) and therefore at odds with Fairclough's critical discourse approach, the perspectives have points of contact. For example, Fairclough acknowledges that he is the beneficiary of Foucault's insights into discourse and power.

Critical scholars traditionally see their research as explicitly documenting the injustices suffered by people for the purpose of effecting social change. Poststructuralists, on the other hand, conceive of the human being as always constituted in discourse/power relations. For critical theorists, the problem with the poststructuralist position is that it surrenders normative, aspirational claims and the autonomy of the human (e.g. Benhabib, 1991). For poststructuralists, the concern with critical theory is that it positions the human external to its context and constraints (e.g. Butler, 1991).

Despite the differences and the debates, synthesis of the two approaches is possible and beneficial. Fraser (1991) argues that synergies can be exploited in ways that complement rather than contradict each other. For example, she maintains it is perfectly possible for the human subject to be both culturally situated and capable of critique. Clegg's (2009) call for more research-based accounts of practice in higher education dismisses the denials of a connection between 'is' and 'ought'. She argues that there is never a need to preclude descriptive social research from critically oriented, normative analysis.

The productive potential of Foucault's theory of social life and Fairclough's theory of social practice lies in their capacity to explain engagement in the everyday lives of international students. Foucault provides understanding of the students as human subjects enmeshed in the social conditions of the Western academy while Fairclough delivers the mechanism for analysing the details of practice. Put another way, Foucault's theories provide a means of explaining what social/institutional life is for the student while Fairclough's socially theorised method provides explanation of how the student does social/institutional life. The synthesis is an approach that reveals the particularities of the everyday: 'through analyses ... to question over and over again, to disturb people's mental habits, ... to dissipate what is familiar and accepted, to re-examine the rules and institutions' (Foucault, 1996b: 462).

## Explaining the human subject

Reviewing his life work shortly before his death, Foucault (1982) concludes that his project was in fact always about the human being. He puts it this way: '(t)he goal of my work during the last twenty years ... has been to create a history of the different modes by which, in our culture, human beings are made subjects' (Foucault, 1982: 208). He explains these modes in the three 'phases' of his work.

The first phase – archaeology – used the mode of inquiry. That is, it inquired into the ways that human beings become the subjects of the human sciences and are 'objectivised'. The social sciences are seen as discourse formations with four principles, including the rules that govern and regulate actors' speech acts. In the second phase – genealogy – archaeology is extended to include power, specifically the relations between systems of truth and modalities of power. While archaeology isolates discursive practices and their rules of production, genealogy concentrates on the relations of power connected to discourse formations. Of interest are the external technologies of power which control the body and mind of the human subject and divide it 'within' itself or from others. Notable examples are the mad from the sane and the sick from the healthy. Finally, in the third 'phase' – ethics – there is continuation of the logic but the focus shifts to the human subject herself/himself. The point of interest is the ways in which the human being makes itself a subject through its practices of self-regulation, that is, the government of the self. The focus is the active self-operating within social and institutional constraints.

Power makes individuals into subjects. Foucault (1982) defines *subject* in two ways: (i) being subject to someone else by control and dependence, and (ii) being tied to one's own identity by a conscience or self-knowledge. In both cases, the meanings suggest a type of power which 'subjugates and makes subject to' (Foucault, 1982: 212). Given this position, it is hardly surprising that Foucault (1996a) rejects the idea of a founding and sovereign human subject. Rather, his investigations are always pointed at the historical conditions that make various types of differentiated subjects possible in the first place. This insight is helpful in understanding the historical moments that generate different representations of international students in the higher education research literature. Foucault's interest is the processes of subject-production, or subjection, and the ways in which they are achieved by modern forms of scientific knowledge. In addition, he is interested in the implications for the individual and her/his subjectivity or sense of self in the social and historical conditions.

The depictions of international students in the research literature constitute an exercise in subject-production. The implications for power and subjectivity are that the individual cannot be conceived as a nucleus that is self-contained and prevailed upon by power which crushes and subdues. Rather, Foucault (1980: 98) posits that it is 'already one of the prime effects of power that certain bodies, certain gestures, certain discourses, certain desires, come to be identified and constituted as individuals'.

## Discourse and how things come to matter

The study of discourse within specific historically situated practices involves the differentiation of historically situated knowledge *savoir* from *connaissance* which is the general domain of knowledge, a distinction not made in English (Foucault, 1996e). Foucault's (1996e: 14) aim is to look for the underlying knowledge (*savoir*) which makes the practices, institutions and theories of this particular society possible: 'the stratum of knowledge that constitutes them historically'. To do this, he goes to the practices, institutions and theories and looks for 'traces' or more specifically, *ensembles* of common traces which constitute a homogeneous domain (Foucault, 1996c).

This approach to inquiry is embedded in his radical redefinition of discourse diverging from traditional linguistic notions of text to four interrogative, disruptive principles: (i) the reversal of the positiveness of 'the author' and disciplines; (ii) discourse as discontinuous; (iii) recognition that discourse produces the things of which it speaks; and (iv) recognition that discourse is best understood by examining its conditions of possibility, that is, the external conditions of its existence, appearance and regularity (Foucault, 1984). Foucault's definition of discourse as discontinuous discursive practices and sets of statements about an object which circulate without authorship and without discursive and disciplinary controls has become the main understanding of discourse in poststructuralist research in the humanities and social sciences (Threadgold, 2000).

The analyst's interest is the way in which one discursive formation comes to be substituted for another. The aim is not to discover the moment of a discourse's birth; rather, its conditions, actions and effects leading to transformation. In his theorisation of the properties of discourse, Foucault (1972) proposes the statement (or *énoncé*) as the unit of a discourse. Relations between statements in a discourse are not necessarily geographically close and continuous; rather, they operate as 'systems of dispersion' and are 'full of gaps, intertwined with one another, interplays of differences, distances, substitutions, transformations' (Foucault, 1972: 37). To account for their interconnections and regularity across dispersed sites, he posits discourse as a discursive formation.

A discursive formation exists according to four rules or conditions of existence:

- the formation of objects;
- the formation of speaking positions about and in relation to the topic at hand;
- the formation of concepts;
- the formation of strategies or thematic choices.

These conditions are a complex group of relations that are in effect the constitutive elements of discourse. A discourse then is a number of dispersed statements for which a set of conditions of existence can be defined (Foucault, 1972). This is an eminently useful tool for examining the constitution of discursive entities such as English and what counts as English in the Western academy. The conditions of existence are presented in more detail below.

### The formation of objects

In the formation of objects, discursive formations produce the object of which they speak (Dreyfus & Rabinow, 1982). This is in opposition to the view that objects exist independently and are simply referred to in a discourse. Objects, as defined by Foucault, are objects of knowledge; they are entities which particular disciplines or sciences recognise within their field of interest and which they take as targets of investigation. Foucault (1972) provides three 'planes of differentiation' in which the particular objects of a discourse may appear: surfaces of emergence, authorities of delimitation and grids of specification.

*Surfaces of emergence* are those places where particular discursive 'objects' may emerge and be accorded status. They are not the same in different types of discourse, different societies and different historical periods. They have a delimiting function in that they have a 'margin of tolerance' and a threshold beyond which exclusion is demanded. The authorities in society which 'delimit, designate, name and establish' something as an object are the *authorities of delimitation* (Foucault, 1972: 42). *Grids of specification* are the systems by which different historically and socially situated ideas are 'divided, contrasted, related, regrouped, classified, derived from one another as objects' (Foucault, 1972: 42). The example that Foucault uses is specifying different kinds of madness as objects within psychiatric discourse.

### The formation of enunciative modalities

The significant point with respect to the formation of enunciative modalities is the relationship between the human subject and the statement, that is, what can be said. The statement positions human subjects, both the producer of the statement and those being addressed, in particular ways. Enunciative modalities are types of discursive activity such as describing, forming hypotheses and teaching which have their own subject positions. For Foucault (1972: 50), the question is about who has the right to speak with the presumption that what she/he says is true: 'What is the status of individuals who sanctioned by law or tradition are able and expected to use such a discourse?'

For example, teaching involves positions such as teacher and student. A university student is subjected to a configuration of enunciative modalities and subject positions that form part of the prevailing discourses of higher education and the student's chosen discipline. The human subject is never considered to be the source of discourse. Rather, the discourse emerges through 'an anonymous field' of practices (Foucault, 1972).

### The formation of concepts

A particular discursive formation achieves its unity through a discernible set of statements and concepts that link to one another (Foucault, 1972). However, concepts shift, incompatible concepts overlap and all are subject to conceptual revolutions (Dreyfus & Rabinow, 1982). To explain this, Foucault diverges from the traditional linguistic reliance on internal rules and describes the external 'anonymous dispersion' of concepts across texts, books and other 'surfaces'. He rejects the notion that one theory replaces another because of its inherent superiority. Rather, conceptual shifts are attributed to the rules of an anonymous truth game.

Foucault defines concepts as the categories, elements and types which a discipline uses 'as an apparatus' in its field of interest. Concepts appear and circulate through the organisation of a 'field of statements' within discursive formations. This strategy gives rise to a rich description of the conceptual relationships within and between texts. These lead Foucault (1972: 98) to conclude that 'there can be no statement that in one way or another does not reactualize others', a point which immediately recalls Kristeva's (1986) notion of intertextuality.

### The formation of strategies

Within the properties of discourse, Foucault considers that unity and discontinuities can be further investigated by looking at themes and their articulation across different fields. For example, the theme of evolution was articulated differently in the 18th and 19th century – same theme, different discourses. If themes change, what then accounts for segments of continuity and change? Foucault (1972: 66) argues that a discursive formation makes available certain points of choice, or strategies: a 'field of possible options'.

This field of possibilities opens up a space for manoeuvre; certain strategies for action emerge, are exploited and then abandoned (Dreyfus & Rabinow, 1982). Not all strategies are possible; the formation rules determine which options can be realised. This insight is extremely useful in explaining transgressive spaces within institutional discourses. It gives recognition to the ways that teachers can simultaneously attend to the assessment needs of second language international students while remaining within the parameters of university policy.

## Discourse at work in educational institutions

Foucault expands his thesis on discourse formation to the ways that discourses operate in society, that is, the procedures by which they are controlled, selected, organised and redistributed. These procedures manipulate discourse in social activities and institutions and are particularly evident in education at all levels, including universities. The first set of procedures are exclusionary and exclude particular discourses from practice by means of prohibition; rejection of the speech of certain social members (for example, the madman); and the determination of what is true and false in a particular historical period, known as the *will to truth*. The will to truth has 'prodigious machinery' (Foucault, 1984: 114) in institutions where it is reinforced by practices such as pedagogy, books and libraries, history and research.

The second set of procedures exercise control internally within a discourse and are mainly concerned with the production and reproduction of particular knowledge. Key procedures include the scientific discipline which defines a domain of objects, a set of methods and a corpus of propositions that are considered to be true (Foucault, 1984). Another procedure selecting and redistributing discourse is the commentary which reproduces major narratives. Education perpetuates certain commentaries thus ensuring their permanence and dominance.

The third set of procedures imposes rules on individuals and prevents certain people from having access to a discourse: 'None shall enter the order of discourse if he [sic] does not satisfy certain requirements or if he is not, from the outset, qualified to do so' (Foucault, 1984: 120). Again, these procedures can be linked to education. The social dimension of discourse appropriation differentiates the uptake of discourses by different individuals in education. This is despite its claim to provide all individuals with access to all discourses.

## Power/Knowledge: Education's Quintessential Relationship

To study power, Foucault investigates 'truth' and the ways that knowledge produced in contemporary society affect human subjects. He labels what he is studying power/knowledge, with the slash suggesting that for his purposes, power and knowledge cannot be separated. For him, power and knowledge imply each other; power relations constitute a field of knowledge and in turn, knowledge presupposes certain power relations (Foucault, 1977). Discourse and truth are central to establishing and maintaining power/knowledge relations. Truth is a 'thing of this world'; it has a history. Regimes of truth are produced and sustained by systems of power. They are produced through apparatuses such as universities and the media and are widely circulated through education.

Foucault (1987) uses the metaphor of 'game' to conceptualise these relations and their machinery for establishing and maintaining certain 'truths'. The subject requires multiple subjectivities to navigate the various 'games' encountered in social life including education. It does not have the same relationships towards itself when it is a political subject as it does when it is attempting to fulfil its sexual desires. Rather, a different kind of subject or a different form of relationship with oneself is operating as the subject constitutes different subjectivities for different games of truth.

## The nature of power

Foucault brings a number of key insights to his retheorisation of power. Firstly, for him power is 'always already there' in that it is coextensive with every social relationship. It follows that power is in fact power relations; to live socially is to be involved in power relations. Consequently, his question about power is not so much *What is power?* but rather *How is power exercised?* He wants to know what happens when individuals exert power over others. He defines the exercise of power as the way in which certain actions modify others. Important to this notion of power is the element of freedom. Relations of power are not possible unless the subjects are free. Freedom is the precondition for the exercise of power; this ensures that a relationship of power is always being 'provoked' by the possibility of resistance and insubordination. His famous term *governmentality* (Foucault, 1996f) refers to the whole group of relations and techniques that allow particular relations of power to be exercised.

## Power in modern society

Foucault conceptualises modern capitalist society as a disciplinary society; an age of social control. It is a society of supervision and surveillance. One of its characteristics is the supervisory regulation of aspects of life and life processes, or biopower. There is a constant supervision of individuals by people who have power over them – the school teacher, prison warden, physician – who as long as she/he exercises power, has the possibility of both supervising and of constructing a knowledge about the person being supervised. This knowledge is concerned with whether the individual is behaving as she/he should, in accordance with a rule or not, and whether she/he is progressing or not. In other words, this new knowledge is organised around the norm of what is normal, correct and what one must do.

The power in the disciplinary society operates through a 'web of microscopic capillary political power' which is established at the level of each person's very existence (Foucault, 2000: 86). This power works within the immediate everyday lives of individuals: it categorises them, attaches them to their own identities, imposes a law of truth on them which they must acknowledge and adhere to and which others have also to recognise (Foucault, 1982). This view of power working in a capillary fashion deviates significantly from Marxist models. Foucault's criticism of 'Marxians' is that they see power as imposed from above by one class (the dominant class) upon another (the workers) and is negative – associated with domination, coercion, manipulation, authority/repression. Foucault (1977), on the other hand, sees power as productive:

> We must cease once and for all to describe the effects of power in negative terms … In fact, power produces, it produces reality, it produces domains of objects and rituals of truth. (Foucault, 1977: 194)

The two major technologies that Foucault (1978) sees operating in the disciplinary society are *discipline* and *confession*. He represents them metaphorically as the panopticon and the confessional. While the technologies handle masses of people at a societal level, their effects work differently. Disciplinary power operates in a highly individual way and has the effect of objectifying people. The confession, on the other hand, works within society as a power that subjectifies them. Foucault (1978: 59) maintains that '(w)estern man [sic] has become a confessing animal'. This refers to the trend in modern society to talk about oneself, especially one's sexuality in an increasingly widening set of social settings (Fairclough, 1992).

The confession allows for the interpretation and reconstruction of events and leads to the development of commentary on them (Foucault, 1978). It is used most readily in the sciences to influence knowledge and also in other discourses about the self where the power relations are unequal and a specific knowledge is produced about a person, for example, in the classroom. In higher education, self-reflection and self-disclosure in group and class discussions are ubiquitous but they bring with them a 'terror' of performance, especially for students speaking in their second language.

## The Active Subject: Crafting a Life

In the final 'phase' of his work, Foucault's interest in subjection remains but moves from the external techniques governing the subject to the internal techniques of self-regulation, or ethics. He does this by looking at ancient Greece and Rome and identifying two key features: (i) that these epochs operated with a sexual ethics different to our own and (ii) that both of these societies, particularly the ancient Greeks, operated with almost no external techniques of control (Foucault, 1996d). Foucault's focus then turns to the internal relation of the self to the self vis-à-vis the question of proper sexual behaviour. He concludes that sexuality is not a human constant and contemplates how and by what route subjects come to subject themselves to particular desires, albeit desires defined and interpreted in a historical period (McHoul & Grace, 1993).

Foucault (1996d) proposes life as 'styles of existence': as an aesthetic; a concern for the self with the subject in the practice of self-formation. The practice involves 'an exercise of the self on the self, by which one attempts to develop and transform oneself, and to attain to a certain mode of being' (Foucault, 1996d: 433). In the context of the ancient Greeks and Romans, this 'mode of being' reflected the morality of the time and was expressed through what Foucault (1996b) calls the 'art of existence', the 'aesthetics of existence' (Foucault, 1996a).

In ancient Greco-Roman lifestyles, a certain austerity was associated with work on the self that was not imposed by law or religion (Foucault, 1986). Rather, it was a choice that the individual made about her/his existence – a decision about whether or not to care for themselves. Foucault concludes that the ancient Greeks and Romans acted so to give their life certain values. Training had to take place of oneself by oneself and took forms such as abstinences, memorisations, examinations of conscience, meditations, silence, listening to others and writing. The measures constituted 'technologies of the self' which allowed people to 'effect by their own means or with the help of others a certain number of operations on their own bodies and souls, thoughts, conduct, and way of being so as to transform themselves in order to attain a certain state of happiness, purity, wisdom, perfection, or immortality' (Foucault, 1988: 18). In this way, one was able to make one's life an object of art.

In this body of work, Foucault (1996d) posits an active subject, albeit one operating within contextual constraints:

> I would say that if I am now interested in how the subject constitutes itself in an active fashion through practices of the self, these practices are nevertheless not something that the individual invented by the individual himself [sic]. They are models that he finds in his culture and that are proposed, suggested, imposed upon him by his culture, his society and his social group. (Foucault, 1996d: 440–441)

Peters (2004) suggests that this position represents a changed sense of agency on the part of Foucault from his earlier work and that here, he has become interested in questions of self-mastery and the ethical constitution of the self. Gubrium and Holstein (2000: 494) maintain that while Foucault is offering a vision of the subject constituted through discourse, he is also allowing for 'an unwittingly active subject who shapes discourse and puts it to work'. Is Foucault suggesting agency? The argument here is that the technologies of the self, including self-mastery, are the bedrock of engagement as the student actively pursues her/his goals, albeit within the constraints (and possibilities) of the contextual conditions.

## Agency and resistance

Foucault's defining of the active human subject resonates with Fairclough's ideas on the subject and agentive action, although the latter places more emphasis on the transformative potential of agency. Fairclough (2003) sees people as not only pre-positioned in how they participate in social events and texts but also as social agents who do, create and change things. *Agency* is a much-used term although Foucault does not use it. Rather, he refers to the subject working in 'an active fashion' within social and cultural constraints.

Fairclough's (2001a) definition of agency resonates with Butler's (1997) work extending Foucault's notion of subjection. Fairclough argues that while social subjects are constrained to operate within the subject positionings set up in discourses, it is only through being so constrained that they act as social agents. Being constrained is a precondition of being enabled. Butler (1997) similarly works with the notion of being constrained in order to be enabled. She argues that power acts on the subject in at least two ways: first, as what makes the subject possible, its formation; and second, as what the subject takes up and reiterates in its own acting. Within the exercise of power, the subject *of* power 'eclipses power with power ... the subject emerges both as the *effect* of a prior power and as *the condition of possibility* for a radically conditioned form of agency' (Butler, 1997: 14–15, emphases in original). Agency exceeds the power by which it is enabled and adopts its own purpose which may diverge from the purposes intended by the power regime. The interesting point is not so much how discourses position people but rather how these positions can be actively taken up and used to advantage (Kettle, 2005).

## Acquiring a discourse: How does it happen?

Various terms have been used to conceptualise the process by which the subject actively fashions itself and takes up new subjectivities, for example, becoming (Grosz, 2004; Kettle, 2011); recrafting and identity transformation (Ichimoto, 2005); resourcing identities (Kennett, 2003); and self-translation and the (re)construction of selves (Pavlenko & Lantolf, 2000). The process involves the discursive transformation of the self through the acquisition of new linguistic, social and cultural practices for a particular purpose. This purpose has been defined variously as the transformation of the self 'in order to attain a certain state of happiness, purity, wisdom, perfection, or immortality' (Foucault, 1988: 18) and the pursuit of legitimacy through discursive assimilation (Miller, 2003).

Crucial insights from Foucault are that these transformations are riven with power, most particularly for members of minority groups. In a democratic community, power is exercised in multiple ways that are not necessarily explicitly brutal and oppressive. Rather, in the exchange and interactions between groups, power is exercised subtly and often concealed beneath the guise of mutually shared benefits (Reich, 2011). For minorities, this can mean that their interests are dissolved and disappear. The discourse of diversity is a relevant example and is discussed in the following chapter. The role of researchers and scholarly endeavours is to investigate how the power relations in taken-for-granted institutional assumptions and practices serve to marginalise certain groups, and conversely how these relations can be manipulated productively from within. In play is the assistance rendered by others, especially those with powerful roles in the institution.

The interest then is the means by which the human subject acquires a new discourse in the process of crafting a new existence. The process of taking on new discourses and associated ways of knowing, doing and being is a topic of great interest in the literature and the wellspring of many different theoretical perspectives and concepts. Change in the international student literature has been variously conceptualised as adaptation, adjustment, acculturation and intercultural competence (Lee, 2015). The problem with many of these perspectives is that they assume it is the responsibility of the student to change.

With Foucault, acquiring a new discourse involves venturing statements associated with the new reality and subject position, with growing rights and recognition as an authoritative and legitimate participant. Fairclough (2003) proposes a three-step process: rhetorical deployment, enactment and inculcation. Inculcation is the complex process of coming to 'own' a discourse by positioning oneself within it. A prior stage to inculcation is enactment which is the way a new discourse or 'possible world' is enacted in real activities, subjects and social relations (Fairclough, 2003). The step towards enactment is rhetorical deployment, when people may learn new discourses and use them for certain purposes but self-consciously retain a distance from them. Fairclough claims that one of the mysteries of the dialectics of discourse is the process by which rhetorical deployment becomes inculcation. Part of the aim of this book is to dispense with the mystery and show how this process is actively managed by international students intent on transitioning to successful academic lives at an overseas university.

## Reinterpreting the International Student

Foucault's work on how the human being is constituted as a subject enables us to move away from the notion of a fixed subject. The subject becomes a site not only of subjection but also of active engagement and resistance. This standpoint challenges the representations in the research literature of the international student as a fixed and culture-bound entity. As well, it problematises the binaries in which the international student is placed in opposition to her/his Australian counterpart. The images of the silent, passive student – deficit and different, or at best, adjusting but still different – become open to question. A new subject becomes possible – a subject with multiple subjectivities who can simultaneously be subjected to existing power relations while actively crafting themselves an academic life on their own terms.

Foucault's work affords insights into three modes by which the international student is made subject within the practices of a tertiary study. The first relates to the ways in which the student is discursively constructed within course practices, with the acknowledgment that these practices privilege certain knowledge, social relations and subjectivities. What subject positions or enunciative modalities are afforded within the course? What is the role of teaching? Second, how do discourses exercise control over the students?; by what means or procedures? How is the student incorporated into the power/knowledge relations of the course and in what ways does the student respond? Third, what goal or motivation does the student bring to the course? How does the subject undertake to fashion a 'life' in response to the discursive requirements of the course?; what technologies of the self are employed? By what means does the student transform herself/himself? What is the assistance of others? Is an 'aesthetics of existence' achieved?

## Defining Social Practice

The concept of social practice is introduced in this section. As noted above, social practice is the means by which the human subject *does* social life. Social life comprises particular configurations of practices for different parts of life, for example, educational, familial and political. By foregrounding social practice, a researcher can gain insights into social structures as well as individual actions and agency (Fairclough, 2001b). Social structures are abstract entities, for example, a social class or kinship system, an economic structure or a language. They present a potential, a certain set of possibilities. The practices that people undertake in the everyday events of their lives instantiate certain structural possibilities and exclude others. Particular networks of social practices form a social order. A social order might be an entire education system or on a different scale, a university course. The ways in which the practices are networked together can shift and change. For example, university teaching and research are increasingly networked with discursive practices of managerialism and standardisation, impacting the practices of lecturers and researchers and changing the social order of the university.

The defining feature of a social practice is that it is relatively stabilised; as noted in the Preface, it has the felicitous ambiguity of being both a *thing* and an *action*. This means that a social practice exists as a thing, a social entity that stands outside people and is identifiable. A social practice is also something that people do; it is their action and engagement in the practice as it exists for them. People *practise* social practices routinely; it can be a family meal or classroom teaching (Fairclough, 2003). Each practice comprises diverse social elements within a relatively stable configuration. The elements include activities; materials and objects; temporal and spatial locations; people and their social roles and relationships; values and beliefs; and semiotic resources such as language (Chouliaraki & Fairclough, 1999). The elements are dialectically related which means they are different but not fully separate and discrete. They 'internalise' each other but are not reducible to each other (Harvey, 1996).

The dialectical relationship between elements has implications for social change. Shifts in one or more elements lead to change in the overall practice. The introduction of a new technology or values from a different discourse impacts the whole practice due to the dialectical relationship between the elements (Fairclough, 2003).

## Social practice: An everyday example

Family mealtimes are highly illustrative of social practice as the realisation of a family's habituated activities, roles, social and economic circumstances, values and cultural affinities. Family meal practices are already, always, enmeshed in the broader social order and while relatively stable configurations, can change comprehensively with the altering of one element. Family meals involve an extensive array of elements working in relation to each other:

- activity (e.g. cooking, preparing the space, eating, cleaning up);
- objects (e.g. foods, eating utensils, condiments, heat sources);
- time (e.g. designated times for particular meals);
- spaces (e.g. table, floor, kitchen, in front of television, who sits where);
- people (e.g. roles: cook, table-setter, dishwasher; family members);
- language (e.g. speakers, listeners, topics, turn-taking rules).

Traditionally, family meals, especially dinner, are highly ritualised with heavily socialised rules about practice in relation to food types and eating behaviours, to name a few. Rules exist about the order of the dishes – the grammar of the meal, for example in a classic Western meal, small servings precede large; hot precedes cold; and sweet follows savoury. The style of food dictates the tools, for example, a fillet of chicken requires a knife and fork whereas chicken stir-fry pieces are small and can be eaten with chopsticks.

The practice of family meals is deeply susceptible to changes in elements and a reconfiguration of the practice, including social impact; for example, changing spatial arrangements such as people eating in front of the television or in bedrooms rather than at the family dinner table can have implications for social interaction and relationships. It also has effects on language use. Clark (2013) in National Literacy Trust research on oracy and mealtimes in the UK found that talk at family mealtimes is a significant contributor to communication confidence and positive attitudes about communication skills among children. The study found that one in four children do not have a daily mealtime chat and that significant differences operate across socio-economic and ethnic groups. The broader social and political implications are that speaking and listening are of current interest to the British government in its revision of the primary

National Curriculum from September 2014. Families are being urged to do their bit by chatting to their children at mealtimes (Clark, 2013).

## Social practice: An academic example

Within education, university teaching is also an example of social practice (Kettle, 2011). Teaching, as the more contemporary counterpart to lecturing, is constituted by a particular constellation of elements. The introduction of a communication technology like PowerPoint has led to a reconfiguring of elements that has transformed the practice of teaching. Knowledge is organised to fit PowerPoint templates while concepts and their relationships are represented using tools such as animation and charts; new objects such as data projectors and computers have been installed in lecture rooms; lecturers have become technology users; and students are expected to be proficient producers and consumers of multimodal learning materials.

The dialectical relationship between the teaching elements means that the change in one element, that is, the introduction of a new mode of content delivery, leads to a shift in others and a redefining of the practice. In the case of PowerPoint, university teachers can provide attractive visual material to enhance student learning. Interestingly, the technology itself has not altered the power relations between the teacher and students nor traditional seating arrangements in many lecture halls. The teaching approach may continue to be teacher led and transmission orientated. PowerPoint is now pervasive and having a profound effect on knowledge construction and presentation. Its introduction has also influenced teacher expectations about the cognitive benefits of visually appealing materials for student concentration and enhanced learning.

## Researching social practice through text analysis

Social practices mediate social structures in everyday events that people undertake in their lives. During social events, people produce texts that instantiate their understandings of the social order. Three types of meaning are produced: (i) representations of the social and physical world; (ii) construction of particular social relations with other people; and (iii) utilisation of textual features to promote coherence and cohesion (Halliday, 1978). Following Halliday, Fairclough (2003) proposes text meanings as ways of representing the physical and social world; ways of acting and interacting; and ways of self-identifying. These meanings are realised linguistically, that is, grammatically and lexically. The logic of Fairclough's model is that linguistic analysis of texts can reveal their social meanings and the social conditions of their production. The focus of the analysis is the discourse element of a social practice.

The nexus between the social and the linguistic is pivotal in Fairclough's method of social analysis. It provides the basis for making claims about the social based on the linguistic. Discourse mediates the link because it is both social and linguistic; discourse in social practice is the linguistic articulation of social meanings. It is the point at which the social transmogrifies into the linguistic. The logic is that analysis of the linguistic provides insights into the social.

The analytical method involves a 'relational view' across several social and linguistic 'levels' (Fairclough, 2003). The key 'level' is that of social practice which is the *meso* level connecting and mediating the *internal* or *micro* level of the text and the *external* or *macro* level of its social context. The text's *internal* (semantic, grammatical, lexical) relations are connected to their *external* relations (other elements of social events, social practices and social structures) through the *interdiscursive relations* of the genres, discourses and styles. Analysis of the lexicogrammatical features of a text is conducted with the understanding that they articulate particular social meanings, that is, ways of acting and interacting (genres), ways of representing the world (discourses) and ways of being (styles) (Chouliaraki & Fairclough, 1999; Fairclough, 2003). These meanings are the person's responses to the social conditions operating in the social event in which she/he is participating. Particular mixings of discourses, genres and styles are the *interdiscursive relations* and constitute the discourse element of a social practice.

My understandings of the relationships between the levels of social life and texts are presented in Table 3.1.

**Table 3.1** Social and discursive relationships in Fairclough's social practice theory

| The social | Discourse elements |
| --- | --- |
| **Social structures** Societal and institutional structures: e.g. a language, a social class | |
| **A social order** Social practices networked in a particular way, that is, the structuring of a social space into domains associated with various types of practice, e.g., an education course in a particular place at a particular time in history. | **An order of discourse** The discursive elements of a social order, that is, the genres, discourses and styles associated with the network of social practices ordered in a particular way. One aspect of this ordering is dominance; some ways of making meaning are dominant and mainstream while others are marginal or oppositional. The dominant ordering can become hegemonic but will always be contested to a greater or lesser degree. The ascendancy of particular ways of making meaning over others is because they represent the ideologies of the dominant group in that place at that time. |

*(Continued)*

**Table 3.1** (Continued)

| A social practice | Discourse (language and visuals) as an element of social practice |
|---|---|
| A relatively stabilised form of social activity. An intermediate entity; mediates the relationship between social structures and events through selection of certain structural possibilities and not others. The elements of a social practice exist in a dialectical relationship: <br>• activities; <br>• subjects and their social relations; <br>• instruments; <br>• objects; <br>• time and place; <br>• consciousness and values; <br>• discourse. <br>Example: classroom teaching. | Discourse features in social practice as: <br>• ways of representing (discourses); <br>• ways of acting and interacting (genres); <br>• ways of being and identifying (styles). |
| **A social event** | **A text** |
| Some highly textual; others not. Shaped by social practices. | Texts are produced in social events. Producing texts involves articulating different 'mixes' of genres, discourses and styles using lexical and grammatical forms (and visuals in some texts). These linguistic forms and their particular manifestations in text are not arbitrary; rather they instantiate the meanings that people bring to the particular social situation. |

## Seeking research rigour

The social practice theory presented above establishes a framework for analysing social life and its relationship to language. Fairclough is intent on ensuring that his method of analysis is scientifically sound and rigorous, where rigour in research is understood as evidence of systematic investigation (Taylor, 2001). To this end, Fairclough (2001a) provides a tri-focal approach to analysis: (i) *description* of the textual features; (ii) *interpretation* of the interdiscursive relations; and (iii) *explanation* of the social context, including power. This approach commits the analyst to 'analysing the relationship between texts, processes, and their social conditions, both the immediate conditions of the situational context and the more remote conditions of institutional and social structures' (Fairclough, 2001a: 21). Luke (2002: 100) calls the process a 'principled and transparent shunting back and forth between the micro analysis of texts using varied tools of linguistic, semiotic and literary analysis and the macro analysis of social formations, institutions and power relations that these texts index and construct'.

At the text level, the *description* stage involves identifying and labelling the linguistic features in the text. The view is that the linguistic (grammar and vocabulary including metaphor) and paralinguistic (rising volume and intonation) features are social in the sense that they are used by people in social settings. As such, they are socially determined and have social effects.

At the level of social interaction, the role of the analyst is to *interpret* the participants' meanings as they manifest in their linguistic choices during an interaction. The participants' discursive choices are seen as responses to the social constraints which they consider to be operating in the particular situation. To do this, people draw on an array of internal psychological resources or 'members' resources' (MR) (Fairclough, 1992) which include language knowledge, language competence, values, and knowledge and assumptions about the natural and social worlds. These resources comprise their understandings of the prevailing social order and the linguistic competence to 'speak' this order.

The third level of analysis, *explanation*, requires the analyst to redescribe the linguistic choices made by participants in theoretical terms. This analysis relates to the third dimension of discourse and the understanding that producing and interpreting texts are influenced by the social and institutional structures that contextualise the situation. Of particular interest to the analyst is how participants' assumptions about culture, social relationships and social identities are manifested in the texts and work ideologically to maintain, challenge or change existing power relations (Fairclough, 2001a).

## Positive critique

The objective of the critical research approach is to make visible social conditions that were hitherto hidden in taken-for-granted practices. Several outcomes are possible: awareness-raising and reflection on social alternatives, and overtly challenging existing practices for the purpose of generating change. As noted above, the approach taken in this book is critical and positive; the focus is affirmative and on the institutional conditions and practices evidenced in the research texts that work to facilitate international student engagement with the demands of the new academic context.

The outcomes of such research are exemplars of transformative practice. After all, how are we to make positive change if we don't know what it looks like? New knowledge and understandings are presented through this approach which will provide policymakers and lecturers with clear examples of what works to promote engagement. Not least will be explication of engagement as a construct – what its various dimensions are and what institutional stakeholders need to know to talk authoritatively about engagement. Positive critique is reconstructive in that it presents evidence of reimagined, reconstituted practices that address prevailing problems and questions. Research on exemplary practice redresses the inadequacy of much of the existing literature on international students' approaches to learning and scholarship. The benefit of the approach is its potential to effect change through the explicit identification of discourses, practices and texts that work in the experiences of international students. Making these transformative examples visible increases the possibility for uptake by stakeholders tasked with the responsibility of ensuring an engaging, participatory learning experience for international students enrolled at their university.

## International Student Engagement

This chapter has presented the key parts of the social practice theory of engagement. The focus accords with calls for greater practice-based research in higher education (Clegg, 2009). Conceptualising international student engagement as social practice foregrounds the institutional conditions that students find themselves immersed in and their efforts to respond. More specifically, the conditions are conceptualised as a social order composed of social practices that are particular configurations of elements such as activities, materials, times, spaces, people, values and discourse. Practices are realised in the specific, localised events experienced by students every day in their overseas university courses.

A social practice theory of engagement sees the international student as a human subject located within prevailing discourses; she/he is subjected to dominant power/knowledge relations but always capable of action and transformation. The theory highlights the cultural, social, academic and linguistic demands in practices and links them to students' responses and efforts. It is interested in the behavioural, cognitive, strategic, affective and social resources that students combine in practices of engagement to meet the institutional demands. In addition, it recognises engagement as a thing, that is, an entity that drives particular achievements and outcomes. For many international students, these achievements and aspirations include academic success; in addition, the study sojourn aboard provides possibilities for personal renewal and cultural exchange.

In summary, the perspective on international student engagement proposed here embraces social complexity; it provides a comprehensive and detailed description of social life as it operates in the higher education context. Engagement is recognised as a triadic experience incorporating the following: (i) antecedents including pre-existing institutional conditions and individual circumstances; (ii) actions associated with cognition, behaviour and emotion; and (iii) achievements including learning outcomes and personal milestones. The argument is that an investigation of engagement requires focus on antecedents, actions and achievements, a complex undertaking which is ably resourced by a theory of social practice.

The explanatory power of this perspective is its capacity to make visible the discursive elements of academic practices as identified by the international students themselves. In addition, it shows their responses to subjection in course practices and their social and academic changes. Social practice theory provides access to students' meanings of the representational, actional/interactional and identificational demands of their course and the array of resources that they deploy to meet them. Recognising the institutional demands, mobilising subsequent actions and shaping achievements are the practices that constitute engagement in a course of overseas study.

# 4 University People and Places: Diversity in Action

## Picturing the University

Internationalisation is changing university spaces and places. Food outlets are the most obvious with refectories increasing their menus to include dishes from Asian countries and the Middle East. Halal options are on offer and banks of microwaves are available for students to heat their meals. Festivals with East-West themes are held throughout the academic year and noticeboards in refectories and other public places are festooned with posters advertising international student clubs and parties, among other things. In other parts of the university, prayer rooms for Muslim students are provided along with washing facilities for men and women. During the Muslim month of Ramadan when followers are required to fast from dawn until sunset, refectory spaces are often rearranged in the evening to accommodate prayer and a communal meal.

Campus chaplaincy services for students feature representatives from all major faiths and denominations, and campus market days are a smorgasbord of colour, music and smells as different student groups sell food and wares. In Australia, increasing diversity on campuses is an outcome of international recruitment agendas and domestic initiatives to widen participation by marginalised groups such as newly arrived migrants, people with disabilities and Aboriginal and Torres Strait Islanders. Life at university presents the opportunity for more exposure to different bodies, languages and cultural artefacts than ever before.

This chapter provides a detailed picture of a postgraduate course at an Australian university: its design, classroom space and assessment. It introduces a group of international students enrolled in the course together with their lecturer. 'Picturing' the course and its participants is an attempt to describe the social order of the course – to detail its rationale, objectives, knowledge, skills, materials and values as the international education context experienced by the students. The course was titled Issues in Education and Leadership (ME5100) and was part of a compulsory suite of courses in a Master of Education programme. Like humanities courses at postgraduate level in many Western universities, it contained a relatively small student cohort. Class sessions were seminar style with an emphasis on dialogic interaction and critical thinking (Kettle & Luke, 2013).

The students were introduced in the Preface and volunteered to participate in the study which followed them during their enrolment in the Issues course. The students were from culturally, ethnically and linguistically diverse backgrounds that meant differences in race, religion, language, nationality and social class. The similarities between the students included levels of previous education, shared aspirations for the future and a common need to align existing educational resources with the new academic demands. The students' stories are presented in detail below.

*Diversity* is a term that is highly prevalent in contexts where difference presents itself. For example, in the *OECD Education Policy Outlook 2015: Making Reforms Happen,* teaching diverse student populations is presented as a common challenge facing the Organisation for Economic Co-operation and Development (OECD, 2015) members. Throughout the document, *diverse* is collocated with *student populations*; the term *diverse* is used, paradoxically, to encapsulate the uniformity of diversity. The following section presents diversity as it is realised in university policy statements and outlines key principles and debates in current theorisations of diversity.

## Problematising Diversity

In Australia, diversity is acknowledged in university policy statements variously as a noun and through the adjective *diverse*; for example in the mission statement for my university, Queensland University of Technology (QUT, 2016): *diverse and complex environment*; *diverse communities*; *diverse groups of students*; *a diverse talent base*. In the case of *diversity*: *QUT's diversity and gender equity goals*; *equity and diversity*; *community diversity*; *seeking diversity in QUT's income base* (QUT, 2016). *Diversity* is often paired with *equity*, although not always; it is also used to refer to the university's income base. The term functions as an acknowledgement of heterogeneity without the compulsion to specify individual differences. As such, the term works as a catch-all that saves on the need to be explicit.

In the late 1990s, after two decades of market-driven internationalisation, Rizvi and Walsh (1998) wondered how university policy commitments to diversity had been realised in practice, particularly in the curriculum. They found that much of the thinking about difference at the time regarded culture as an add-on consideration in the curriculum with little relevance except as a site for uncritical celebration. Internationalisation of the curriculum was largely seen as broadening vocational and life opportunities, primarily for domestic students. Some years later, Bullen and Kenway (2003) noted that change in the curriculum was still slow in coming, even negligible, despite the rhetoric about commitment to cultural diversity.

Internationally, cultural diversity has been identified as an opportunity for personal enrichment and the development of globally relevant cultural and communicative resources (OECD, 2008). Despite these projected benefits, Smart *et al.* (2000) found in a study of social cohesion in Australian universities that international and domestic students have little social contact. Rather, the groups proceed through their university courses as two parallel streams, in close proximity but with little or no interaction. The authors suggest that instructional methods and classroom intercultural interaction are areas where changes can be implemented. The issue of social interaction between international and domestic students remains an issue. The 2015 'Draft National Strategy for International Education (For Consultation)' published by the Australian Government (2015a) identifies one of its key actions as improvements in the experiences of international students. This strategy is to be demonstrated through higher levels of satisfaction among international students achieved by increased opportunities for contact with Australian students and communities.

Some researchers have problematised the term *diversity*. For example, Nichols (2003) argues that *diversity* in the discourses of higher education has come largely to refer to international students. *Diversity* references multiculturalism and foregrounds tolerance and celebration. In addition, understandings of what *diversity* means are contextually situated: different contexts ascribed significance to different attributes of diversity (Rizvi, 2011). In higher education classrooms, key markers of diversity ascribed to international students are language and academic resources. Indeed, reference to international students in relation to course assessment and quality continues to be code for concerns about language and academic capability.

Multiculturalism as a state-sponsored policy has had much to do with understandings of diversity in countries such as Australia and Canada. Despite its political motivations to accord migrants rights and access to economic, social and cultural resources, multiculturalism often juxtaposes cultural heterogeneity as a goal against homogeneity as the norm. In this context, cultural differences are essentialised to visible, uncontentious forms such as dress, dance and food. At the level of the nation, the arrival of people who are culturally, racially and linguistically different is often presented as a threat to cultural homogeneity, as discussed in Chapter 1. Policies of assimilation are designed to ensure that the cultural homogeneity of the nation is preserved through initiatives that transform immigrants into 'one of us' (Rizvi, 2011). The exhortation to the nation as a homogenised entity was demonstrated in Australia in 2014 when the then Prime Minister Tony Abbott, referring to Australians travelling as recruits to overseas wars, called for all Australians to be 'on Team Australia'. The comment raised questions (and eyebrows) about what he meant given that most of the young Muslim men travelling overseas were already Australians and therefore part of Team Australia (Summers, 2014). The politics of homogeneity and the presence of heterogeneity continue to be sites of struggle and contestation in a culturally pluralistic country such as Australia.

*Diversity* then is a contested term. Bhabha (1994) argues that the concept of diversity can be used to provide an illusion of pluralistic harmony but is tolerated by the dominant cultural norms, social orders and practices only so long as the latter remain unchallenged. Cameron (2002: 69) notes that the contradictory but favoured 'trope of the new capitalism' defining the late 20th century–early 21st century is 'unity in diversity'. Bhabha makes the powerful distinction between *diversity* and *difference*, and claims that where *diversity* paradoxically masks ethnocentric norms, *difference* does not. Rather, the cultural politics of difference does not assume consensus and problematises the norms that create difference (Bhabha, 1990). Globalisation is a powerful incubator of diversity across multiple sites. Within education, Rizvi (2011) argues that the diversity being generated by globalisation demands a more dynamic relational definition of cultural diversity. Such a definition of diversity should emanate from the changing conditions of interculturality, that is, intercultural relations. Diversity originates in intercultural relations; it does not precede them.

## The fluidity and hybridity of contemporary social life

Globalised, networked and developed economies such as Australia and other education host countries are characterised by plurality and fragmentation in social life (Chouliaraki & Fairclough, 1999). In Western societies, institutions are charged with providing a social order that, to a greater or lesser degree, promotes political pluralism, capitalism, scientific method, the rule of law and property rights, and democracy (Ferguson, 2011). Yet, change is afoot and shifts in geo-political and economic relations are contributing to the reorganisation of civilisations. The institutions that promulgated Western civilisation and its ascendancy are no longer monopolised by the West; indeed, on most measures including educational attainment and research output, the West is losing its ascendancy to the Rest, notably China (Ferguson, 2011).

Within Western social life there are growing social and economic inequalities driven by rapacious and unregulated financial institutions. In his historical analyses of economic systems across three centuries, Thomas Piketty (2014) shows that a major feature of the 21st century is the dramatic accumulation of capital in the hands of an elite. He argues that capitalism in its current form is threatening the general interest and the meritocratic values of democratic societies. Capitalism has become separated from democracy and is generating deep social and economic inequalities (Piketty, 2014). Change, contestation and opportunity are accompanying these new fluidities of people, products and practices and the hybridised knowledge, interactions and identities they are creating across globalised contact points. Heterogeneity is the new norm but remains a perplexing problem for many institutions and individuals rooted in social orders of the past.

As new forms present themselves, the dominance of the prevailing social order is threatened. Change becomes possible but is always contested by those invested in the existing order. For many universities, and indeed societies at this time of mass mobility around the globe, the challenge is to reconcile difference with sameness. But how is the will to sameness and commonality reconciled with the right to difference and diversity in pluralist societies? At the university level, which elements in institutional practices are decision-makers and teachers prepared to change in response to diversifying student profiles? Garrison (2011) maintains that sameness, difference, and pluralism are crucial 21st-century issues. For him, democratic participation in diverse, pluralist societies is best handled by embracing a paradox: there should be enough sameness in the community to ensure a common conversation and enough difference to make the conversation necessary and worthwhile. Indeed, differences in a community are important for democracy and the lesson for majorities is that they always benefit from the ideas of minorities (Eldridge, 2011; Reich, 2011).

## The Course

The students introduced in this book embody the fluidity of movement by people to universities around the world. Theirs are the new hybridised ways of knowing, doing and being that characterise globalised knowledge interactions in academic contexts such as universities. The six students were enrolled in a Master of Education (Leadership) programme at a public university in a major Australian city. The course that was the focus of the study was the compulsory ME5100 Issues in Education and Leadership.[1] The university – to be known here as The University – like many metropolitan universities, has a student population of about 40,000. The Issues course was worth two credit points in a programme requiring either 16 or 24 credit points depending on prior qualifications, and was offered in the first semester. The semester started officially in early March and continued for 13 weeks until the beginning of June. Students continued to submit assignments and meet with the lecturer after this date. The final assignment was due on 21 June.

The internal enrolment in the course was 21: 10 international students and 11 home, or domestic, students. The course had almost equal numbers of women and men: 11 women (4 international and 7 domestic) and 10 men (6 international and 4 domestic). All of the domestic students worked in schools, mostly at the secondary level and were teachers, deputy principals or principals. The backgrounds of the international students were more varied as shown in Table 4.1. The lecturer was a senior academic with a reputation for excellence in teaching. She was aged in her fifties with a background in social justice and educational reform. She had held leadership positions in education faculties in a number of countries and was in a leadership role at the time of the study.

The Issues in Education and Leadership course was described in the Postgraduate Coursework Student Handbook as follows:

**Table 4.1** Profiles of the international students

| Names of participants | Nationality | Sex | Age | Occupation |
|---|---|---|---|---|
| Javier* | Argentina | M | 35 | Merchant banker |
| Anna* | China | F | 29 | Civil servant in a government education department |
| | El Salvador | M | Not available | |
| Grace* | Mozambique | F | 36 | Training officer at a subsidiary of a multinational beverages company |
| | Singapore | M | 30–35 | High school teacher |
| Erica* | Singapore | F | 29 | High school teacher |
| Sonny* | Thailand | M | 33 | English teacher at a sports institute |
| | US (exchange student) | F | 29 | Teacher/manager of a children's clothing store |
| | Vietnam | M | 37 | University English teacher |
| Hanh* | Vietnam | M | 26 | Business English teacher at a foreign trade university |

* Indicates those who volunteered to participate in the study and are named using a pseudonym.

> This course critically examines the nature of educational leadership and the challenges posed by globalisation. It views leadership in relation to broader social and value contexts, examines different historical and theoretical debates in leadership, and considers alternative approaches based on equity, networks, collaboration and critical and constructive thinking.

The course outline was the official description of the course. The role of the document is to set out for the student the design and priorities of the course:

(1) Welcome and introduction.
(2) Aims and objectives.
(3) Course outline.
(4) A study plan.
(5) Reading resources.
(6) Assessment.
(7) The lecturer.

The document was prefaced by a generic introduction to the faculty and department by the head of department, followed by statements of policy on assessment submission, submission extensions, plagiarism and disability. Throughout the outline, the lecturer 'speaks' directly to the individual student through the use of the personal pronoun 'you'.[2] For example, in the section on aims and objectives:

> This course locates itself within leadership studies in education and more broadly. Its aims are:
>
> - To review major theoretical debates on leadership, so that you are able to develop your own theoretical position;
> - To analyse the current context of leadership in education, so that you have a better understanding of the possibilities and constraints of leadership actions; and
> - To consider the skills, competences and knowledge needed for leadership in new times, so that you have a fuller understanding of what leadership entails at the start of the 21st century.

The lecturer provides advice to the student, for example, in the section on reading resources: 'Please read as widely as you can' and indicates her willingness to be flexible around student needs. For example, in the assessment section, she notes that alternative assignment topics are possible but must be negotiated with her. She highlights the critical orientation of the course: 'Ideally, you should be debating with the text, and using other references to dialogue' and prioritises conceptual challenge in her final statement: 'I hope the course gives you a lot to think about!'.

Like many Education Master's courses, the assessment requirement was 5000 words in written tasks or the spoken equivalent. The assignments for the Issues course were as follows:

---

### Assignment 1

This assignment is intended as an ***extended literature review***, where you have the opportunity to pursue your reading and thinking on two or three issues that the course has touched on. You are encouraged to provide arguments and analyses of texts intermixed with your own experiences and journal reflections.

*It is essential for you to engage with the Learning Guide and Course Reader for the assignment, and you are encouraged to draw on other readings as well.*

The following topic provides a focus for your literature review:

'Leadership and management refer to complementary but distinct actions'.

Critically discuss this statement.

**Due date**       **28 April**
**Length**          **2000 words**
**Weighting**    **40% of course grade**

---

> ## Assignment 2
>
> This assignment is intended as a **critical analysis** of key issues that have been touched upon in the course. Using the Learning Guide, Course Readings and other literature, critically discuss the following:
>
> 'Leading learning should be the major focus of school leadership in new times'.
>
> *It is essential for you to engage with the Learning Guide and Course Reader for the assignment, and you are encouraged to draw on other readings as well.*
>
> **Due date**      21 June
> **Length**        3000 words
> **Weighting**     60% of course grade

## The Physical Space

The teaching space for Issues classes was a standard-sized classroom, not a large multitiered lecture theatre. It was not new and showing some signs of age but at the time of the study was undergoing incremental refurbishment. Space in the university was at a premium and the department was bartering rooms with other departments to ensure that its staff, students and storage needs were being met. The furniture was regulation rectangular desks designed to seat two students with plastic chairs.

There was no differentiation between the students and the lecturer; the lecturer placed her books and resources on one of the desks at the front of the room but frequently moved them when the space was needed for students. The desks were arranged in a large square with the front row mainly occupied by the lecturer. Often, there were several desks in the middle of the square which were used for group work. During the study, I placed an external microphone on one of these desks while videoing the class sessions. To keep myself as unobtrusive as possible and in consultation with the lecturer, I videoed from a corner at the back of the room.

## The Pedagogical Space

The class sessions for the Issues course were scheduled from 5pm to 8pm each Monday evening. The sessions were usually divided into two core topics or tasks with a tea break in the middle. Each week, different students were assigned the job of bringing milk and biscuits for the tea and coffee.

The size of the room meant that the physical distance between the students and the lecturer was always close. This spatial arrangement appeared to have implications for the pedagogy. As Foucault (1977) notes, the organisation of institutional spaces and bodies is not benign but heavily implicated in relations of power. The close spatial arrangement meant that the lecturer was able to look at the students individually and call on them to speak using their names and hand signals. She was also able to initiate interactions between particular students using hand gestures that were clear and visible to all. The lecturer used a number of modes of delivery including monologic lecture-style and more dialogic seminar-style interaction patterns. At times, she set up group work tasks which were assisted by the portability of the furniture.

## The Participants

In this section, I introduce the participants using their own words as much as possible. It is an attempt to echo their voices, how they sound and who they are. Table 4.1 presents an overview of the backgrounds of all the international students in the class.

### Sonny

Sonny was a 33-year-old, single Thai man who worked as an English communication teacher at a sports institute in northern Thailand. There are 17 such institutes across Thailand, which are dedicated to training athletes, coaches and referees. His family were rice farmers who lived in the north-east near the border of Thailand and Laos. At the time of the study, he was in his first semester of the Master of Education (Leadership) programme at The University and studying with the help of an Australian government AusAid scholarship. He was part of the last cohort of Thai students to be awarded AusAid scholarships to study in Australia. Sonny completed a Bachelor of Education (English) in Thailand in 1997. His first language (L1) was Thai, with English as his second language.

As part of his study programme application, Sonny had to show proof of proficiency in English and consequently sat for the International English Language Testing System (IELTS) exam in Bangkok. IELTS is a suite of internationally recognised exams which test a candidate's English proficiency in speaking, writing, listening and reading. The tests calibrate the candidate's overall proficiency on a nine-point scale; 9 is the highest score and is rated as a 'competent' level of proficiency (IELTS, 2003).[3] Sonny scored 6 on his speaking and writing tests and 7 on reading and listening, giving him an overall IELTS score of 7 – a proficiency rating of 'good': 'Has operational command, though with occasional inaccuracies, inappropriacies and misunderstandings in some situations' (IELTS, 2003: 4). In his first semester, he enrolled in four courses, Issues in Education and Leadership being one. It was the first time he had been overseas.

During his first semester, Sonny shared a house with seven other students, mostly from Asia, including China, Vietnam, Taiwan and Singapore; one student was Australian. Everyone did their own shopping and cooking and Sonny reported that they got on well. The lingua franca of the house was English. Initially, Sonny found some Australian foods hard to eat: 'I can't get familiar with the Western food because I don't get familiar with the bread, butter or something' (Sonny: Interview 2). He joined four clubs on campus: the Australian Space Association, the romance languages club (because of the free movies), the Thai student association and the Taiwanese student club. He preferred to use his anglicised name 'Sonny' and said that all his good friends called him that name.

Sonny talked about how he loved his students at the sports institute in Thailand and wanted to help them express themselves in English. Despite enrolling in the Leadership strand of the Master's programme, he had no desire to become a principal. He believed that such a move would distance him from his students, which he was most reluctant to do. In his second semester, he took a job cooking in a Thai restaurant. He regarded his sojourn in Australia as possibly his only chance to go overseas and saw it as an important opportunity to learn and gain new understandings of a different culture.

Sonny found studying in Australia difficult particularly because of English, but took the view that: 'everything is not just like a smooth road so that everything has problems itself, so how we can pass this point in order to just like complete our goal and achieve our goals' (Sonny: Interview 1). He failed the first assignment for the Issues in Education and Leadership course but passed on resubmission. He also failed the second, larger assignment for the course and rather than resubmit, chose to repeat the whole course the following year. He said that repeating would help him to learn more.

During his second attempt at the Issues in Education and Leadership course, he rarely went to lectures. Instead, he simply submitted his assignments when they were due. The lecturer, who was the lecturer in the study presented here, was interested to know why Sonny was not attending lectures. The research project was generative in developing not only important insights about international student engagement but also personal relationships between myself and the participants. I maintained contact with the lecturer and students after the study had ended and was able to ask Sonny about his lack of attendance in the Issues classes. He replied that the course was better suited to someone who was in administration which held little interest for him. He passed the first assignment but failed the crucial second one. He asked me to help him edit the assignment, which I did and he passed on resubmission, going on to graduate successfully from the programme.

On his last day in Australia, Sonny visited to thank me for my help and also to give me a birthday card. It was my birthday and as it is at the end of July, it is often the day when AusAid students fly home after completing their programmes mid-year. Sonny said he was sad and excited; sad to be leaving Australia and excited to be returning home. His travel plans were to fly to Bangkok and then change planes to northern Thailand where his parents would be waiting for him. He had asked his mother to prepare special food for his homecoming: a spicy Thai pickle, curry paste, papaya salad and sticky rice using rice grown by his parents. His plans were to recommence teaching at the sports institute in August.

## Hanh

Hanh was a 26-year-old, single Vietnamese man who worked as a business English teacher at a university in Ho Chi Minh City and in a multinational Information Technology (IT) company. His programme at The University was the Master of Educational Studies; he was in his first semester at the time of the study. He enrolled in the course because of what he described as his 'lifelong career commitment' to education:

> before I actually applied for the scholarship, I decided to do educational studies. Again, my background is a teacher. So I want to further down into how to get to know the ropes of education, the rope of teaching. (Hanh: Interview 1)

Hanh had already completed a Bachelor of Education and a Master of Arts in teaching English to speakers of other languages (TESOL) at the Vietnam National University in Ho Chi Minh City with English as the medium of instruction for all courses except those on Vietnamese culture and learning styles. Many of the teachers on his Master of Arts programme had been Fulbright scholars from the US and had impressed Hanh with their teaching styles. He was interested in and impressed by many aspects of American culture. His study in Australia was financed by an American philanthropic organisation, Atlantic Philanthropies, which had provided scholarships to a number of Vietnamese students for study at The University. Hanh's Australian studies were not the only time he had studied overseas. He had already undertaken six-month exchanges to Tokyo University and Nanyang University in Singapore, the latter to learn Mandarin Chinese. He named Vietnamese as his L1, and Mandarin and English as his second languages.

During his first semester, Hanh shared a house with two other Vietnamese students whom he met during their five-week academic English preparation course. Early in the semester, he got a job as a cleaner at the Hilton Hotel, working from 6am to 11am Monday to Thursday. His responsibilities were the glass panels in all public areas and some housekeeping duties. He thoroughly enjoyed the work, not only as an opportunity to meet people and to speak English but also because it provided him with meals. He referred to himself as a 'self-starter'. He was conscious of time and being time-efficient, and was proud that he had found himself a job.

After Hanh finished his Master's programme at The University, he travelled to the US to investigate the possibility of a PhD programme there or in Australia. He visited a number of universities but returned to Australia confused. On the day he was to leave Australia he visited me, excited that he had made the decision to apply for an international student scholarship to do a PhD at The University. That night, he flew to Ho Chi Minh City, where his parents were to pick him up in a friend's car. The family did not have a car of its own. From the airport, he expected that they would return to the family villa where his parents and sister lived. His parents owned a coffee production business and grew coffee trees in the garden and on some land in a nearby province. The business was successful which accounted for the family's large house and garden. Hanh attributed his self-starter quality to his family:

> I think my father and mother are self employed, we have our own business. So I think I catch up with that fast, moving environment. It's something to do with your life ... something you plan your life, you have things like that, and you can relax along the way, ... but at least you just go ahead with your life. So I have been that way. (Hanh: Interview 1)

Hanh returned to his university in Ho Chi Minh City to teach business communication. His application to The University failed but he was awarded a scholarship to another Australian university and commenced his doctoral studies the following year.

## Erica

Erica was a 29-year-old, single Singaporean woman. She came to the Master of Education (Leadership) programme as a mathematics and geography teacher in a Singaporean high school. She was in her first semester at the time of the study. Before embarking on her Australian study programme, she completed a Bachelor of Arts/Social Sciences and a postgraduate Diploma of Education in Singapore. Her plans were to pursue her postgraduate studies to doctoral level, possibly with the aim of becoming a university lecturer. Her reasons for doing the Issues in Education and Leadership course were professional development and career advancement. She saw herself as an educational leader but wanted to learn more. The programme also provided her with the chance to take a sabbatical from work.

Erica was an enthusiastic and confident participant in class discussions and was named an inspiration by another international student who was concerned about her English. For Erica, the people in the course – the lecturer and her classmates – made the course a 'terrific learning experience' (survey data). In some ways, the course was a life-changing experience for Erica. She had been teaching in the Singaporean education system for six years and represented herself as somewhat of a 'rebel' – as someone who wanted to make changes to the system but was constantly presented with difficulties. The critical focus of the course resonated with her and gave her a sense of vindication that her approach was legitimate. Her mother and aunt were school principals in Singapore and she was proud to be a teacher. Her 'passion' was to excel at teaching. For her it was important to be challenged and she wanted to immerse herself in Australian culture. She enjoyed the 'global village' feel of the campus.

Erica said that she felt more herself and more relaxed in Australia: 'I feel that when I'm here I'm less inhibited' (Erica: Interview 1). As a Singaporean student, she was not required to provide The University with proof of her English language proficiency. English was her L1 with Mandarin and Cantonese Chinese her second languages. She said that many families in Singapore with graduate parents used English as their L1 at home. Towards the end of the semester, she worked in an ironing shop, communicating with customers and looking after orders, and thoroughly enjoyed the experience. She returned to Singapore at the end of her Master's programme.

## Anna

Anna was from China where she worked as a civil servant in a government education department. She was 29 years old and married; her husband joined her in Australia three months after she had started her studies. Prior to his arrival, she shared a house with two other Chinese women in a suburb adjacent to the university. She was enrolled in a Master of Education (Leadership) and studying with the assistance of an AusAid scholarship. The Issues in Education and Leadership course was part of her second semester enrolment.

Anna's motivation for enrolling in the Master's programme was as follows: 'I first applied for this program because I think there is something lacking in myself. I need to promote my theoretical things' (Anna: Interview 1). When she first arrived in Australia, she felt timid and 'incredibly nervous' about speaking in English:

> my first language crisis when you want to approach someone. At the very beginning when I arrived here, I don't think much more confident or I'm not actually comfortable to talk with the native speaker and sometimes you know I think the language. (Anna: Interview 1)

At the time of the study, with one semester of study already completed, she said she was feeling much more comfortable and no longer nervous about her English.

Anna's previous study was a Bachelor of Arts (English) at a university in southern China. Her English name was in fact the English name closest to the name of her town on an island in her province. She anglicised her name because 'I think I found that people it's hard for them to pronounce my name … so I just choose my English name easier for them to pronounce' (Anna: Interview 1). Mandarin Chinese was Anna's L1 and English her second. By the end of the semester, Anna had two part-time jobs: one waitressing in a Tibetan restaurant and the other waitressing and cleaning in a sushi bar. In an email, she told me that she was keen to learn how to balance study and work because this was a challenge for her. She returned to China at the end of the year.

## Grace

Grace was a 36-year-old woman from Mozambique, completing a Master in Education (Leadership) programme with the assistance of an AusAid scholarship. Before taking up the offer of the scholarship, she worked as a training officer at the South African franchise of a large multinational food and beverage company. Her initial interest in the Master's programme was its focus on administration but by the time she had been accepted into the programme, the focus had changed to leadership. Later in the programme, she enrolled in courses in the business faculty on human resource management, and organisational behaviour and management, in order to retain some relevance to her work.

Grace's previous qualifications were an honours degree in English Teaching as a Foreign Language, completed in Mozambique and a postgraduate diploma in Public Management in South Africa. She said it was common for people in Mozambique to send their children to South Africa for education because it was conducted in English. She felt that the experience of living away in South Africa had prepared her for life in Australia, although during her 18 months in Australia she went home only once – at Christmas to see her two-year-old son.

She identified her main motivation for doing the programme was to gain a qualification that would ensure a good job for herself and the means to provide for her son: 'It's for him. I'm doing it for him. My parents give for me. I'm doing it for him' (Grace: Interview 1). It was hard for women in Mozambique and having a Master's degree would help her in the workforce:

Now people looking for more knowledge, more advanced academic level. I can't stop otherwise I will be back. And being a woman in my country, it will be worse so always thought I have to do my Master's degree. (Grace: Interview 1)

When Grace received her first offer of a scholarship to study in Australia, she was pregnant and turned it down. After her second application was successful, her sisters persuaded her to accept and said that they would look after her child. Grace said that while it is hard to be away from her son as a toddler, it is probably better than when he is older. When she went home for the Christmas break, she emailed me to say that her son was calling her 'aunty' and her sister 'mum'. She said she accepted the situation but was looking forward to returning to Mozambique and being reunited with her son.

Grace's mother tongue was Chuabo, a local language in Mozambique. She learned Portuguese at school and then English later in high school. In Australia, she was sharing a flat with a South African man whom she met at the airport on the day of her arrival. Her friendship group included other students from Mozambique and her South African flatmate, as well as two Australian women she met when swimming at the university pool. Generally, however, she had little contact with Australians. At the end of the Issues in Education and Leadership course, during semester break, she and a friend travelled to a provincial city where they joined legions of students and backpackers, picking fruit and vegetables. She said that she enjoyed the experience although the money was poor and the work back-breaking.

In the final semester of her Master's programme, Grace's mother died. Grace faced the difficult decision of whether to return to Mozambique or stay in Australia. In the end, at the insistence of her family, she stayed and completed her studies but organised a special church service to celebrate her mother's life. In her final semester, she asked me to be her academic mentor, an AusAid-funded position, to help her complete her research project. She graduated successfully from the programme and returned to Mozambique and her son.

## Javier

Javier was a 35-year-old Argentinean man who was in his second semester of the Master of Education (Leadership) programme. As part of his programme, he was enrolling in all available counselling courses with the aim of becoming a school counsellor. He had studied a course with the lecturer in the previous semester and was enthusiastic about her teaching style which he describes as 'fantastic' (Javier: Interview 1). In Argentina, he had worked as a merchant banker in the finance industry for 15 years, 12 in a 'big big bank':

> And I get really tired and sick of it, so I wanted to change my career. But as you know, I have a big family and I still have to feed them. So I thought that I can't just start it over and be an architect or something really new. And I have to find out something that is has to do with something that I'd done before. And I think just searching the web, I found these Educational studies here, it's something that I didn't know that existed. (Javier: Interview 1)

The move to Australia had been significant for Javier because it included his family – his wife and their four children. At the time of the study, the family was in the process of applying for permanent residency in Australia. Both Javier and his wife were interested in living abroad, especially in an English-speaking country with an extra incentive being their concerns about the social and economic situation in Argentina. They chose Australia on the recommendation of a friend and despite offers from other universities, Javier chose The University because it was 'supposed to be the number one in education' (Javier: Interview 1). While he and his wife were happy with the move, he said that the children were missing aspects of Argentinean life, particularly their big house in Buenos Aires and their maid, and also the money which had meant treats such as trips to fast-food outlets.

At the time of the study, Javier was doing a counselling practicum at a boys' high school and was thoroughly enjoying it. His secondary education in Argentina had been at a similar institution and he felt an affinity with the place. He had been offered a permanent position as counsellor at the school, a position he described as his 'dream job':

> For me, working as a counsellor was a dream ... That was something that I would never thought I would ever do. That was my dream back at home. And I didn't come here to do that, but I've learned that that I can do that. And in a way ... it's like I would be able to fulfil my dream here. (Javier: Interview 1)

Javier's first language was Spanish but he felt confident in his English. He began learning English in kindergarten when he was three years old and was able to further practice his English during regular holidays to the US and the Caribbean when he was a child. At 18, he travelled to Cambridge in England to study English intensively. His previous tertiary qualifications were an undergraduate degree in Business Administration and Master of Business Administration (MBA). Many of the readings in his MBA programme were in English.

## The lecturer: Helen

As noted above, Helen was in her fifties and a professor. A South African by birth, she first came to Australia in the 1970s, and had since spent substantial periods of time in both countries. She continued to carry out research and postgraduate supervision in South Africa. Her L1 was English, with Afrikaans as a second language, reflecting the education policies of apartheid. Within the Faculty of Education at The University, Helen had a reputation for being an excellent teacher. She attributed much of the formative influence on her pedagogy to her years of working in South Africa with Black students in the campaign against apartheid.

Though not formally trained in second language teaching, she had, in fact, spent much of her academic life teaching second language speakers, in both South Africa and Australia. She had worked in Adult Education as a materials writer where she said it was always clear to her that the limited language of second language speakers did not automatically mean a limited understanding of concepts (Lecturer: Interview 1). She applied this insight to her teaching of international students. During the 1980s, Helen worked in a so-called 'open university' in South Africa. The university was one of eight that actively resisted the apartheid regime and received lower levels of government funding. Helen's work was with African students who were teachers, principals and school inspectors. A major focus with the students was critical analysis of the Bantu education system and the development of an 'analytical understanding' of how the segregated education system worked and could be changed. For Helen, 'the most empowering thing that people could experience was how to get a theoretical understanding of their lives' (Lecturer: Interview 1).

During the 1990s, Helen became Dean of the Faculty of Education and professor in the field of education policy and management. Her work at The University focused primarily on educational leadership and school change, particularly in disadvantaged schools. Helen coordinated the Issues in Education and Leadership course. She wrote and prepared the materials and lectured all the sessions on the course except for one workshop on teamwork.

## The Study

The research study was a case study of the MEd Issues in Education and Leadership (ME5100) across a semester although the contact with many of the students and lecturer continued for longer. The research approach was to generate a 'thick' description of course practices using ethnographic tools that comprised the following:

- interview data from students and teacher: an interview at the beginning of the course and after it was completed with transcriptions incorporating prosodic features such as rising intonation and volume; participants were asked to verify the accounts in the transcriptions;
- classroom video data of all three-hour seminars for 13 weeks of which I watched all twice and transcribed several lessons in detail including one from Week 2 and another from Week 3;
- an archive of written materials: international student orientation pack from the university; course materials; student assignments with teacher feedback; emails between the teacher and students; lectures from selected students; and teaching evaluation forms;
- field notes: I kept a detailed researcher journal in which I recorded observations of classroom activity and a separate column for reflections and ideas.

University ethics procedures were followed carefully in which I sought participants' consent and de-identified all data. The students self-selected for the study although all completed the consent form to be filmed during the class sessions. The research participants were informed that they could withdraw from the study at any time. Indeed, the issue as the course progressed was not withdrawal but other students wanting to join based on the positive reports they had heard from colleagues. It seemed that the interviews acted as a form of 'safe house' (Canagarajah, 1997) for some of the students where they could address the interview questions but also seek advice on assignment topics and discuss personal matters such as family and living arrangements in Australia.

The design of the study was driven by the excellent teaching reputation of the lecturer and her preparedness to participate in the study. While the genesis of the study lay in exclusionary classroom practices for a group of international students, I decided to investigate 'good practice' in the study rather than 'bad' practice. The research objective was to access a course where the lecturer had an established reputation for excellence in teaching and to discern the features that characterised teaching excellence. The approach was to identify how students evaluated the teaching practice and if they considered it helpful to their learning, explore its characteristics in depth. The study would provide useful outcomes on what international students regarded as effective teaching for learning. The approach accords with Luke's (2004) call for research that describes and documents affirmative discourses, practices and texts in the belief that they can provide ways of redressing inequitable practice. My position was that while inadequate and exclusionary teaching practices should be named, it is more ethical and useful to provide examples of effective practice. These examples can act as exemplars and contribute to pedagogical change that promotes international student participation and engagement.

## Issues impacting engagement

The major themes that emerge in the research are practices related to English, teaching and participation, learning and strategies and issues of the self. These findings do not suggest that each theme exists in isolation from the others. For example, English does not exist as a separate theme; rather, it operates in dialectical relationships with teaching, class participation, learning and identity issues related to self-representation. Performing publicly in a second language in an unfamiliar context is risky business and has profound implications for identity (Kettle, 2011; Miller, 2003; Norton Peirce, 1995).

The practices emergent in the data related to English, teaching and participation, learning and strategies, and issues of the self and are heavily implicated in student engagement as posited in the social practice-based model of engagement discussed above. The following chapters present the practices as they align with the three dimensions of engagement: (i) the institutional antecedents involving English and the mediational practices of the teacher to promote student participation and learning; (ii) the students' self-regulatory practices to action their own learning; and (iii) the students' achievements and outcomes including academic success and personal transformation.

## Notes

(1)  The course title has been changed.
(2)  Single quotation marks indicate the words, phrases and sentences of interest. Italics are reserved for highlighting and emphasis, and for the titles of policies, documents and sections of documents. Double quotation marks denote direct speech from study participants and quotes from authors of cited texts.
(3)  The minimum IELTS entry score required by most Australian universities is 6.5.

# 5 English: What Counts in the Academy

## Introduction

The pursuit of an English language education is contributing to major flows of international students to English-speaking countries such as Australia, the UK and the US. English has become a source of capital, a fact that universities are keen to exploit. English permeates most discussions on international higher education in Australia and is a recurring theme in the international students' accounts of their study experiences. English in the university is often presented as benign, merely the neutral vehicle for communicating knowledge. For international students undertaking university studies in English as their second or additional (ESL/EAL) language, language is far from benign, especially at the outset. The pervasiveness and naturalness of English invites what Foucault (1972) calls a suspension of its continuity and a disturbing of its tranquillity. This chapter presents the state of English in the world and in higher education more specifically. It then moves to English in postgraduate international education and the contextualisation and recontextualisation of English across multiple university documents from institutional-level policy statements to course-level assignment feedback. The aim is to reveal the conditions forming English within the English-speaking university and their instantiations in high-stakes course practices such as assessment.

Language has an amplifier effect in all aspects of academic life. Cazden (2001: 3) argues that language in teaching and learning environments has a tripartite core of functions: (i) the communication of propositional information; (ii) the establishment and maintenance of social relationships; and (iii) the expression of the speaker's identity and attitudes. From a social practice perspective, it follows that language is overdetermined in its relations with other elements in academic practices. The dialectical relationships between elements means that language as the semiotic element impacts exponentially on the other elements; in education, knowledge, tasks, people and values associated with ways of proposing knowledge; establishing social relationships; and expressing oneself in classroom settings.

These principles are relevant to higher education. In the English-speaking context, English and other elements in the academic practices constituting courses must be seen as interrelated. 'Doing' academic work is very much 'doing' English. For limited proficiency users of English (Horwitz, 2012), albeit emerging bilinguals with developing competence, engagement in high-stakes practices such as assessment tasks and class discussions is challenging and difficult. The students' English language competence is overdetermined in its effect on their capacity to participate in important course practices.

Following Foucault, these practices can be seen as the everyday realisations of institutional discourses characterising the contemporary social order of the English-speaking academy. The practices are networked in particular configurations to form courses such as Issues in Education and Leadership. For students and teachers, course practices contain certain rules and norms, or 'truths', about acceptable disciplinary practice, that is, the 'game' (Foucault, 1987). Failing to comply with these rules represents a transgression beyond the threshold of acceptable practice, incurring social repercussions and possible exclusion.

For the students in the study, English and its relationship to their academic practice in the Issues course preoccupied them greatly – some of them overwhelmingly. They were aware of its power, including its exclusionary power, and were highly exercised by trying to discern its 'rules of engagement'. This chapter examines what the students recognised to be the institutionally preferred ways of 'doing' English, that is, what counts as English in the English-speaking university. It also presents an example of the way that discursive norms and practices can be strategically exploited to assist second language users struggling to meet the English language part of valued course practices. Together, these analyses provide insights into the magnitude of English as a condition impacting international student engagement in the English-speaking academy.

## English and Global Higher Education

Within the globally competitive higher education market, English has become a highly prized good (Marginson, 2006). This situation has afforded English-medium universities particular opportunities and has also led to the displacement of other languages in education and research. In research, English has become the language of publications and databases which means that dissemination of findings to an international audience is based on knowing how to write and understand academic English (Ammon, 2001). Studies of higher education literacy practices in four European countries have found that academics often rely on assistance to write their research findings in English and consider English to be very important in the publication and distribution of research around the world

(Hewings, 2012). Moreover, while China is currently second only to the US in terms of scientific output, a significant gap exists in the international citations of Chinese research (Ferguson, 2011). Publishing in English – or not – is a major contributor to this situation.

In 2016–2017, the top eight universities in the Times Higher Education World University Rankings with performance in the core missions of teaching, research, knowledge transfer and international outlook are in the US and the UK (TES Global, 2016). The top three are (from number one in descending order): University of Oxford (UK); California Institute of Technology (US); and Stanford University (US). At number nine, the Swiss Federal Institute of Technology Zurich is the first representative from a non-Anglophone country. The first Asian university to appear on the list is the National University of Singapore (#24). The 14 universities ranked from 10 to 23 between the Swiss Federal Institute of Technology Zurich (#9) and the National University of Singapore (#24) are from either the US or the UK. The first Australian university is the University of Melbourne (#33). The global concentration of research in English-speaking countries has been noted and is described by Marginson (2006) as 'disturbing'.

## English in the construction of knowledge

Some scholars have examined the ways that the grammar of the English language itself impacts on views of the world and how this might have implications for research designs and findings. For example, Baldauf and Kaplan (2014) argue that one way that English structures the world is in the individualisation of mass nouns (e.g. a glass of water) and the measurement of mass nouns (e.g. a litre of water). These wordings and their associated meanings operate as metaphors and create a world view that fragments the unity of entities such as water. (I discuss metaphor in more detail in Chapter 7.) As a result, it becomes difficult to understand the pervasiveness of a problem such as water pollution because water is fragmented and seen as discrete entities rather than a whole. Equally, segmentation and counting mean that noun units can be pluralised, obscuring the plight of the whole. Baldauf and Kaplan (2014) argue that this English language world view causes people to see *things* rather than *processes* (italics in the original), which has implications for research objectives and approaches.

The pervasiveness and dominance of English in global knowledge systems is impacting not only on research but also researchers and the social order. Aligning with points raised above about the advantage of English-medium universities in market-driven higher education, Kaplan (2001) argues that English-speaking nations hold a type of cartel on scientific information because much of the information is organised technologically according to English-based knowledge systems. For nations pursuing development agendas, this means dealing with the dual demands of accessing scientific information in English and understanding the conceptual relationships in English-based knowledge systems. A whole new cadre of scientifically and technologically savvy information managers has become necessary to interpret and operationalise this information.

The association between English and economic advancement is a political and ideological one, and has different meanings and consequences depending on the contexts in which it is encountered (Seargeant, 2012). In some settings, the association informs government language policy and is the driver of development projects and initiatives such as sending students overseas to study at universities where there is expertise in areas of national need, as discussed in Chapter 1. In other cases, the relationship between English and economic advantage is personal, tapping into the values of consumerism, entrepreneurialism and English as 'cool'. For others, learning English is unavoidable. For example, Nigerian scholar Ayọ Bamgboṣe (2009: 648) makes the point that for many people, it is not so much a case of wanting to learn English because of the advantages that it brings; rather it is *needing* to learn it, because not learning English is not really a choice'. English is perceived as the prerequisite to improved wages, opportunities and living conditions, a perception which is realised in certain cases (e.g. Grin, 2001).

## English going global in universities

Given the benefits and lucrativeness of English, it is not surprising that more and more universities in non-English-speaking countries are offering courses in English. The increased availability is particularly prevalent in countries where English is already used extensively as a lingua franca, that is, a contact language, for mediating purposeful communication. Hence, in Denmark, Finland, the Netherlands and Sweden, many university courses are now offered in English (OECD, 2013a). Countries offering some courses in English are: Belgium (Fl.), the Czech Republic, France, Germany, Hungary, Iceland, Japan, Korea, Norway, Poland, the Slovak Republic, Switzerland and Turkey. The level of study can play a role: for example in Belgium, English-medium courses are available at Master's level only (OECD, 2013a). In the Asian region, The Philippines has become a budget destination for students from countries such as Vietnam who want to learn English but are reluctant or unable to pay the fees demanded by institutions in the US, the UK, Australia and other English-speaking countries (McGeown, 2012). The widespread offering of English-medium courses has raised the question about whether English has become the lingua franca of higher education around the world (Rigg, 2013).

The push for English as the medium of instruction (EMI) has led to questions about the recruitment of academics with both disciplinary content knowledge and English language competence. The concerns are about the displacement of local content specialists and the implications for the quality of students' learning experiences. Anecdotal accounts from international students point to changes in university recruitment policies in response to the demand for English. For example, a Taiwanese postgraduate student who recounted how the business course at her university in Taiwan had mandated EMI and recruited overseas lecturers from European countries rather than local academics because of the latter's lower English language levels. Local expertise was being replaced by globally mobile academics capable of teaching the disciplinary content in English.

Universal English language instruction operates in countries such as Australia, Ireland, New Zealand, the UK, the US and Canada, although French-medium courses are also offered in Quebec. Strikingly, many of these Anglophone countries share common approaches to higher education. Australia, New Zealand and the UK are all commercially driven education-as-export countries (Marginson *et al.*, 2010). They bear similarities to other English-speaking countries such as Canada and the US in that they favour a monocultural approach and have a resolute commitment to English (Bailey, 2013; Lee & Rice, 2007). It is through strategies such as these that university markets are able to reproduce 'the hegemony and homogeneity of English' (Marginson, 2006: 37).

# English and the World

English is the language of globalisation: it mediates and facilitates interactions and transactions all over the world. Within the global English phenomenon, English has been transformed by its multiplicity of uses and users. The question in current English studies is what does it look and sound like across this new linguistic landscape? In their *Companion to English Studies*, Leung and Street (2014) take the view that English is a 'protean entity'; it is constantly being shaped and reshaped in multiple ways. English is both fixed and in flux; it is consistently stable in writing but more varied in the spoken form. While the English spoken as a contact language around the world remains discernibly English, it is localised in sounds, vocabulary and occasionally grammar. As such, English is now Englishes, or different dialects that retain the markers of English but absorb features derived from the local language.

## Devising terminology for English use and users

These myriad manifestations of English have generated a profusion of terms that are designed to capture its multiplicity of forms and functions. World Englishes and global English highlight the changing forms and range of English. English as a lingua franca (ELF) and English as an international language (EIL) focus on function and the features of English when it is spoken by speakers for whom English is not their first language (L1). Indeed, most of the world's English communication is now occurring between people using English as their second or additional language without a native speaker present (Jenkins, 2003). Possibly as a counterpoint to the elevated status of English, some scholars are arguing that the world is experiencing a 'multilingual turn' (May, 2014) and highlighting the plurilingual nature of most people's lives. In educational jurisdictions in Australia and the UK, learners are now often referred to as 'English as an additional language (EAL)' rather than 'English as a second language (ESL)' while 'language background other than English (LBOTE)' has been substituted for 'non-English-speaking background (NESB)'. In Australia, 'English as a dialect (EAD)' recognises the fact that many Aboriginal and Torres Strait Islander students use Standard Australian English as an additional dialect of English to their L1 of Aboriginal English or a creole, also written as Kriol. The rationale is political and advocatory: the new terms promote the understanding that learners are highly resourced in languages and should not be depicted as linguistically deficit because they are learning (Standard) English. Indeed, most people in the world are multilingual, or at least, bilingual with monolingualism a condition largely confined to the Anglosphere (Wardhaugh, 2010).

One of the most influential attempts to capture the diversity of English use has been Kachru's (1992) typology using three concentric circles: the Inner Circle, the Outer Circle and the Expanding Circle. These circles are geographically orientated and represent dominant groupings of users who speak English, respectively, as a native language (e.g. Australia); as a second language (e.g. Singapore); and as a foreign language (e.g. Thailand). The initial large-scale catalyst for the spread of English was the British Empire and colonisation of swathes of territory around the world. Subsequent to large-scale decolonisation after World War II, nation-building in former colonies often led to language planning initiatives for local languages as well as the retention of English as a means of ensuring economic and political links to the former colonial power (Iyer et al., 2014). An interesting feature of English in the former colonies is that it has 'indigenised' into local varieties (Sonntag, 2003). In Kahru's Expanding Circle countries, English is a foreign language (EFL) with little or no official status but is, nonetheless, used extensively by people in business, trade and diplomatic negotiations, and accessed readily via mass and online media. Initiatives such as the consolidation of the Association of Southeast Asian Nations (ASEAN) into a single trade bloc in 2015 are propelling the learning of English in EFL countries such as Vietnam. ASEAN has chosen English as its official language for group meetings and negotiations between members (Kirkpatrick, 2012).

## The power of Standard English

The ascendancy of English in areas such as science has sparked much political debate, particularly around issues of standards, exclusion and new forms of imperialism. Concerns have been raised that in this age when the predominant users of English are non-native speakers, the continued supremacy of native-speaker models is a form of linguistic prejudice (Ammon, 2000). The model of the native speaker as the ideal language user persists through a number of means, mostly notably the privileging of Standard English. Standard English is defined primarily by its formal grammar and lexis which are most evident in written English. Written English is remarkably standardised across even highly differentiated dialects pointing to the strong relationship between the two: Standard English is achieved significantly through standardisation in writing. Widdowson (1993: 164) refers to Standard English as 'a kind of superposed dialect' which most native speakers are not born to but rather learn at school. And while Standard English is not the naturally acquired L1 of most English native speakers, native speakers remain the yardstick for linguistic correctness (Ammon, public lecture, 24.08.04). The assumption is that English speakers from Kachru's Inner Circle are the 'correct' model. Chowdhury and Phan (2014) argue that native-speaking English varieties are often considered the most desirable standard for international education. These varieties form an approach to English referred to as BANA: British, Australasian and Northern American (Holliday, 1994, 2006).

Part of the power of standardised English is that it becomes the standard; Standard English is the standard required for entry into particular communities. At universities in Australia and elsewhere, the gatekeeping role of Standard English is evident in the policies dictating language requirements for international student enrolment.[1] The result is English language levels working to either afford or deny access to educational opportunity. These conditions of possibility and impossibility also extend to domestic conditions involving English use and education. Tupas (2006) argues that *inner circles* exist in both 'native' English-speaking and 'non-native' English-speaking countries where social advantage ensures access to the standard variety of English. For example, in Kachu's Outer Circle countries, local elites with links to the former English colonial power have retained the privilege associated with access to English education (Iyer *et al.*, 2014). The growing middle classes in Outer and Expanding Circle countries are also investing in English language education in the belief that it will accrue economic and social benefits, as discussed in Chapter 1. The beneficiaries of these English language investments continue to be the education institutions in BANA countries including universities, although these flows are being challenged by the emergence of alternative English language providers in 'non-native' English-speaking countries as discussed above. The changes and the inherent responsibilities of institutions to their students mean that complacency, especially in teaching and learning experiences, is not an option (Ryan, 2011).

## English in the Academy

This section proposes English as a discourse, where a discourse is formed through the regularity of statements across dispersed practices and 'surfaces of emergence' (Foucault, 1972). It is within the practices on these 'surfaces' that the domain of the discourse is delimited and defined, thus giving it the status of an object. For most international students, English is a familiar entity long before they arrive at their overseas, English-medium university. For the students in the case study, English is a global entity with a number of them linking English to the future development and prosperity of their countries. For example, Erica from Singapore connected English to international business and Singapore's economic survival. Grace acknowledged the benefits to herself of speaking English, especially in Mozambique which is Portuguese speaking but surrounded by English-speaking countries.

The global dispersion of English manifested itself in various ways in the students' lives at home before coming to Australia. Most of them were heavily involved with English at work. For Erica, English was her L1 and the medium of instruction in her mathematics and geography classes. Javier from Argentina began learning English at kindergarten and spent extensive time as a child travelling with his family to English-speaking countries such as the US. He attended English classes in Cambridge, England, when he was 18 and continued to travel to Europe regularly. Two of the other students worked as English language teachers: Hanh as a business English teacher at a university in Ho Chi Minh City and Sonny as an English communication teacher at a sports institute in Thailand. Sonny regularly used American pop songs in his teaching and said that most of his friends used his anglicised name. Grace trained as an English teacher but moved into workplace training at an international company in Maputo, Mozambique. The company's official policy was that English language proficiency was not compulsory for workers; nonetheless, among the workers themselves, it was understood that speaking English was an advantage as the company was South African. English language ability was linked to better job prospects within the company.

All of the students in the study had had some exposure to academic English and to the expectations of studying in English; indeed, some had previous study experiences in English-speaking contexts. Erica completed undergraduate and postgraduate degrees in Singapore in English and Javier's Master of Business Administration (MBA) programme in Argentina comprised many readings in English. Anna majored in English in her

Bachelor of Arts degree in China as did Sonny in his Bachelor of Education in Thailand. Hanh's Master of Arts in teaching English to speakers of other languages (TESOL) in Ho Chi Minh City was mainly conducted in English by Fulbright scholars from the US. Grace had experience as an international student in South Africa having travelled there to complete an English language postgraduate diploma in public management.

The privileged place of English in Australian universities was immediately evident to the students when they began applying for enrolment in the Master's programme at The University. English language proficiency requirements came into force and English language academic preparation programmes were mandated for the AusAid and other scholarship-sponsored students. The gatekeeping role of English was evident in the minimum entry requirements of English as an International Testing System (IELTS) 6.5 and Testing of English as a Foreign Language (TOEFL) 570. The students' IELTS scores are listed in Table 5.1.

For the scholarship students, Anna (China), Sonny (Thailand), Grace (Mozambique) and Hanh (Vietnam), compulsory attendance in the academic English preparation programmes meant arriving in Australia two to three months before the commencement of the Master's course. The preparation programmes were provided by The University and intended as an introduction to academic English and the foundational skills needed to study in Australia.

The argument being made here is that a discourse comes into existence and assumes power within the practices of institutions and other 'surfaces of emergence'. The elements constituting English within the academic practices of the course became evident to the students once the course began as did the power and regulative function of English. In the next section, I shift from the coherence of geographically dispersed themes about English to English at the practice level in the students' experiences of the Issues in Education and Leadership course. I investigate The University's mission

**Table 5.1** The IELTS scores of the participants in the study

| Erica | Language proficiency test not required[a] |
|---|---|
| Javier | 7 |
| Hanh | 7 |
| Anna | 7 |
| Grace | 6.5 |
| Sonny | 7 (with 6 for speaking and writing and 7 for reading and listening) |

[a] Erica's English language undergraduate and postgraduate qualifications from Singapore exempted her from the need to show proof of English language proficiency. The first language status of English and previous degrees from Singaporean universities are regarded as proof of the requisite level of English needed for study at The University.

statement and strategic plan as well as enrolment policy documents for representations of what counts as English from an institutional perspective. I then map the articulation and rearticulation of these representations of English across a chain of Issues course documents including assessment criteria and lecturer feedback on written assignments.

## What counts as English in The University

The mission statement of The University foregrounds the creation of a community dedicated to national and international levels of excellence in teaching, research and scholarship, and the importance of contributing to the state and nation. Within its plans for teaching and learning, The University identifies one of its strategic objectives as a commitment to curriculum that delivers an international focus. It also identifies what it considers to be the key capabilities of graduates, namely independence, creativity, critical judgement, effective communication, ethical and social understanding and knowledge of a designated field. These capabilities are repeated in policies on graduate attributes, the student charter and academic integrity and plagiarism. The recurrent wordings and statements contribute to the formation of a discourse on the preferred ways of being a student at The University.

In terms of English, The University's strategic plan makes no explicit mention of language. The only explicit references to English are in the policies on admission requirements and support programmes for international and Australian NESB students. Within the general mission and vision for the university, there is no specific awareness of language. By its very absence, English is assumed. Its existence as a default state of affairs without mention indicates hegemonic status within the institution.

The privileged role of English within the university mirrors the place of English in the wider Australian community and for that matter, the rest of the Anglosphere. In countries such as the US and Australia, English remains the taken-for-granted language, irrespective of the settlement of generations of migrants and refugees. Home-based languages have minority status and English remains the norm in the mainstream, despite the linguistic diversity. Most people are monolingually English; in the Australian context, 81% of people speak only English (ABS, 2013a). Despite this dominance, nearly one in five people speak a language other than English at home, not including Indigenous Australians who speak a dialect of Australian English. Referring to the US, Fishman (1981: 517) argues that 'The greatest American linguistic investment by far has been in the Anglification of its millions of immigrant and indigenous speakers of other languages'. Equally in Australia, English monolingualism is unconscious and hegemonic (Ozolins, 1993). Government immigration and settlement policies have moved through phases from assimilation to multiculturalism but with every phase resolutely committed to English.

English has no official status in Australia yet its centrality is rarely challenged (Smolicz, 1995).

## Assessment

The specification of academic attributes and practices is most obvious in course assessment criteria. The criteria rearticulate the norms mandated in the university policies; they are policy rearticulated for practice. The continuity of statements across dispersed 'surfaces of emergence' is shown in Table 5.2. Key capabilities for graduates are mapped against the criteria for written assignments in the Issues course. The table highlights the ways in which a discourse is formed through the coherence of themes across disparate sites.

The clear patterns of reproduction are not surprising; it is after all the role of courses to apply the values espoused by university policy. What is interesting is the consistency with which the themes are rearticulated across the chain of genres comprising policy statements, course assessment criteria and lecturer feedback. Genres are socially situated, purpose-driven text types that provide a useful means of analysing the reinterpretation of a theme across a chain of different text types (Fairclough, 2003). Analysis

**Table 5.2** Key student capabilities recontextualised across institutional texts

| The University strategic plan: Key capabilities for graduates | The Issues course outline: Criteria for written assignments |
|---|---|
| Independence and creativity | A thorough analysis of recent and relevant ideas from a variety of sources. A highly creative synthesis of appropriate ideas. |
| Critical judgement | Evidence of ability to think in critically reflective ways in a variety of theoretical and practical educational situations. Taking ownership of ideas. |
| Effective communication | The student's work shows:<br>(i) clear and logical structure;<br>(ii) fluency and written expression of a high order;<br>(iii) accurate referencing procedures. |
| Ethical and social understanding | Sensitivity demonstrated in obvious situations, and also in more subtle situations. |
| In-depth knowledge of field of study | Extensive reading of appropriate literature. Reading ranges broadly beyond 'set' texts. |

of a genre chain shows the resilience of a theme as it moves from context to context via text. It can indicate the emergence of a new discourse or the continuity of an existing one. The analysis showing continuity of statements across various university documents points to a powerful discourse on what constitutes valued academic attributes at The University: independence and creativity; critical judgement; effective communication; ethical and social understandings; and in-depth knowledge of a field.

Significantly for second language users, academic attributes have a performative dimension: the Issues written assessment criteria exhibit a high density of nominalised verb forms, that is, actions that have been written as nouns (*a thorough analysis*; *a highly creative synthesis*). The predominance of verb forms constitutes a type of performativity in which the emphasis is on 'doing', that is, *doing* academic practice as described in Chapter 3. It is the habitualised *doing* of academic life which is co-constitutive with particular types of *knowing* and *being*. Successful academic practice is doing, knowing and being within the institution. The criteria both shape the performances of the students and measure them. In the Issues course at The University and at most other Australian universities, assessment criteria are elaborated in descriptors across seven standards from High Distinction (HD: Grade 7) to Pass (P: Grade 4) to Fail (F: Grades 3–1). The criteria and standards form a 'grid of specification' (Foucault, 1972) that objectify and measure student performances including those at the threshold of exclusion. The criteria operate as a 'regulative ensemble' (Aglietta, 1979) that reproduces the university 'regime of truth' about the performative attributes of the ideal student.

## English in assignment presentation guidelines

The recontextualisation analysis of English in multiple texts from university-level policy statements to course-level assessment criteria revealed no explicit reference to English, as noted above. Rather, reference to English appeared only in policies about plagiarism and the enrolment of international and domestic ESL students. At the course level, the only explicit reference to English was in the guidelines for Assignment Presentation in the course outline. The Assignment Presentation section is of interest because it establishes the norms and expectations for written assignments, including the role of English in academic writing.

### A critical discourse analysis of what counts as English

The following section presents detailed analyses on what counts as English in the academy as represented by a Master of Education (MEd) course at an Australian university. The analysis provides the means of making visible the often-hidden features of this particular English. It is also an exemplar of evidence-driven discourse analysis and how it can be reported in scholarly writing.

The section on Assignment Presentation comprises three paragraphs and covers two-thirds of an A4 page. The paragraph that I present here is the first; it deals with written communication and contains the reference to English. The other two paragraphs refer to correct forms of citation and referencing, and word-processing and formatting, respectively. The first paragraph containing the reference to English is reproduced below.

---

### Assignment Presentation

Assignments should conform with word limits, be neatly presented and demonstrate a level of written expression that enables readers to understand the points being made. Successful written communication requires a level of adherence to the conventions of our common language. Attention should be paid to the conventions of standard written English, sentence structure, grammar, usage, appropriate style, and correct punctuation and spelling. If you experience difficulties in this area you should contact us some weeks before the posting date so that we can discuss assistance which may be available.

---

The paragraph constructs meaning about what constitutes 'successful written communication' in the course, and by extension, The University. Of interest is how 'successful written communication' is linked to 'standard written English'. Mostly, the links are achieved through semantic and grammatical resources and a chain of lexical references. Themes are introduced and sustained across sentences in a set of relations creating cohesion and coherence across the text. Coherence operates across the following:

> a level of written expression that enables the reader to understand the points being made → Successful written communication → adherence to the conventions of our common language → Attention ... to the conventions of standard written English → sentence structure, grammar, usage, appropriate style, and correct punctuation and spelling → this area.

Grammar is a tool for making meaning and in this paragraph the grammatical relations construct 'successful written communication' as dependent upon 'adherence to the conventions of our common language' which in turn are represented as 'the conventions of standard written English'. The relations between the 'things' (in noun phrases) are elaborative; each elaborates upon the other in the previous sentence. In this way, a logic is built whereby successful written expression is equivalent to standard written English: 'standard written English' incorporates conventions on 'sentence structure, grammar, usage, appropriate style, and correct punctuation and spelling'.

What is happening is that the organisation of the text is establishing a logic of equivalence (Laclau & Mouffe, 1985). The aim of such logic is to collapse and subvert difference. In the analysis, a logic of equivalence is established between 'successful written communication' and 'standard written English'. The relation of equivalence allows the discourse on successful academic practice to appropriate standard written English as a defining part of itself. Successful written practice becomes constituted by adherence to the standards of standard written English. It is at this point that these two concepts internalise one another: successful written practice becomes standard written English. Their relationship is dialectical and it becomes difficult to prise apart the issues that relate separately to English and to academic writing. The implications of this relationship are twofold: (i) standard written English becomes assumed in university academic practices; it is hegemonic and 'invisible'; and (ii) standard written English becomes the marker of academic success. There are numerous implications for these findings, not least being the problem that academics regard written text as the marker of scholarly endeavour but neglect to make the features of such valued disciplinary texts explicit. Rather, it is incumbent upon academics to teach not only the content of their discipline but also the linguistic and textual means for communicating that content (Biggs, 2003; Kettle, 2011; Neff-van Aertselaer, 2013).

The university's commitment to the relationship between 'successful written communication' and 'standard written English' is a system of 'obligations' (Halliday, 1994) articulated through the modality of the text. The most prevalent modality marker is the modal verb *should*, for example, *should conform, should demonstrate,* where *should* is a type of deontic modality related to meanings of necessity and obligation. *Should* has low-medium level obligation; the recipient of an instruction carrying the word *should* is not highly obligated to follow. However, in the Assignment Presentation paragraph, the low-medium level modal auxiliary verb *should* is often juxtaposed with high-obligation main verbs such as *conform* and *pay attention* (written in the passive form). Also, the high-level obligation, non-explicit modal verb *requires* is used. A disjuncture immediately presents itself in the use of these contradictory forms: one establishes the level of requirement as low-medium; the other as high. Such disjunctures, or cruces, are of interest in discourse analysis because they can indicate unexpected meanings in the text, often linked to power relations (Fairclough, 1992).

Despite the use of low-medium level modality in the paragraph, the authority of the author is preserved by other devices in the text. Genres are ways of interacting and, as such, constitute particular social relations between the participants (Fairclough, 2003), in this case, the author of the Assignment Presentation guidelines and the reader. Various features of the text indicate that the authority of the author is unchallenged, despite the use of *should*. The verb *requires* points to the authority of the writer. In addition, the sentences are highly impersonalised: they are mostly devoid of social actors (except the last one with *you, us, we*) and often passivised. These textual features are indicative of an author who assumes the right to mandate conditions without the need to identify herself/himself. In this light, the choice of *should* in the text cannot be seen as offering compromise and negotiation. Rather, as Swan (1995) notes, *should* can function as a way of making orders and instructions more polite. The meaning of high obligation still operates but *should* is a pragmatic device chosen to establish particular social relations with the reader. Modality choices in text are significant in the process of 'texturing' self-identity (Fairclough, 2003). By choosing to use *should*, the writer (whose identity remains ambiguous: is this section on Assignment Presentation written by a representative of The University, the Faculty of Education, or the lecturer?) is able to build a less authoritarian identity for herself/himself. The desire for such an identity may relate to the institutional context in which postgraduate classes in departments such as education often involve small cohorts of students with classes conducted as seminars rather than formal lectures. In this setting, the social relations between the lecturer and students are more intimate and informal, hence the need for less authoritative forms of address.

The final feature of the paragraph as an institutional text is the choice of pronouns. Pronouns are a particular way of representing social actors and their divisions (Fairclough, 2003). The paragraph on assignment presentation guidelines contains four pronouns, three appearing in the final sentence:

*our* (common language)
*you* (experience difficulties)
*us* (some weeks before)
*we* (can discuss)

The use of *our* in the sentence 'Successful written communication requires a level of adherence to the conventions of our common language' is particularly noteworthy. In the grammatical and semantic relations of the text, 'our common language' equates with English. The collective possessive pronoun *our* establishes solidarity between the writer and the reader around the common language of English. Ambiguity is created on a number of fronts: is the assumption that English is an L1 and therefore *our common language* refers only to English native speakers, thereby marginalising non-English-speaking students; or is English as our common language inclusive of all students. Whatever the case, the ambiguous use of *our* works ideologically: it sets up social divisions between particular social groups. The approach to set up divisions was markedly out of kilter with the social advocacy of the lecturer and led me to wonder about the conditions of text production. A check with the lecturer revealed that the guidelines had been authored by administrative staff; they were available for all lecturers to insert into their course outlines.

And in the same way that *our* is ambiguous, so are *we* and *you* in the final sentence: 'If you experience difficulties in this area you should contact us some weeks before the posting date so that we can discuss assistance which may be available'. Who is *you* and who is *we/us*? *You* can be singular or plural in English while *we/us* is collective. The sentence proposes you – and we-communities where the former have the problems and the latter have the solutions. In the final clause 'we *can* discuss assistance which *may* be available', the modal auxiliary verbs *can* and *may* indicate epistemic modality, that is, future ability and capability: The level of capability for assistance and help offered by *we* is flagged as low.

Overall, in the analysis we see how standard written English is internalised in academic practice with regulative mechanisms that preserve the ongoing status of English. In an era of international higher education and sensitivities to inclusion and equity, it is not surprising that an Australian university offers support services to students in academic need. Interestingly, the analysis shows that it is the students who must initiate assistance and there is the indication that it *may* – or may not – be available within the institution. In line with the orientation to social change, the implications for these findings are to consider how institutional practices might be modified to improve the international student experience. As noted above, one outcome is to problematise the propensity of some academics to blame students' English levels for their academic difficulties. While language thresholds do play a role (and are evident in the student accounts below), recognition must also be accorded to the responsibility of academics to teach the ways that the disciplinary knowledge is expressed. After all, no one is born with innate knowledge of science texts; it must be taught and learned.

## Written feedback

This section focuses on lecturer feedback as one genre in the chain constituting the discourse of English as academic practice. In providing written feedback to students on their assignments, the lecturer is interpreting the assessment criteria and instantiating them in practice. In this way, the feedback provides another text in the reproduction of The University's academic values and priorities. The investigation of the lecturer's feedback is focused on the ways that English is authoritatively delimited by the lecturer, that is, the ways in which the 'grids of specification' (Foucault, 1972) are activated to classify what is 'in' and what is 'out' of desirable academic practice in the Issues course. To conduct this analysis, I examine Sonny's failed assignment to identify the features that pushed it over the 'threshold beyond which exclusion is demanded' (Foucault, 1972: 41). The analysis also looks at the strategies that the lecturer used to provide assistance to the international students having difficulties with meeting the assessment demands. The course assignments were presented in Chapter Four; Assignment 1 is reproduced here.

---

### Assignment 1

This assignment is intended as an extended literature review, where you have the opportunity to pursue your reading and thinking on two or three issues that the course has touched on. You are encouraged to provide arguments and analyses of texts intermixed with your own experiences and journal reflections.

It is essential for you to engage with the Learning Guide and Course Reader for the assignment, and you are encouraged to draw on other readings as well.

The following topic provides a focus for your literature review:

'Leadership and management refer to complementary but distinct actions.'

Critically discuss this statement.

| | |
|---|---|
| Due date | 28 April |
| Length | 2000 words |
| Weighting | 40% of course grade |

---

The lecturer provided two sets of written feedback on Sonny's assignment. The first was a general statement of evaluation which is presented below.

Sonny

I can see that you have a sound grasp of key ideas, and that you build and sustain your argument.

However, it is very important for you to have your grammar and expression corrected – take advantage of the assistance offered to international students. I haven't corrected any of this, but it needs to be done. When you have done this, I'll assign a final mark to your essay. It passes in terms of content, but not in terms of expression. Also, I think you could refer a little more extensively to the readings and literature as you make your points.

(Signature)

(Date)

The second set of written feedback was a list of points that were numbered and indexed to specific points in the assignment. The points relevant to this discussion are reproduced here:

1.   These statements are self-evident, and don't add anything much to our understanding. You use these kinds of statements at several points in your essay, and my advice is to find other ways of making your points.
3.   You need to indicate by referring to literature, or by making an argument of your own, why this is the case. It isn't sufficient simply to assert the points.
4.   This is getting a bit repetitive.
5.   Try not to use quotes as long as these ones; try to make the points in your own words and save quoting for special points.
6.   Participation is a very broad concept. A teacher can participate in the school's goals by teaching in the classroom, but this need not entail participation in the school's leadership or management. Try to be more specific about what you mean here.

Analytically it can be seen that each point of feedback is constructed in two parts (except # 4): first, the assertion of a problem and second, the solution to the problem in the form of advice. Point 4 contains only an assertion. The couplets are arranged in Table 5.3.

This interaction is a knowledge exchange between the lecturer and Sonny. The problem statements directly index the general categories of 'grammar' and 'expression' in the criteria and indicate what the lecturer considers to be *not* acceptable academic practice. The statements of advice effectively teach Sonny what is required; they are instructional. The lecturer's approach to assessment is both formative and summative; she uses feedback to teach as well as to evaluate. Through these means, she is effectively introducing Sonny to institutionally sanctioned English language expectations, that is, the antecedents that precede and determine the required course of action. Through her feedback, she provides him with strategies to assist his engagement with the task demands and the means to meet institutional expectations.

The lecturer further assists Sonny by delaying her final grading of his assignment until he has had it edited. Through the use of the 'causative have' (Swan, 1995) in her feedback, she openly suggests that he seek expert help to 'have' his grammar and expression corrected; she recommends the support services offered to international students. She does not see it as part of her role to make the corrections. Once the corrections have been made, the lecturer indicates that she will grade the assignment. Her approach buys Sonny time and provides him with an opportunity to refine his assignment with assistance from a student counsellor. She scaffolds his learning to the point where his paper achieves a Pass standard (Grade 4).

**Table 5.3** Problem and solution feedback from the lecturer

| Assertions of a problem | Suggestions for overcoming the problem |
|---|---|
| (1) These statements are self-evident and don't add anything much to our understanding ... | (1) ... and <u>my advice</u> is to find other ways of making your points. |
| (3) It isn't sufficient simply to assert the points. | (3) You <u>need to</u> indicate by referring to literature, why this is the case;<br>(3a) (you <u>need to</u> indicate) by making an argument of your own, why this is the case. |
|  | (5) <u>Try not to</u> use quotes as long as these ones;<br>(5a) <u>try to</u> make the points in your own words;<br>(5b) <u>(try to)</u> save quoting for special points. |
| (6) Participation is a very broad concept. A teacher can participate in the school's goals by teaching in the classroom, but this need not entail participation in the school's leadership or management. | (6) <u>Try to</u> be more specific about what you mean here. |

Two discourses are at work in the lecturer's assessment feedback. The first rearticulates the policy line about standard written English as the realisation of successful written communication. The lecturer takes up a particular speaking position in and through which she asserts her authority about what constitutes acceptable practice. The second discourse foregrounds English language issues and is evident in the lecturer's feedback; for example, references to support services for international students; opportunities for editing and resubmission; detailed suggestions and advice; and priority given to communicative intent and content.

Interviews with the lecturer indicated that her approach was a response to the English language needs of international students in her course. For her, the extra support was not directly about 'affirmative action' but rather to do with teaching: 'I do it as a teaching thing' (Lecturer: Interview 1). She attributed her approach to work with African educators in apartheid South Africa and to her own experience of studying in university where she felt she received little or no help with 'knowing what the disciplines were and how knowledge was constructed' (Lecturer: Interview 1). Her view was that international students come to Australia with interesting lives and backgrounds but in some cases, are disadvantaged by English.

Her approach to assessment as exemplified in Sonny's paper resonates with Foucault's (1972: 67) point about the existence of strategies in a discourse to create 'a modification in the principle of exclusion ... due to the insertion of a new discursive constellation'. His argument is that other options are always possible when new discourses present and insert themselves into a prevailing discourse. The presence of students such as Sonny with capabilities at odds with the assessment criteria prompted the lecturer to devise new methods for helping the students.

Not that she reneges on 'standards'. She does not 'soft mark', that is, award grades that massage and misrepresent the standard of an assignment. Indeed, Sonny's second assignment in the Issues course failed on similar grounds to his first. Rather than resubmit the assignment, he declined the lecturer's advice and chose instead to fail the course. He said he wanted to 'learn more' (personal communication) and repeated the course successfully the following year. The lecturer's approach can be explained through the understanding that all discourses include strategies for continuity and discontinuity. The lecturer was able to perpetuate the discourse of acceptable academic practice while also assisting a student whose academic capabilities at the beginning of the course were developing but just below the Pass standard, or seen another way, just beyond the threshold of exclusion. The lecturer took action to not compromise standards while also finding possibilities for manoeuvre in the time frames and submission procedures for Sonny's assignment. The lecturer made available new ways of achieving the desired forms of practice for students such as Sonny. Mediating students' access to new practices is a key theme in the lecturer's pedagogical approach and is examined further in the next chapter.

### Feedback and second language writing

Within research on second language education, feedback is recognised as a highly effective way to expand student capabilities in second language writing (Ferris, 2011; Hyland & Hyland, 2006; Leki *et al.*, 2008). The enactment of new writing practices takes time and requires extensive feedback and practice (Duff, 2010; Ivanič, 2004). Two approaches to feedback have been identified in the treatment of second language writing errors: indirect feedback and direct feedback (Sheen & Ellis, 2011).

Indirect feedback is output-prompting and involves the teacher in underlining, circling or using codes to indicate an error without correcting it (Hyland & Hyland, 2006; Storch, 2010). The pedagogical rationale for this approach is that learners are engaged in solving their own writing problems and acquiring greater independence and learning (Ferris & Roberts, 2001). Direct feedback, on the other hand, is input-providing and occurs when the teacher identifies an error and makes an explicit correction. It is considered better suited to beginners who do not have the requisite language knowledge to self-correct errors. The argument is that direct correction is efficient and provides the student with an accurate and immediate model (Ferris, 2011; Hyland & Hyland, 2006).

The lecturer's feedback on Sonny's first assignment indicates a pedagogical intervention that is quite input-providing, as is appropriate for a beginner. While she does not provide specific examples, she is nonetheless explicit in her feedback, for example, saving quotes for special points. The feedback is formative and guides Sonny through the steps he needs to take to resolve the problems in his assignment. The effectiveness of the feedback was evident in Sonny's successful resubmission of his assignment.

## The Students' Experiences of English

The final texts on English belong to the students. They are the students' statements about what counts as English in their experiences of the Issues course. This section highlights the enunciative modalities (Foucault, 1972) available to international students in the pervasive discourse on English and academic practice. In other words, what are the speaking rights and speaker statuses afforded and/or denied to international students about what constitutes English and how it impacts them?

### Erica, Javier and Hanh

Erica, Javier and Hanh were the students most conversant with English at the outset of their studies in the Issues course, thanks to the respective factors of home language context (Erica), travel (Javier) and previous study (Hanh). Their accounts are presented in order below.

English was Erica's L1 – she said that English tends to be the L1 in Singaporean families with graduate parents. Erica's reflections on her frequent contributions to class discussions link participation to confidence and competence in English:

Because I'm competent in English, it's not a problem. I would imagine if Mandarin was my first language, I'd be very hesitant because I would imagine that people that were proficient in class would want to get ahead with the subject and I would be holding them back, with my stumbling words and that. I would probably be more threatened, feel more insecure if English was not my first language. And then I would probably find another mode of communication with Helen, maybe through email or through phone calls where it's more private and I don't feel potential criticism coming my way. (Erica: Interview 2)

For Erica, the challenges in the Issues course were not about comprehension and performance. Indeed, she became somewhat of a leader within the class, initiating activities and offering help to other students. Her challenges were content and the specialised vocabulary and concepts of leadership theories.

The newness of the concepts and the complexity of their wording impacted on her reading practice, forcing her to slow down and reread constantly.

Javier was also confident in his English capability. While he defined English as his second language, he felt comfortable with it: 'I'm very confident in my English' (Javier: Interview 1). He began learning English at kindergarten in Buenos Aires and spent a lot of time travelling with his family to English-speaking countries. As noted above, most of the readings in his MBA in Argentina were in English. For him 'English – it's not a problem for me'.

The skill which presented Javier with most difficulty was writing: 'the only problem I have here is the writing because it was the first time I have to do massive writing in English. But I coped with it' (Javier: Interview 1). For him, writing an assignment along with other tasks such as choosing a topic and reading widely were linked together in what he called a 'system'. Much of his learning in the Issues course was associated with learning this 'system'.

Hanh was also confident in his English ability: 'I think I'm happy with that (spoken and written English)' (Hanh: Interview 1). His self-belief may have contributed to his unhappiness with the five-week English preparation programme that he had to attend as a condition of his scholarship. He considered the course to be irrelevant and a waste of time: 'I hate the teachers. I hate their program, I hate everything over there. It's bad' (Hanh: Interview 1). He says that he learned more once his Master's studies had started and he began to 'explore the library at night'.

With confidence and pride in his English level, Hanh was extremely frustrated with his inability to discern a useful approach for completing assignment tasks. He missed the conferencing support he received with Fulbright scholars during his Master's degree in Ho Chi Minh City and railed against the isolation and independence demanded in the Australian experience: 'I think the problem is that I need more conference time with the lecturers especially on the assignment topic, to narrow it down to a workable doable load. That's it' (Hanh: Interview 1). His frustration was palpable at the end of the semester when he referred to another course on marketing as 'junk' because the lecturer had given him a grade of 5, or Credit, for the course: 'I expected it turned out to be much better than that. I got 5, 5 is not me' (Hanh: Interview 2). He was relieved, however, with his result in the Issues course. He received 7 or High Distinction for his second assignment, an improvement on 6 for his first, and 7 for the overall course. Both Erica and Javier also attained a grade of 7.

## Anna and Grace

Anna was the student who, along with Sonny, most frequently referred to English. Her account was heavily indexed to time, especially transitions from past to present with associations of sacrifice and change. Anna was in her second semester of the MEd at the time of the study so her insights had a longitudinal dimension:

> At the very beginning when I arrived here, I don't think I'm not actually comfortable to talk with the native speaker … so at the very beginning it's a bit hard but now I get used to it … but at the same beginning you know, whenever I want to use the language, I was incredibly nervous but now I'm not. (Anna: Interview 1)

Anna's representations of her use of English on arrival in Australia are characterised by past time markers and negative forms. They evoke the literature on anxiety in second language use presented above; attempting to communicate in a second language with native speakers of that language is a highly face-threatening act. The anxiety is doubled with concerns about the intelligibility of one's own utterances as well as fears about comprehending native speaker responses, especially if the person is insensitive to language. On arrival in Australia, Anna experienced immense emotional difficulty with being a second language user of English. She felt timid and afraid. As time passed, however, she found herself changing: 'I begin to think in a slightly Australian way. I feel much more comfortable to live here' (Anna: Interview 1). She attributed her increasing comfort to improvements in her English:

> Of course language is one thing. I realise that my listening improves a lot actually and sometimes I don't know when I speak to Australians I think I can adopt their accent sometimes at the end of the sentence I tend to use the up-tone … that kind of thing. (Anna: Interview 2)

In the light of Anna's concerns about her spoken English, it is not surprising that a major concern for her in the Issues course was participation in class discussions. At the end of the course, she said that her two take-away things were 'to think in a more critic way' and 'what you call voice'. For her 'voice' was: 'You put yourself in an embarrassing situation virtually like you have to say in a discussion; while you think that you don't have anything to contribute, I think that's very important for me, this kind of good feeling' (Anna: Interview 2). For her, voice was integral to her desire to be herself in the course: 'I really want to be myself. I mean to be a true self'. Her lack of participation in the first semester bothered her immensely because she found herself hampered by two factors: (i) English and (ii) academic knowledge. With regard to English, she recalled: 'for the first semester I just try to make up any sentences I can speak out, I mean to help myself out of that embarrassment and I think I'm saying nonsense all the time'. She calculated that in her first semester, 50% of her thoughts were about English; the other 50% was ideas and content.

Anna's second concern related to academic knowledge and what she called 'old thinking': 'You know, the stuff in your mind. Because before we never think of this kind of issues'. She conceptualised the learning process of integrating new knowledge into her existing knowledge using the metaphor of flying in the air and getting down to the ground. I discuss the students' extensive use of metaphor in Chapter 7. The teaching approach of the lecturer was instrumental in scaffolding the learning process for Anna. By her second semester in the MEd programme, Anna found that English and the practice of claiming speaking rights in class discussions were no longer a problem. She made few, if any, references to anxiety about 'speaking nonsense' in class and the conscious division of labour between English and ideas. Rather, her sole focus was ideas; ideas were paramount and prevailed over her apprehension about English: 'If you really want to talk; you really want to contribute, I mean you really want to discuss about your ideas and check if it's right, check, so that's what I'm thinking this semester' (Anna: Interview 2).

Anna's account of English, her academic practices and her ways of self-identifying reflect transition and change. She indicates increasing confidence at being able to perform the academic practices integral to the Issues course. Her account highlights the enunciative modalities inherent in the prevailing discourse in which English is co-constitutive with performative practices. Anna successfully 'read' the elements of these practices as antecedents to engagement, and then made conscious efforts to enact them. She was highly successful in the Issues course. She received a 7-, or High Distinction (minus) for her first assignment and a High Distinction for the overall course.

Like Anna, Grace's representations of her gradual acquisition and enactment of English-medium academic practices in the Issues course were heavily referenced by time. She identified difficulties with English, particularly with the quantity of reading and comprehending English language texts. For her, the South African postgraduate programme was not as demanding and she found the Australian programme 'at a higher level'. Despite the difficulties and similar to the other students in the study, Grace was committed and aspirational, and expected that with time, she would be able to overcome the difficulties:

> I'm still having difficulties but I think I will overcome along the time. I'm grasping quickly the content when I read. I have to read thoroughly. We have a lot of course readings. We're reading a huge amount of material but I can follow it that way otherwise I would get lost. (Grace: Interview 1)

At the end of the semester, Grace received a grade of 4, or Pass.

## Sonny

Sonny referred constantly to English and his home country of Thailand. He 'read' the ways of 'doing' class in the Issues course as favouring participation but initially felt that he was unable to do this. His representations of English as academic practice remained heavily indexed to Thai practices. He linked his difficulties to the unfamiliarity of Australian classroom practices as well as to personal anxieties about his English capabilities, especially managing interactions and interruptions.

Sonny referred to himself on arrival in the Issues class as 'nobody' because of his inability to participate in class and express his ideas. His account was emotional punctuated by loudness, false starts and repetition:

> Here (Australia) I think for the first time, it was very difficult to get myself involved in class activity. In Thailand, there's no problem it's OK if a student just sits and listens ... but here I feel just like ... this was very ashamed for myself ... I don't have any participation in class just like I am nobody. I can't even express my ideas in class. It's very hard and very ... uncomfortable.

Like Anna and Grace, he asserted that the passage of time was significant and that he had made progress: 'but right now I think I'm better' (Sonny: Interview 1). He identified a developing understanding of what was required in the course and what the other students were saying in class, and indicated that at a time in the future, when he has more confidence, he would have 'more action, more reaction in class'.

Sonny expressed surprised that some 'Asian' students were participating as much as 'Australian' students. Interestingly, he used the word 'nonsense' in the same way as Anna to refer to fears about being incomprehensible and judged negatively by classmates: 'I worry I don't understand so my English is ... like how to do in class ... if I say something that's irrelevant ... it's nonsense'. One of his strongest representations of English and its association with academic practices was his advice to a prospective student from his Thai province coming to study a Master's degree in Australia. He identified key practices as independent study, large quantities of reading, extended written assignments and class participation. Crucially, he stressed the need for 'very excellent English especially speaking' on arrival.

Sonny appeared to position himself outside of the practices of the Issues course. He believed that engaging in particular practices was contingent upon English but because of his limited English and the difference to practice in Thailand, he was unable to participate. In line with Fairclough's (2003) model on the ways that discourses take hold within practice, Sonny 'imagined' and projected a 'possible' world which involved acceptable

English academic practice. He listed key attributes and practices for successful study and indicated a desire to acquire them. While not at the stage of inculcation or 'owning' the discourse, he was at least at the stage of being able to name key practices. In this way, he was showing a level of what Fairclough calls rhetorical deployment, even though this did not extend to enactment in the classroom. As noted above, Sonny failed the Issues course but repeated it successfully the following year.

# Speaking and Writing in a Second Language

## Second language speaking

The students' experiences of speaking in a second language recall work by Miller (2000, 2003) on language use, identity and social interaction among ESL high school students in Australia. Miller argues that self-representation for ESL students in an institutional setting depends heavily on the ways that the students are 'heard' and given legitimacy. Students represent themselves and are represented in social interactions. Powerful social interactions in a postgraduate course are classroom discussions and smaller group work sessions. Students' access to these interactions is linked to their linguistic resources and the opportunities they are given to participate. One of the problems for ESL students is that limited English resources can lead to marginalisation in the main group and a lack of opportunity for participation (Miller, 2003). Instances of marginalisation are evident in the MBA student experiences presented in the Preface and Leki's (2001) research with international students at an American university in Chapter 2. Language is a key part of self-representation; indeed, in classroom contexts, Cazden (2001) argues that language is foundational not only for engagement with curricula content but also for establishing social relationships and expressing self-identity. Central to these classroom functions is participation and pedagogies that promote interaction and opportunities for all students including those from minority groups.

With language heavily implicated in self-representation, it is little wonder that the negotiation of classroom talk in a second language generates deep anxiety and reticence for second language students. Speaking publicly in a second language, especially when native speakers are present, makes the speaker vulnerable to not only being misunderstood but also not understanding others. The situation is face-threatening with the potential loss of both self-esteem and esteem in the eyes of others. Second language speakers are constantly subjecting themselves to the possibility of negative evaluation. In classrooms, language anxiety is a widespread phenomenon caused by learners having to perform in a language they are still trying to master (Horwitz, 2001; Tsui, 1996). Learners often feel that their intelligence and personality are not fully represented when they communicate in a language in which they have limited resources.

## Writing academically in a second language

For students such as Javier who are confident in their English, academic practices involving writing become a core concern. Writing continues to be a major component in higher education assessment programmes, despite the emergence of oral-based assessment (Doherty *et al.*, 2011; Kettle & May, 2012). The continuing predominance of writing is due to its associations with knowledge and knowledge building. Through particular lexical and grammatical features, written language is able to present the world as a product, an entity that can be attended to and examined (Halliday, 1985). Moreover, writing features enable the concrete, specific experiences of the individual to be rendered in abstract and universal terms, for wider application and inspection. These characteristics align writing with the academy and its focus on knowledge reproduction, construction and dissemination. For these reasons, written texts have long been associated with the presentation of scientific knowledge (Halliday, 1985); they continue to be heavily represented in high-stakes assessment tasks evaluating students on their knowledge and understanding of a disciplinary field.

Writing is a skill learned consciously. Its principles for use are deeply embedded in culture and reproduced in the socialisation systems of schooling and higher education (Uysal, 2008). In the Western academy, written tasks, particularly at postgraduate level, are often in-class and out-of-class; lengthy and protracted; related to reading; requiring use of scientific concepts and terms; comprising extensive cognitive demands including summarisation, synthesis, evaluation and speculation; demanding argument and author positioning; and compliant with disciplinary conventions on structure, formatting and expression (Bailey, 2013; Hale *et al.*, 1996; Kettle & Luke, 2013).

Writing remains a vexed area for higher education academics and students alike, as found in research in Chapter 2. For students, especially those from non-mainstream backgrounds such as international and indigenous students, academic writing tasks present unfamiliar organisational, rhetorical and textual demands (Kettle, 2011; Rose *et al.*, 2003). Research from English-speaking countries that host high numbers of international students has found that many academics blame poor writing performances on low English language levels and consider marking international student writing difficult (Auditor-General, 2002; Bailey, 2013; Foster, 2012; Lee & Rice, 2007; Samuelowicz, 1987).

Notwithstanding the well-meaningness in the academics' concerns, the views conflating English levels and writing competence are problematic for a number of reasons: (i) they fail to recognise the arbitrary nature of disciplinary texts and writing practices and the responsibility of university teachers to make these explicit to all students, not just those from overseas (Kettle, 2011); teaching genres and language should complement teaching content (Biggs, 2003; Neff-van Aertselaer, 2013); and (ii) they ignore transitions and the dynamic processes that drive changes to students' epistemological and methodological capabilities across the length of a course.

## The Formation and Operation of English in the Academy

This chapter has looked at the English language conditions contextualising international student engagement in the Issues in Education and Leadership course. The conditions are characterised by a discourse that overdetermines English in relation to other academic elements in high-stakes course practices. This discourse might be called English as academic practice or following Foucault's use of the slash, English/academic practice. The point is that practices involving doing English and doing academic work instantiate a powerful discourse that has significant effects – both productive and punitive – on international student engagement.

The lecturer's strategies mitigated the power of the English/academic practice discourse through supported learning for newly enrolled second language students. She was able to rearticulate accepted norms to make available new ways of achieving desirable academic outcomes. For the students, English was the element most amplified in prized course practices such as extended reading, lengthy essay writing and class discussions. The 'terror' of performance as emergent English bilinguals derived from the propositional, social and expressive demands to produce meaningful arguments in a language that they were simultaneously striving to master.

The findings from the chapter on what counts as English in the English-speaking, Western university can be summarised as follows:

- A preferred form of English, academic practice and academic human subject are evident.
- English is taken for granted and unproblematised in policy documents and course materials, indicating hegemonic status.
- The themes including silences about English cohere into common meanings across disparate 'surfaces' within the university.
- Standard written English is equivalent to successful academic writing, a mechanism that establishes and maintains written English as favoured academic practice. This relation is sustained by assessment criteria and grading protocols.
- English is just one element in course academic practices but is amplified, or overdetermined, in relation to the others.
- The students' interpretations of the speaking positions afforded by the English/academic practice discourse are contingent on their own experiences and performances. Students with confidence in their

English level are primarily focused on academic practices while others remain preoccupied with English.

- Concerns about English are often related to self-representation and fears about ways of being 'heard' and socially positioned by peers.
- Teaching can be highly transformative by applying new strategies to existing institutional conditions, thus affording opportunities to uninitiated international students and alternatives for teaching practice.

These insights lead to teaching and further exploration of its mediating role in student engagement with course practices, as identified by students themselves. English is not dismissed; indeed, the students' accounts and the analyses above point to the complexity of English/academic practice as a discourse: its dispersed presence; its ways of marshalling ideas and concepts; its regularity of practice and enforcement of thresholds; its impact on student subjectivities; and its inbuilt strategies for change and manipulation. The lecturer's recognition of the complex interrelationship between English, successful academic practice and assessment enabled her to shape the conditions to meet the needs of the students.

## Note

(1) The main proficiency tests are the English as an International Testing System (IELTS) and the Testing of English as a Foreign Language (TOEFL).

# 6 Teaching: Generating Learning and Participation

## Introduction

This chapter turns to teaching as it was enacted in the Issues in Education and Leadership course. The reasons are numerous: the consistently high student evaluations; the generative impact identified by the students in the study; the rich insights offered by the lecturer about her own teaching; and the interest of this book in pedagogies of engagement. Overwhelmingly, students in the Issues course, including those in the study, rated the teaching highly on end-of-course evaluation forms. Examples of anonymous comments about the lecturer's strengths included:

> [Helen] is an outstanding teacher. She is able to move everyone forward in their thinking in a completely inclusive and unthreatening way. Would recommend this course highly.
>
> The lecture is well-organized, well-informed with up-to-date information of the field concerning the lecture. The lecturer respects students. It is worthy to sit in the lecture.

Teaching is clearly external to the individual student's 'internal' actions and the research was interested in how the lecturer 'moved everyone forward in their thinking in a completely inclusive and unthreatening way'. The comments point to teaching that generated thinking, participation and personal safety. These attributes go to the goals of education and the core concerns of classroom life: propositional, social and expressive objectives that operate with language at the heart (Cazden, 2001). They also invoke the processes and actions of engagement. The research aim was to make visible the lecturer's practices of activating and supporting international student engagement, that is, teaching as the institutional condition for possibilities of engagement. Which teaching practices activated student thinking, participation and self-expression? What were the component parts of these practices: the actions, interactions and relations; or in methodological terms – the approaches, methods and techniques that she used? What role did English and talk play in the teaching? From the student side, what worked? What was the process? How did the teaching incorporate international students into the life and learning of the classroom?

The previous chapter examined English in the experiences of international students. It found that English is an overdetermining semiotic element in student engagement with academic practices. If English is a powerful *semiotic* element in practice, then teaching is the powerful *social* element. The findings in the research indicate that teaching mediated the students' actions in course practices, in other words, it was the social element that enabled engagement in unfamiliar but high-stakes practices. The lecturer played a powerful, transformative role in being both the custodian of established practices and the agent providing access to these practices by students who had little previous exposure to them.

This chapter addresses the questions above by presenting a theory of teaching and exemplars of how good teaching looks from an international student perspective. These are powerful tools for reflecting on, talking about and enacting transformative teaching that benefits international students communicating in English as a second or additional language. It is likely that the teaching approach will also be beneficial for majority group domestic students also struggling with the practices of postgraduate study. The focus on exemplary teaching will hopefully go some way to addressing the calls of Ryan (2011), Chowdhury and Phan (2014) and others raised in the Preface and previous chapters for research that illustrates new approaches to teaching and international student engagement in learning.

## What is Teaching in Higher Education?

Teaching and learning are increasingly emphasised in universities. In Australia, particular attention is being paid to quality and outcomes (Devlin & Samarawickrema, 2010). The emphasis comes at a time when the nature of teaching in universities is changing. Academics are required to take on new teaching agendas which include degree rationalisation, curriculum change and assessment standardisation – 'not to mention coping with more students, accommodating more international students and teaching courses more flexibly' (Brew, 2007: 75). Export-driven internationalisation and domestically oriented social equity programmes aimed at promoting participation among traditionally marginalised student groups (Gale & Tranter, 2011; Gillard, 2008) have contributed to increases in the numbers and profiles of students. In universities, diversity has become the new norm. For higher education teachers, change and diversity have become ever-present companions.

In terms of the emergent priority on teaching and learning, a number of scholars have argued that this has not always been the case.

Ramsden (2003) maintains that higher education has traditionally seen learning as the responsibility of students, outside of lectures and formal classes. Biggs (2003) argues that academics have always been teachers but their first priority has been to keep pace with developments in their disciplines rather than teaching. Teaching was directed at transmitting the disciplinary content related to the academic's field of expertise rather than efforts to ensure student learning of that content. His argument is that while developing content knowledge is important, academics also have a responsibility to develop teaching knowledge: 'This is where many tertiary teachers are lacking; not in theories relating to their content discipline, but in well-structured theories related to *teaching* their discipline' (Biggs, 2003: 7, italics in the original). Teaching is an intervention to promote learning for a greater range and number of students. It involves getting as many students as possible to use the higher cognitive level processes necessary for learning – processes that the more academic students use automatically.

According to Biggs, education is about conceptual change, not just the acquisition of information. It develops 'functioning knowledge' that enables hypothesising and retheorising for application to problem-solving in new situations. Functioning knowledge is the synthesis of other knowledge: academic/theoretical knowledge of a discipline (declarative knowledge); skills for implementation (procedural knowledge); and knowing the conditions under which declarative and procedural knowledge can be used (conditional knowledge) (Biggs, 2003: 42). The challenge for university teachers is to provide teaching activities that extend students' knowledge beyond the declarative and procedural to 'deeper' knowledge that functions to reflect, evaluate, relate, apply, theorise and problem-solve.

The question of how to enact these principles in practice – in curriculum and pedagogy – continues to resonate throughout the literature. For example, research in Australia has found that postgraduate international students regard teaching methods and curriculum to be largely Australian and English language oriented with little recognition of their knowledge and experiences (Ryan & Viete, 2009). Similar views have been found among international students at universities in the UK (Sovic, 2013). Even with initiatives to promote effectiveness and excellence in university teaching, concerns have arisen. Research on effectiveness in the Australian context found that the question of *how* to teach effectively is often not addressed in criteria (Devlin & Samarawickrema, 2010). In the UK, the teaching excellence initiative has raised the profile of teaching among academics but has been used politically to reduce funding (Skelton, 2007: 1): 'excellence shifts responsibility away from the state to enthusiastic and self-regulating individuals, teams, and institutions'.

# Theorising Teaching _

## Teaching, pedagogy and culture

To talk about teaching, one has to know the relationship between *teaching* and *pedagogy*. The terms are often used interchangeably, but Alexander (2008: 4) usefully differentiates them: 'pedagogy ... is the act of teaching together with the ideas, values and beliefs by which that act is informed, sustained and justified'. Teaching, on the other hand, is the observable act which involves the use of a particular method $x$ to enable a student to learn $y$ (Alexander, 2005). Through the lens of pedagogy, the intricacies of classroom teaching are revealed. It enables teaching to be seen as a cultural artefact, deeply embedded in cultural values about knowledge, teacher–student relations, classroom interactions and the role of talk in learning. Cultural beliefs about how people should relate to each other manifest themselves in educational settings, notably in the relationships between the teacher and students.

In a large-scale comparative study of culture and pedagogy in classrooms at primary level in Russia, France, England, the US and India, Alexander (2008) found that three types of social relations operated between teachers and students: (i) individualism (prioritising the self and personal rights above the collective), (ii) community (prioritising human interdependence, caring for others and collaborating) and (iii) collectivism (also emphasising human interdependence but only in the service of larger societal needs). In short, focus on the child, the group or the class (Alexander, 2005). In the study, Alexander (2005, 2008) found discernible patterns in the continental classrooms of Russia and France that favoured the collective principle. Classroom talk was very public with children speaking loudly and clearly to colleagues and the teacher. Problems and correct answers were dealt with publicly, thus collectivising the responsibility for the learning task. The aim was the collective learning of a body of valued knowledge deemed to be fundamental to society; in the case of France – the civic values considered fundamental to the republic.

In contrast, the English and US classrooms displayed different social relations and cultural priorities. The orientations of the teachers were more towards the individual and community which saw teachers working hard to protect students from public mistakes. The approach put a great deal of value on the correct answer and led at times to ambiguous feedback rather than clear correction and modelling. Indeed, Alexander (2005) argues that in US classrooms, values of self-fulfilment and sharing were constantly at odds with commitment to the curriculum and the collective good. An antipathy to transmission teaching meant that interactions were pushed ineluctably into questioning mode with all student responses accepted as valid. The ambience was conversational but coloured by ambiguity and dissonance because while the tone appeared conversational and accepting, content and control were also very much in operation (Alexander, 2005). Teachers were indeed looking for particular answers and actively seeking them through questioning that at times involved relentless rephrasing, cuing and even mouthing the desired answers for the students. A key finding from Alexander's (2005) research was the relevance of context and the cultural distinction between English and US teaching practices that favoured the individual and her/his self-fulfilment in contrast to the French approach that foregrounded subject matter and interactions kept on the desired 'epistemic track'.

## The importance of talk in classroom teaching

While Alexander's research cited above was in primary classrooms, I argue it has salience for university teaching in that cultural values permeate all levels of education. Questioning and therefore feedback, as well as the maintenance of epistemic integrity, are crucial facets of university classroom teaching. Questioning within higher education classrooms cannot be conversational, that is, disjointed and localised; rather, questioning and answering need to be understood as dialogue. Dialogue is teacher managed. Dialogic teaching means that teacher questions and responses operate continuously and cumulatively in a chain of meaningful and cognitively demanding exchanges: the emphasis is on engagement, participation and thematic continuity (Alexander, 2005). Learning is generated by the continuity of the interaction in which teacher questions and student responses build cumulatively on each other to generate understandings of new concepts.

For Alexander (2005), cumulative knowledge building is blocked in classrooms when teacher–student interactions prioritise conversation and repetition over theme building. Classroom talk, especially questioning, needs to give precedence to both participation and intellectual engagement; its functions need to be social and cognitive. Alexander (2005, 2008) argues that social priorities such as building students' confidence are a major tradition in English classrooms with participation often used as the key criterion for evaluating outcomes. However, the emphasis on the social can be to the detriment of the cognitive if questioning and feedback are not focused on learning.

Recognising talk as a crucial dimension to learning is a key argument here. Questioning and answering are major types of talk in a teacher's skill set. Murray and Christison (2011) differentiate two types of questions for the classroom: lower order and higher order. Lower-order questions are factual and elicit recall, comprehension or application; they should be asked when students are being introduced to or reviewing new information. Higher-order questions are thought-provoking such as those requiring analysis, synthesis and evaluation, and are best used once the knowledge base is established and students are progressing towards manipulating information. Higher-order questions help the students to analyse phenomena into categories and to realign and reassemble information in particular ways to solve problems, make predictions and produce judgements.

## Reasserting the centrality of the teacher

Clearly, the teacher stands at the centre of the classroom practice and a theory of teaching would not be complete without reference to the teacher. Yet, in some quarters concerns have been raised about the demise of the teacher and the end of teaching (e.g. Biesta, 2013). The argument is that constructivism has become a dominant approach in schools and universities, and its principles have simultaneously promoted student learning through facilitation and scaffolding while discrediting explicit teaching and input (Biesta, 2013, 2014). Teacher-centred, didactic teaching has gotten a bad name. What Biesta (2013) calls the 'learnification' of educational discourse points to a shift away from teaching to learning. The shift raises questions about the role of teaching and the identity of the teacher.

The battle to define teaching is ongoing. In Australia, a recent report to the federal government titled *StudentsFirst* (Commonwealth of Australia, 2013a) lambasted the quality of teaching graduates and also identified the need for pre-service teaching students to have greater skills in literacy and numeracy. Government attempts to implement improvements include mandated literacy and numeracy tests for all pre-service teaching students from 2016. Students will need to complete the tests successfully in order to graduate and gain employment in a school classroom. The goal is to ensure that teachers are in the top 30% of graduates for literacy and numeracy. Much has been made in the media about the 2015 pilot of the test which found that 8% of 5000 students failed the literacy component and 10% the numeracy (Boyle, 2015). Calls for greater regulation have been rejected by the government on the grounds that the sector is already heavily regulated (Borrello, 2015).

The efforts to define teaching come at a time when teachers are often conceived of as guides and facilitators; the emphasis is on support and drawing out what already exists in the student. Biesta (2013) argues against this view of teaching and proposes instead a view of the teacher as someone with something to give. By this, he means teacher agency and the reassertion of the teacher in education. The teacher's authority is reinstated in the sense that she/he can offer the student something revelatory and new – the teacher is an external presence through which the student's thinking is transcended: 'To receive the gift of teaching, to welcome the unwelcome, to give a place to inconvenient truths and difficult knowledge, is precisely the moment where we *give authority* to the teaching we receive' (Biesta, 2013: 458, italics in the original).

Recognition of the power of teaching does not mean an unrelenting diet of transmission teaching. But nor does it preclude transmission when it best serves the purposes of learning. Teaching is served optimally by a repertoire of approaches, methods and techniques. The university teacher in the study was manifestly present in the classroom and from student accounts, deployed an extensive array of teaching methods, including the explicit teaching of reading skills most often associated with academic English preparation programmes. She was directive and authoritative, but not authoritarian. Her teaching approach and identity as 'giver' were recognised and highly praised, especially by the international students. Indeed, the students' accounts of teaching in the Issues course indicate large-scale transcendence in which 'old thinking' and 'old selves' were transformed into new academic identities through the intellectual, social and personal opportunities provided by the teacher. The classroom was a dynamic and at times risky place for international students, as I show in Table 6.1 and Chapter 7. The remainder of this chapter is dedicated to analysis of the Issues classroom teaching and the in-class interactions that were identified by the international students as mediating their academic engagement, participation and legitimation as class members.

To put it simply: if the students thought that the lecturer's teaching was good, what made it good? How did she equip the students with the resources to enact preferred academic practices? What was the relationship between the students' existing cultural and academic resources and the demands of the new university context? Above all, what teaching exemplars can we take from the Issues course that might be instructional for other academics teaching in university classrooms with diverse student cohorts? These questions invoke issues of access, participation, opportunity and transformation.

## Transformative Teaching in Higher Education: Lessons from the Classroom

The teaching exemplars are two lessons: one in Week 2 that I have titled What is Leadership? and the other in a Week 3 session titled Academic Reading and Writing. The lessons were 31 and 23 minutes, respectively. I define them as lessons because although they were part of a larger programme of class activities, they were 'marked off' by distinctive interactional patterns between the teacher and students (Mehan, 1979). Once set up, the lessons moved sequentially through a number of predictable

**Table 6.1** Students' representations of good teaching in the Issues course

| Themes | Teaching approach | Teaching methods and techniques |
|---|---|---|
| Content | Challenging. Engages me and classmates.<br>Very interesting. Engaging.<br>A role model and content wise. | Readings she chooses are very good.<br>Very clear on her concepts – when she says something, we understand.<br>Normal ways of teaching. Speak for a while; uses some slides but lots of people interaction.<br>Manages time accurately. |
| Interaction and participation | Very active. Very interactive. Motivates students to participate in lessons.<br>Less distinction between a lecturer and the student. Encourages open two-way communication.<br>Keeps control of what is going on there. | Pulls strings like a puppeteer. Pulls the strings of everybody, like she knows who to ask at the right time. A conductor; she allows everybody to participate.<br>Teaching methods and content more flexible [than China]. |
| Explicit teaching of academic skills | Very explicit. You know what she expects from you.<br>[Her explicitness] helpful. Narrows me to one specific pathway that I know that that's what she wants, that's what she likes. Don't fly about. | One of her unique methods: teaching like techniques of reading or writing. Through this method, judge whether it's right or not. Realise author is organising this way and then you understand it in a better way.<br>Talking about the [course] book, talked much about structure then left contents out. |
| Care and concern for students | Loves her students. Really care about her international students – whenever she has a question, she asks every nationality.<br>Takes the best of everyone. Always tries to get opinions for everybody.<br>Easy for international students; easy to understand her. Can help beginners. | Outgoing and very spontaneous in her expressions, full of hand gestures, very expressive body language. Way we interact with her similar.<br>Doesn't speak fast, even very strong South African accent. |

stages: an opening phase, an instructional phase which was 'the heart of the lesson' (Mehan, 1979: 36) and a closing phase. The foundational unit of the instructional phase is the 'topically related set' (TRS) which is a set of coherent interactions dedicated to a particular topic.

The social practice view of classroom interaction recognises that classroom interactions are dialectically related to other elements of teaching such as teacher and student roles; types of talk; implicit and explicit curriculum knowledge; values; and space/time arrangements. As discussed above, these configurations are the education enterprise itself that is shaped by historically honed links to culture, society and nation. So-called traditional classroom interaction patterns (Cazden, 2001) are characterised by the three-move set of initiation-response-evaluation (IRE) in which the teacher assumes the primary roles of initiator and evaluator in the transmission and reproduction of knowledge (Edwards & Westgate, 1994). In non-traditional classroom settings (Cazden, 2001), initiation and evaluation, along with responses, are often undertaken by students, leading to greater distribution of interactional turns and student participation as well as more process-oriented knowledge building and higher-order thinking.

In many classrooms, the latter is a dominant teaching approach, especially in postgraduate higher education (Kettle & Luke, 2013). It is often realised through teacher-led elicitations and/or group work and team projects. While highly lauded by institutions in the promotion of attributes such as knowledge construction and collaboration, it is not always productive in practice and can be derailed by unequal participation and inadequate allocation of roles by the teacher. The latter experience is not unfamiliar to many international students and was the case for Chinese students at an American university (Leki, 2001) and the students at an Australian university introduced in the Preface.

My justification for choosing these two lessons is that they are representative of the teaching qualities that students identified as beneficial in the Issues course. The first lesson, What is Leadership?, was highly interactive with the lecturer using open-ended questions to elicit responses from the students, gradually accumulating concepts and establishing understanding of the complex constructs defining leadership. The Academic Reading and Writing lesson, on the other hand, was a teacher-centred exposition of academic reading and writing skills which was reminiscent of a language-focused academic preparation programme and widely appreciated by the students in the study.

As noted above, Cazden (2001) argues that the three main functions of language in the classroom are the communication of content and curriculum; the establishment and maintenance of social relationships;

and the expression of identity. Analysis of lessons can provide insights into the ways that these functions are accomplished – or not – and can also generate further questions about 'what is it a member knows in knowing how to participate' (Cazden, 2001: 40). She conceptualises the interactions between teacher and students as performance, a metaphor that resonates with the students' accounts. For example, Javier described the lecturer's teaching approach using the performance metaphors of puppeteer and conductor. There is a strong sense in the students' accounts of 'doing' classroom life; the performance is public with heavy demands around the articulation of knowledge, social relationships and self-representation.

## The students' views

The approach in the research involved eliciting students' views on the teaching as the starting point for the investigation. The student interview questions at the beginning of the semester sought their initial impressions of the content and teaching methods in the Issues course and their other Master of Education (MEd) courses as well as the types of teaching that helped them best. The second interview after the completion of the course asked similar questions and also their reflections on class participation and the differences between studying in Australia and at home. The views were analysed with the following themes emerging as the most consistent across all student accounts of teaching in the Issues course: challenging content taught through clear explanations and tightly managed class interactions; highly supported opportunities for participation by international students; explicit teaching of academic reading and writing that clearly established expectations; and care and concern for international students. Evident in the student data is the discourse of transition: (i) in knowledge about the discipline of educational leadership, (ii) in academic reading and writing skills, (iii) in class participation, (iv) in English language proficiency levels and (v) in legitimacy as a member of the class. The students' words and thematic analyses are presented in Table 6.1.

The remainder of this chapter is dedicated to what good teaching looks like in the Issues classroom. It draws on the science of classroom discourse. The intent is to provide university teachers with the metalanguage to 'word up' their practice and to assemble a heuristic for good teaching that can be adopted, adapted and applied in other courses. The authority and effectiveness of the teaching are made visible through detailed interactional analyses that can contribute to efforts to explicate excellence in university teaching.

## Authority in Teaching

The authority of the teaching derives from the strengths attributed to it by the students. They value the lecturer's masterful grasp of disciplinary knowledge; her extensive repertoire of teaching approaches, methods and techniques; her dexterous management of classroom interactions; her explicitness and clarity of meaning; and her conscious inclusion of international students. Teaching approaches included both highly dialogic lessons with extensive interaction and more monologic lessons with explicit instruction and little interaction. Both were teacher fronted but with the teacher acting as guide and facilitator in the first approach, and sage and expert in the second. One does not predominate the other; both co-exist in her teaching toolkit for deployment at the appropriate time. This dexterity presumes extensive knowledge and skill in teaching informed by clear philosophies on knowledge, student roles and teacher responsibilities – the sociocultural dimensions to teaching and pedagogy discussed above. The lecturer's repertoire can be represented as a pedagogic continuum. At one end is the teacher as sage and expert with the lessons largely monologic and the students primarily in reception mode, while at the other end of the continuum is the teacher as guide with the lessons dialogic and the students engaged in high levels of continuous and cumulative knowledge production. Lessons incorporate the techniques and methods associated with the respective approaches. As changes occur in the curriculum, student needs and time/space, so does the teaching approach. The pedagogic continuum and the features of the different approaches are presented in Figure 6.1. They represent the repertoire of teaching tools utilised by the lecturer in the Issues course.

The lecturer, Helen, defines herself as 'a passionate academic ... I love ideas, concepts, and I want to show people that. And I believe enormously

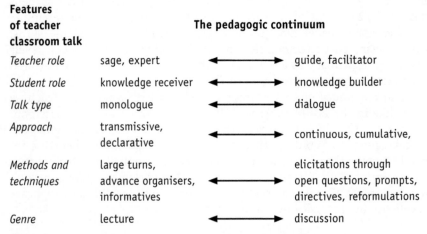

| Features of teacher classroom talk | The pedagogic continuum | | |
|---|---|---|---|
| *Teacher role* | sage, expert | ←——————→ | guide, facilitator |
| *Student role* | knowledge receiver | ←——————→ | knowledge builder |
| *Talk type* | monologue | ←——————→ | dialogue |
| *Approach* | transmissive, declarative | ←——————→ | continuous, cumulative, |
| *Methods and techniques* | large turns, advance organisers, informatives | ←——————→ | elicitations through open questions, prompts, directives, reformulations |
| *Genre* | lecture | ←——————→ | discussion |

**Figure 6.1** The pedagogic continuum of teacher classroom talk

in the power of conceptual structures etcetera, thinking. And I really want people to have access to that'. She links her emphasis on access to her experience of working with Black educators in South Africa and the need to make explicit the constructs and conventions of Western academic knowledge. She describes it as a game in the sense of Bourdieu and Foucault:

> One of the things which I have become completely aware of in the past years teaching particularly Chinese students is that – I wouldn't begin to say that I know for sure that a Confucian style and rote learning are in any way inferior and may well be superior – but these are the traditions of the Western academy and what I have to do is to show people how those traditions work ... but I feel quite clear actually that ... in a game sense rather than a trivial sense, it's about playing a game ... in fact let's stay with Bourdieu much better – it's about learning the rules of the game.

For her, explicit instruction is a key means of introducing and inducting students into the 'game':

> I have a strong view based on my South African experience plus research that everybody benefits from the more explicit. So I don't do it as an affirmative action thing, I do it as a teaching thing.

Her approach recalls Ryan's (2011) point about the need for academics to explicate the 'rules of the game' to international students. Helen identifies a crucial part of the Western academic game as critique and links critical practice to notions of 'voice'. She saw her teaching practice as political with voice integral to the distribution of power:

> an important part of voice ... it's actually to make the classroom or the lecture room a place where non-dominant voices of all sorts can be encouraged or made space for. (Lecturer: Interview 2)

She identified a triadic model of voice in her practice:

i.   voice as the physical resources to produce audible words and ideas;
ii.  voice as the right to speak as a minority person in the dominant culture;
iii. voice as demanding the right to speak in one's own culture, in the face of entrenched gendered and hierarchical opposition.

The centrality of the teacher is a feature of the two lessons presented here; indeed, the teacher frontedness of Helen's Issues lessons was not a problem for the students. As noted in the evaluations above, the students highly valued her approach. Javier, for example, attributed much of his learning in the MEd to Helen's teaching and the contributions of his peers. In relation to peers, he said: 'I think it's very, very good to have other people in the class ... very different points of view, very different experiences'. With regard to Helen, he acknowledged the autonomy that she granted the students in their choices of assignment topics while also maintaining high standards about argument and written expression. For Javier, the two positions did not preclude each other; rather they were complementary and generative.

Moreover, he was derisory of another Master's course that had no main teacher and consisted of different guest lecturers each week. He expressed his dissatisfaction through the metaphor of TAPAS[1]: 'In teaching, tapas is nice but tapas is like an entree. Sometimes you have a very nice meal with tapas but not every meal'. His point was that a course with different lecturers is neither satisfying nor sustaining; he preferred the steadfast presence of the lecturer in the Issues course. Not that the teaching in the Issues course was all teacher fronted. Student-centred small groups were also organised, often after key concepts had been established in class discussion. Students then worked together on a task such as identifying the relevance and application of the concepts to their professional practice. In another task, the students were required to reach consensus on questions about aspects of the topic at hand.

## Dialogic teaching

The instructional phase of the What is Leadership? lesson comprised eight TRSs generated after viewing a video of former South African President Nelson Mandela talking about the complexities of leadership. The topics were initiated by students following lecturer prompts such as 'What did Mandela say about leadership? What do you remember?'. The resulting topics can be demarcated as: work environment; hierarchy; vision; culture; empowerment; followership; influence; and management/headship/leadership. The lesson exhibited high levels of student interaction, with students initiating and contributing to topic development. Despite the variety of student contributions, the TRSs are highly consistent in their structures: a clear introduction; elaboration of the topic; a summary; closure of the topic; and initiation of a new topic. Each topic is clearly delineated and exhausted conceptually in the interactions before being terminated and the next one begun. The question is 'how?'.

The answer is boundary marking, which is the closing off of a TRS and the beginning of a new one (Mehan, 1979). Boundary marking in the What is Leadership? lesson was consistently the prerogative and responsibility of the lecturer. The lesson transcript shows the lecturer guiding the cumulation of concepts in each TRS through elicitations, open-ended questions, reformulations and directives. Much of the teacher work is intellectually orientated and directed at knowledge-building (elicitations, questions, reformulations, informatives). She did intervene in the interactions on occasion, however, to issue a directive for an international student to take the turn. Her intervention usually included scaffolding the response as a means of supporting the student's participation in the discussion. Closure of a TRS indicated the end of a topic and marked the boundary between it and the next topic. The lecturer usually signalled impending closure through markers such as 'OK' and 'good good' accompanied by falling intonation. Closure of a TRS and the elicitation of the next one occurred mostly in the same turn. This coupling is evident in the bold text in Table 6.2 – in Turns 4 and 7. In Turn 4, the lecturer closes TRS 1 (Work environment) and elicits TRS 2 (Hierarchy). In Turn 7, she ends TRS 2 (Hierarchy) and invites contributions on a new topic.

The lecturer's final turn in each topic set is often an extended monologue (see Turn 7) in which she synthesises key concepts; notes important terminology; and relates the topic to others in the current and future lessons. Her explicit links lace the topics together in a conceptual framework that extends across the lesson to other lessons and the entire course. During this informative step, she covers not only disciplinary concepts and theories but also learning strategies that the students can adopt. For example, in Turn 7 at the closing of TRS 2, she promotes cognitive engagement by encouraging 'noticing' through the following directive:

> Now this is a very important idea that you are going to come back to and back to and back to throughout the leadership course ... Next week and the week after we will be revisiting this idea so hold it in your minds for then.

Noticing is a second language concept that is foundational to learning (Schmidt, 2001). It is a cognitive process whereby the learner notes features such as semantic and linguistic qualities and cultural differences and similarities (Liddicoat, 2011). The learner then integrates these into her/his knowledge as the initial stage in learning. Noticing may not be naturally occurring for some learners, and a mark of good teaching is encouraging noticing as demonstrated in the lecturer's turn above.

Mehan (1979) argues that boundary markers demonstrate that classroom activity is a cooperative activity with a particular rhythm. Shifts in language forms, gestures and intonation patterns indicate that something new is about to happen, and students must be aware of the signalling value that these shifts have on the lesson content: '(S)uccessful interaction occurs when teachers and students synchronise the rhythm of gesture and speech with each other, while breakdowns in communication occur in the absence of this synchrony' (Mehan, 1979: 79). The transcripts

**Table 6.2** Boundary marking between topically-related sets (TRS)

| TRS | Boundary markers | Turn | Transcript (L: Lecturer; S: Student) |
|---|---|---|---|
| TRS 1: Work Environment | Initiation and student response | 1. | **L:** What did Mandela say about leadership? What strikes you? What do you remember? (looking from side to side, smiling) What do you remember, Heather? (using hand to indicate Heather) |
| | | 2. | **S:** Leadership creates a good environment for good men and women to work in. |
| | | 3. | **L:** OK. Just say that again. I don't know if everyone ... Justine, did you hear that? She didn't so tell her more loudly. |
| | Closing markers | | *(Interactive sequences forming the body of the TRS)* |
| | | 4. | **L: But it's very important. Good good.** |
| TRS 2: Hierarchy | Initiation and student response | | **L:** What else? Javier? (gestures to Javier) |
| | | 5. | **S-Javier:** I like the part when he said no leader puts himself above the people and above the team, meaning that the leader is no more than the people that he or she leads. |
| | | 6. | **L:** Do people agree with that? Julie, have a comment back. |
| | | | *(Interactive sequences forming the body of the TRS)* |
| | Closing markers | 7. | **L: Ok, that is the significant distinction – you might be at the top but that doesn't make you more important than everybody else. So basically he is talking about a certain set of values and assumptions. What I remember about the video is how much emphasis he was putting on morals, the common good and leading for the betterment of others. That for me was a very strong message he was putting out – that leadership is a moral act and he was also talking about vision – something greater than the individual. Now this is a very important idea that you are going to come back to and back to and back to throughout the leadership course – and that is the extent to which leadership is about vision and the extent to which it is a moral kind of action. Next week and the week after we will be revisiting this idea so hold it in your minds for then.** |
| TRS 3: Values | Initiation and student response Response | | **L:** Anything else strike you about what Mandela said about leadership? |
| | | 8. | **S:** I think the quality but also the leader, they must be looking for freedom. |
| | | 9. | **L:** So that's his vision and his values ... |
| | | | *(Interactive sequences forming the body of the TRS)* |

of the Issues classes show the participants in the lesson adhering to the rhythm and patterns of the interaction. Of the international students in the study, Javier is a major contributor to interactions with Hanh and Erica also initiating topics. For culturally and linguistically diverse students, complying with the rhythm of the interaction while marshalling the linguistic resources to present ideas comprehensibly and 'audibly' (Miller, 2003) can be challenging. For Anna, participation demanded language, thinking and critique: 'It [the Issues course] helps you to be more critical because when I participate in the discussion in class, I begin to think'. For other students such as Sonny, the language demands of interaction were intimidating and he was dependent on the interventions of the lecturer to assist his participation. Naming was a powerful way that she nominated and supported his turn; examples are provided later in the chapter.

## Monologic teaching

Towards the other end of the pedagogic continuum is the Academic Reading and Writing lesson which was conducted in Week 3 (one week after the What is Leadership? lesson) and slightly shorter in time than the Leadership lesson (23 minutes as opposed to 31 minutes). The characteristics of the Academic Reading and Writing lesson are that it was largely monologic and instructional. Where monologues often function as informatives marking the boundaries of TRSs in highly dialogic lessons, it was the primary mode of instruction in the seven TRSs comprising the Academic Reading and Writing lesson. The lesson was a teacher-led exposition of the course textbook with the aim to 'look at it as a text'.

Immediately obvious in the lesson are the long turns by the lecturer – in some cases, extremely long (30 and 42 lines of transcript). The seven TRSs are initiated and closed by the lecturer. They draw on the chapters in the book and cluster around the following topics: an overview of the book; academic writing; chapter one: identifying the purpose of the introduction; chapter one: identifying the structure of the argument; academic reading of chapter one and the whole book; the roles of headings and sub-headings including topic sentences and note-taking; and finding your own voice and writing an argument.

The topics and turns are commensurate with a lesson explicating the strategies for academic reading and writing, and are more akin to an English for academic purposes (EAP) programme than an MEd course. The students recognised the approach and were surprised but appreciative. Anna remarked:

> One of her unique methods is she's teaching you something like techniques of reading or writing. That's good especially for those Asian or international students who are not quite used to this kind of writing style. She's helping us gradually to adapt this kind of writing.

The lecturer for her part argued that explicit teaching benefits both international and domestic students because while the latter are advantaged with English, they also need help intellectually: 'I actually believe that explicit pedagogy benefits everybody' (Lecturer: Interview 1). Explicit teaching expedites students' uptake of practices and gives them access to the expectations of the academy and its 'game'.

# Teaching Features

As noted above, the role of language cannot be underestimated in classrooms. For students communicating in their second language, negotiating key propositional, social and expressive functions in front of peers can be daunting. The following section outlines ways that the lecturer provided support to second language students in their efforts to engage with the course.

## Formulating knowledge

Within the dialogue of class discussions, the lecturer formulates new knowledge by reconceptualising student ideas in the terminology and concepts of the field. Pedagogically, this involves the lecturer taking the student's language, knowledge and understandings, and reformulating them in more 'culturally mature formulations' (Cazden, 2001: 76). The lecturer's reformulations act as models of discipline-based ways of thinking and talking about a topic. Reminiscent of Biesta's (2013) point that the authority of teaching derives from its power to help student thinking transcend the old to something new and revelatory, the lecturer uses the metaphor of 'stretching' students' knowledge. Her metaphor is TEACHING EXTENDS and EXTENSION IS LEARNING:

> I find that there's nothing more exciting for me than to connect with how people are thinking and help them step ahead. It's got nothing to do with international or local … it's just actually to be excited by helping people's minds extend. (Lecturer: Interview 1)

An example of a student formulation and lecturer reformulation in the What is Leadership? lesson is provided in Table 6.3; pedagogical implications are included. A hallmark of effective English as a second language (ESL) teaching is offering students authentic and meaningful learning challenges while also extending support for second language expression (Hammond & Gibbons, 2005). This approach enables the students to become co-participants in the construction of the disciplinary discourse, thereby building knowledge, participation and legitimation within the class community. These were highly valued features of the teaching in the Issues course that accorded it authority in the eyes of the students.

**Table 6.3** The lecturer's reformulations of students' contributions

| Student formulation | Lecturer reformulation | Pedagogical implications |
| --- | --- | --- |
| … through her position, marrying into the royal family, she [Princess Diana] was able to initiate lots of charity work – you know, all the things that she did – and yet if she'd never actually had that position, she would never have been able to achieve so much. | OK OK so that's a really important point and it relates to this. What Tom is suggesting to us is that there are two parts to this – one is the actual position that you hold in an organisation, and that relates to what Javier was saying that it is actually easier to lead from a position of power – so there's the position that you hold and then there's your attitude towards your position. OK. | The lecturer marks the point as important. She then indicates that she is referring to Tom's comment and explicating it further. She links it to an earlier point from Javier and delineates two clear propositions, about (i) position and (ii) attitude. Her language is an academic reformulation of Tom's – depersonalised, field-specific with more concentrated information (Gibbons, 2002). |

## Explicit teaching of academic genre

The Academic Reading and Writing lesson was clearly orientated to the explicit teaching of academic skills and genres using the coursebook as a reference. The target audience was not only the international students in the class but also those domestic students who were new to postgraduate study. Within the seven TRSs, the focus was the features of the coursebook as well as reading strategies and models of writing. The book authors' intent was also investigated; for example, the lecturer directed the students' attention to rhetorical considerations in the authors' choices of words: 'What are they [the authors] doing there?'. She also directed the students to 'notice' the top-level organisation of the book: 'Notice that in sentence two, they have introduced some of their key ideas when they say it will have strategies, structures, and cultures; in fact what the book is going to be unfolding'. As discussed above, she is directing the students to notice – a necessary step in the cognitive process of learning.

Another device used by the lecturer to promote noticing was the clear identification of important content using the conjunction 'so'. Her use of 'so' worked discursively as the marker of the *dénouement*, or culmination of a TRS; for example, 'So there's an example of an introduction which is trying to capture your interest at the same time as setting out some key themes that will be developed'. Fairclough (2003) identifies 'so' as a conjunction that establishes consequence as a causal semantic relation between clauses. Throughout the lesson, the lecturer constructs a chain of consequences with the 'so' clause at the end of each TRS signalling strategies the students can take to improve their academic reading and writing.

The lecturer's approach is explicit and more often associated with genre teaching in academic preparation programmes than content-based discipline-orientated degree courses. It aligns, however, with arguments from researchers such as Delpit (1988, 1998), Hammond and Gibbons (2005) and Walqui (2000) that explicit instruction is necessary to ensure minority groups such as ESL students have access to dominant academic genres. While these advocates for explicit instruction direct much of their focus on minority groups in schools, the lecturer in this study was teaching in the higher education context. She was equally adamant that explicit instruction in the favoured genres of the discipline were an issue of rights and access for minority group students. Within her class, these students included not only international students but also women who had returned to study after long absences raising their children.

The international students in the study acknowledged the power of the instruction. For example, Grace observed about the teaching approach: 'I find her explicitness helpful … it's kind of narrowing the step; the way we look to the thing. You don't fly about' (Grace: Interview 2). Anna was equally mindful of the benefits of the explicit teaching of genre: 'Through this kind of style (of teaching), you realise the author is organising this way and then you understand it better' (Anna: Interview 1).

The lecturer is authoritative but she can in no way be considered authoritarian. Indeed, she works hard in her instructional talk to mitigate her power. She does this through strategies such as the use of inclusive pronouns (e.g. *we*) and low-level modality (e.g. *shouldn't*) that function to create what is known as a 'we-community' (Fairclough, 2003):

> Now I know when you write, you are also often tempted to use these dots; we all are tempted. *We shouldn't* give in to the temptation too much because when you do, it produces this rather disjointed effect. So a few dot points now and then you can just about get away with it.

### Critical thinking: The West is not always best

The we-community is also invoked when the lecturer demonstrates a critique of the coursebook. She states explicitly that she wants to show the students what she considers to be 'the less good part of the chapter, the less good writing'. She returns to this critique at the end of the lesson as a demonstration of her point about the need to develop a critical voice when writing: 'to find … your own voice and your own argument'. Her overt demonstration is intended as a model for doing critical work and to highlight the importance of questioning and critique. She encourages the students to take a similar position in relation to the Issues course: 'Why I'm emphasising that is because I want you in some ways to feel free to do the same and to feel free to do the same with what I tell you [in the Issues course]'.

A deep concern for the lecturer about the course was what she called its culture boundedness:

It really, really worries me that the leadership literature is so culture bound. And I haven't got an opportunity myself to explore what leadership might mean in Chinese cultures, what it might mean in non-dominant Western cultures.

Her hope was that the constructs were robust enough to translate into other cultures although a number of the students noted the Western orientation of the course. For example, Anna remarked that despite the lecturer's invitation to international students 'to think, relate this kind of issue to our own context', the content is 'mainly focus on developed countries – globalisation in Western countries' (Anna: Interview 2).

Grace made the salient point that to think critically means thinking independently and having an opinion, but the course assignments required evidence and 'outcomes from literature': 'Because you can't have a view that is not backed by the literature. If it's not backed by a literature, you can't put it in your assignment' (Grace: Interview 2). For her, an added conundrum was that there were few books and accessible materials in the library catalogue about education in her country, Mozambique.

She also noted the paradox between the priority on critical thinking and the need to comply with academic conventions:

I don't know if I can call it the format, the approach for the writing assignments. It's like something that is set. It narrows our perspective with something that is set and we have to follow it. For me, it's like contrasting the encouragement that we are being given that we have to think critically and analytically, and at the same time there is a very established way of doing things. (Grace: Interview 2)

The lecturer for her part believed the two were mutually inclusive rather than exclusive:

I'm trying to build an academic habitus [for the students] and part of that could be summed up in the word 'critical' and part of critical in that sense means assessing, evaluating, judging, contributing to knowledge. Knowing the conventions whereby it is done. Knowing them to be conventions but outside of them; you'll get further in them than you will outside of them until you are very well versed in scholarship.

It appeared that while the students were invested in gaining an English language, Western education, they were not necessarily wedded to the idea that 'West is best'. Anna and Grace were conscious of the relevance of their home contexts to their studies but they were also aware of the lack of resources available at The University. Functioning in the new Western academic community did not mean losing their home values and identities, a point also raised by Delpit (1998) in the context of US minority education.

## Promoting social relations and class participation

Participation is related but different to interaction. High-level dialogic interaction between teacher–students, teacher–student and student–student is the vehicle by which participation occurs in the What is Leadership? lesson. Participation evokes additional dimensions of social relations, speaking rights (Cazden, 2001) and the social capital necessary to impose reception on the group (see Bourdieu, 1993). In other words, participation is not just a matter of jumping into an interactional sequence but is contingent upon a raft of social considerations. The analysis in Chapter 5 shows how operating in ESL is a significant variable in determining how and if a student participates in an interactive lesson. Many of the favourable student views about the teaching practice in the Issues course refer to the lecturer's management of participation in the class sessions.

The analysis shows the lecturer using two prominent strategies to promote social interactions and participation in the two sample lessons: (i) turn management and (ii) namings. Turn management is one way that the lecturer orchestrates participation by international students in the interactive, dialogic processes of knowledge construction. An example from the What is Leadership? lesson involves interaction between Grace and Javier. Within the interactions of the lesson transcribed below, the lecturer nominates Grace for a turn responding to Javier's point about differentiating a leader from a boss (Turn 29). Before Grace is required to respond, the lecturer inserts a scaffold to support her: she indicates that Javier should repeat his point (Turn 32). The repetition gives Grace the opportunity to re-hear the point and prepare her response (Turn 33). The lecturer's intervention buys her thinking time.

27  **Lecturer**:    OK ... Javier

28  **Javier**:    He tried to make a differentiation between the leader and a boss.

29  **Lecturer**:    OK, do people get that? Grace, did you get that?

30  **Grace**:    Are we talking about the leader in general or the organisation?

31  **Lecturer**:    We were talking about what Javier thought was one of the most important parts of the speech so get him to tell you again and then see if you agree with him. (Grace nods in the direction of Javier)

32 **Javier**:   I like the part where Mandela says that no leader should put himself or herself above the people which he leads.

33 **Grace**:   I agree with it. Most of the literature is trying to open our mind to this issue when they think of the good of the organisation and not themselves.

34 **Lecturer**:   OK, so there's an aspect in it where Mandela is talking against hierarchy …

The lecturer's approach of providing certain students with scaffolded support has been recognised as a strategy for promoting participation, especially for students who are reluctant to speak for linguistic and cultural reasons (Hammond & Gibbons, 2005). Without assistance, it is easy for these students to disappear in the 'noise' of the classroom. For their part, the students in the study recognised the importance of participation but responded differently, often because of concerns about English. For example, in a lesson on post-structuralism in Week 5, Erica as a first language user reported the interactions between the lecturer, herself and colleagues as 'quality and people were really contributing and the learning was very focussed'. Javier referred to the lecturer affectionately as a puppeteer who 'tries to take the best of everyone' and 'who pulls the strings of everyone, like she knows who to ask at the right time' (Javier: Interview 1). For Anna on the other hand, her language concerns meant that at times she felt 'uncomfortable because the question [the lecturer] is asking I'm not quite familiar with, I don't know how to answer but that feels good. It's a big challenge for me'.

The second method adopted by the lecturer to promote international student participation especially among reticent students was what Sonny called 'namings'. Namings are when the lecturer nominated a student for a turn using her/his name. Nomination can occur in a lesson in many ways including non-verbal signals such as hand gestures and verbal signals such as the use of a student's name. This form of 'cued elicitation' (Mercer, 1995) brings with it risks, especially for students: they might be uncomfortable being 'spotlighted' and feel unsure about how to respond – as evidenced by Anna's comment above. Nonetheless, the nomination and opportunity to participate were widely welcomed by the students. Sonny with his deep concerns about being 'nobody' in the class (see Chapter 5) was highly appreciative of the lecturer's approach:

I found that the lecturer tries to motivate students to participate in lessons just like she names somebody to say something. And I think it's very, very good because it stimulates the ideas for students. She makes me try to say something that will show my idea. (Sonny: Interview 1)

Sonny claimed that English speakers know how to interact in class, but Asian students did not: 'From Asian countries, they have to think what they want to say [in English], want to express'. The lecturer's approach provided assistance for students such as himself: 'I think this way is very helpful. [Naming is good] because sometimes I have any ideas what to say, but don't have a chance to say that'. He strongly linked participation and legitimacy:

> Everyone in the class participates and if we don't participate in class [there is the] assumption we are nobody. Nobody asks about my country, my background. Nobody know how different if I don't explain my context. So I feel I have to. (Sonny: Interview 2)

Elsewhere I argue (Kettle, 2005), following Davies (1990), that the lecturer's naming provides Sonny with access to 'interactive others' who listen to him and accord him reception (Bourdieu, 1993). She is affirming his identify as a legitimate member of the class by making him a space in the interaction and allowing him to share his ideas. The lecturer considered it crucial that second language users are accorded the right to speak: 'it's about me as a teacher making sure that those voices should be there ... it's actually to make the classroom a place where non-dominant voices of all sorts can be encouraged or made space for' (Lecturer: Interview 2). She saw her role as helping both the international and domestic students to develop an academic identity that was achieved by 'just doing it and doing it, and having somebody mentor you on your own work and somebody model for you'.

## Legitimation and self-identification

The legitimation afforded to Sonny by the lecturer's actions is evident above. Much of his account refers to the impact on his identity and his self-representation in the class: participation enables him to present his knowledge and his country and is also a means by which he can configure his ideas and learning. Given Sonny's language concerns, participation at the class level is only possible with the support of the lecturer.

The lecturer also accords student legitimation through attribution. Attribution differs from nomination in that it involves attributing a valuable concept to a student but not calling on her/him to speak. The lecturer's moves can be seen in Table 6.3 when she links ideas initiated by the students Tom and Javier:

> ... What Tom is suggesting to us is ...

She then 'textured' her reformulation of Tom's point to link it to Javier's:

> ... and that relates to what Javier was saying that it is actually easier to lead from a position of power.

By taking up the students' points and weaving them into the discussion, the lecturer is achieving two objectives: (i) synthesising discrete concepts into a coherent framework of disciplinary knowledge and (ii) acknowledging the substantiveness of the students' contributions. The strategy confers legitimacy on the students as members of the group and is particularly affirming for international students. 'Revoicing' students' contributions not only builds an increasing stock of common knowledge; it also creates 'an ever-more-powerful community of learners' (Cazden, 2001: 91).

For their part, the students recognised and respected the lecturer's efforts to include them in the class community. Anna noted about the lecturer:

> I think she loves her students. She's quite considerate. She really cares about her international students and whenever she has a question she asks every nationality. (Anna: Interview 1)

The lecturer took the position that the international students were a resource in the class, able to provide rich and diverse accounts of experience. Her aim was for domestic students to 'value the unique perspectives they're getting on the international in the class space' (Lecturer: Interview 1).

## Discussion

The teaching approach used by the lecturer can be characterised as generative: it generated knowledge, interaction and participation by international students and positive self-representation within the class group. The students interpreted the lecturer's efforts as a commitment to helping them become successful within the Issues course. Delpit (1995) argues that with support and commitment, teachers can make a difference in transforming students' practices, thereby helping them to become academically successful.

In one sense, the lecturer's teaching of the corpus of largely Western-orientated knowledge about educational leadership and the conventions of Western academic work constitutes a reproduction of the dominant regime of knowledge. Foucault's insights about the productivity of power are useful here. Foucault (1987) states:

> Power is not an evil ... Let us ... take something that has been the object of criticism, often justified: the pedagogical institution. I don't see where evil is in the practice of someone who, in a given game of truth, knowing more than another, tells him what he must do, teaches him, transmits knowledge to him, communicates skills to him. (Foucault, 1987: 18)

The power inherent in the lecturer's practices is productive in enabling the students to incorporate new ways of knowing, doing and being into their 'funds of knowledge' (Moll *et al.*, 1992). Her use of power is not about domination or authoritarianism. Rather, her motivations and rationales align closely with those researchers orientated to the social change of educational institutions and the students within them (e.g. Delpit, 1995; Giroux, 1992; Norton & Toohey, 2004). Despite the lecturer's claim that she knows nothing about language teaching, her approach in fact aligns strongly with that advocated by researchers working for the success of ESL students in mainstream contexts (e.g. Delpit, 1995; Gibbons, 2007; Hammond & Macken-Horarik, 1999; Ryan, 2013; Ryan & Viete, 2009). In the US context, Delpit (1995) argues that explicit instruction is necessary for minority group students such as African American children to access the codes of power. These codes are rules that include linguistic forms such as conventions of writing, communicative strategies, assumptions about school and presentation of the self. She argues that entering a culture is easier, both psychologically and pragmatically, if information is made explicit rather than conveyed through implicit codes, as it would be for those students born into the dominant group.

For teachers, this means a responsibility to *teach* the dominant codes of power to students who do not already possess them. By gaining access to dominant discourses and economic power through practice, minority students transform their own economic and political prospects while also transforming the discourses themselves. In the Australian context, Hammond and Macken-Horarik (1999) argue that ESL students need to be provided with opportunities to access the dominant discourses and genres of mainstream education. They insist that the teaching of established forms does not preclude critical analysis; rather, control of genre and linguistic resources is a vital foundation for critique. Access to genres of power (Luke, 1996) changes who is 'inside' and who is 'outside' of established practices; it redefines who has the right to power.

Despite the work of scholarly advocates, debates are waged in liberal, progressivist education about the place of pedagogies that present dominant genres to minority students. My own experience of presenting the above teaching data and analyses at a local conference has provided a glimpse of the ongoing relevance of these pedagogical debates. A colleague questioned how the international students could find the lecturer's teaching helpful when it reproduced dominant forms of Western knowledge. In another forum, she railed against Education Department policies calling for more explicit teaching of methods in pre-service teacher training courses. Her point seemed to be the repudiation of all forms of established knowledge but with little consideration of what this might mean for minority students struggling to gain access to these very discourses and practices.

The debate gave me insights into the difficulties for ESL students in classrooms where there is no pedagogical consciousness about the power of language and culture in high-stakes academic practices. It calls to mind Ellsworth's (1989) chastening critique of critical pedagogy when it fails to acknowledge its own inherent assumptions about the needs and agency of students. Notwithstanding the argument that all students have the right to access foundational knowledge, texts and practices, it is important to recognise that once established, students can continue to flourish in generative conditions. The following chapter presents the decisions, strategies and 'aesthetics of existence' that the international students in the study activated to craft their overseas study experience.

## Note

(1)   The convention for writing metaphors is in capitals.

# 7 Crafting Lives: Action, Austerity, Aesthetics

## Introduction

This chapter turns to the students and their individual actions of engaging with the academic practices of the Issues in Education and Leadership course. The felicitous ambiguity of practice is most evident: the focus is the students' efforts to practise the established practices of the course. The students' practices can be understood as the actions of engagement; it is at this point that the behaviours, cognitions and emotions of the student become relevant. The aim of this chapter is to show in detail the strategies that students invoke 'in the moment' of doing key academic practices: what are the metacognitive, cognitive and social/affective strategies that they deploy to accomplish tasks? What do they say they do to engage with the high-stakes practices constituting the Issues course?

### Student engagement: Prioritising actions and achievements

The two previous chapters highlighted two powerful antecedents to international student engagement in an English-speaking university context: English as an overdetermined element in academic practices and the mediating role of teaching in generating learning, participation and legitimacy. The lecturer's assessment practices and orchestration of interaction in class discussions were examined in detail. This chapter turns to student action, especially in relation to high-stakes written assignments involving protracted task management and extended reading and writing – a practice that is often deeply unfamiliar to many international students (Bailey, 2013). As noted in Chapter 5, written texts are heavily implicated in scientific knowledge because of writing's capacity to render an aspect of the world in abstract and general terms. Writing at length is often the medium used in postgraduate study to demonstrate knowledge and to argue a critical position on a topic relevant to the field. Within the Issues course, the lecturer, like many academics, was insistent on students 'doing the intellectually demanding work and ... I make sure that that happens in assignments' (Lecturer: Interview 2).

This chapter also presents the students' views on achievement, that is, the accomplishments that derived from their engagement in the course.

This is engagement in association with outcomes. What actions did they take to enact the new ways of doing, knowing and being; what sacrifices were involved; were their goals and expectations achieved and how; were their lives and identities changed?

These questions required the students to reflect on their experiences and to re-present them in the research interviews. One discursive strategy that was strikingly evident in the students' accounts was metaphor. Metaphor is a highly effective strategy for representing one's experiences and realities. It enables social interactants to produce meanings about abstract and unfamiliar concepts by drawing on understandings of other, more familiar objects. Not surprisingly for international students attempting to conceptualise new experiences in an unfamiliar overseas university, metaphor was a useful discursive strategy. In this chapter, I utilise metaphor analysis to investigate the complex meanings that the students brought to their descriptions of engaging with academic work in the Issues course.

The students' accounts are their personalised, 'internalised' responses; their representations of 'self' within the practices and discourses of an overseas university course. The students' selves are differentiated from each other and provide insights into the ways that different international students make sense of themselves and the unfamiliar social, linguistic and academic conditions. Following the theorisation of the human subject in social life in Chapter 3, the student is foregrounded as an agent of her/his own change within the constraints and affordances of the institutional context. Through practices and technologies of the self, she/he is engaged in crafting an academic life that incorporates austerity as well as personal transformation and attainment.

The chapter makes visible the students' actions and achievements. Illuminating these dimensions of engagement provides three powerful insights for university policymakers and lecturers: (i) it offers an insider view of how international students respond to the high-stakes practices of the new academic context; (ii) it identifies the actions, decisions and strategies undertaken by students to progress their learning and academic success; and (iii) it highlights student agency and repudiates the themes of passivity and deficiency inherent in some discourses on international student learning approaches presented in Chapter 2.

The chapter profiles the actions of Javier as a mini-case study. The rationale for the detailed focus is as follows: first, there is a longitudinal dimension to Javier's experiences because he was in his second semester at the time of the study; second, he was successful in his Master of Education (Med) programme, hence the interest in the decisions and actions he took to achieve his success; and third, Javier used metaphor extensively to conceptualise his academic practices, thus providing a rich and informative account of engagement over time.

## Javier's Story: The Act of Engaging

In the transcript below, Javier explains how and what he is learning in the Issues course. The meaning that emerges is that the course presents a new way of learning, one that emphasises autonomy, albeit within constraints. The approach contrasts to the more reproductive, authoritarian one demanded in his Argentinian Master of Business Administration (MBA) programme. In the transcript, Javier's turns are marked as 'Javier' and mine as researcher and interviewer are 'MK'. Every effort has been made to retain Javier's 'voice' although with fillers, false starts and repetitions removed for ease of reading. Javier: Interview 1:

1 **Javier**:   One thing that helps me to learn a lot of is the fact that I don't have to care much about the subject of the assignment. I know I can write about anything I like and if it's something related to the subject, she will say yes OK go that way. So I can pursue what I'm really interested in and not just the cold theme of the assignment. I remember last year [in another MEd course], what I write was really different of what I'm supposed to write but I learned a lot about it. And I think that that way, I learned to get into books and new groups and new things. The way I study here is really different the way I study in Argentina. Maybe because of the subjects I was doing. In an MBA course, you have like a set reading and you just need to read about that, that's it. And we have more classes, like a lecturer sitting there and giving the class to the rest, giving the knowledge and not much participation … So that's why I'm learning. I'm learning a lot to write. I didn't use to write, even in Spanish, I was terrible in that. But I'm learning to research a little which is good for me too. So I think I'm learning more on the way of studying than on what I'm studying. Is that clear?

2 **MK**:   Yeah it is. So more an independent approach to study. It's more driven by your ideas, your interests, your skills.

3 **Javier**:   In my case at least. In my case at least.

4 **MK**:   And so the assignment topics and the way Helen sets up the course allows you to do that?

5 **Javier**:   Yes. She sets the main theme, but going back to the musical metaphor, you could do a jazz theme, you would have a main theme, but you can play the way you like … You have a main theme, but you can jazz around it, which is good. And you're encouraged to do that by Helen.

Javier's statements can be categorised into three propositions, or sets of meaning: (i) discernment of the elements in writing as a practice in the Issues course; (ii) identification of his responses highlighting thinking, acting and learning; and (iii) referencing the new academic context through his previous experience in Argentina. The statements and propositions are categorised in Table 7.1.

**Table 7.1** The propositions in Javier's account of his 'new' academic writing practice

| Javier's statements | Propositional categories |
| --- | --- |
| One thing that helps me learn a lot is the fact that I don't have to care much about the subject of the assignment.<br>　It's more driven by your ideas, your interests, your skills.<br>　So more an independent approach to study<br>　If it is something related to the subject, she will say yes OK<br>　She sets the main theme, but going back to the musical metaphor, you could do a jazz theme, you would have a main theme, but you can play the way you like. | Discernment of the elements in writing as a practice in the Issues course |
| I know I can write about anything I like<br>　I can pursue what I'm really interested in<br>　I think that that way, I learned to get into new books and new groups and new things<br>　I'm learning a lot to write<br>　But I'm learning to research a little which is good for me too.<br>　So I think I'm learning more on the way of studying than on what I'm studying. | Identification of his responses highlighting thinking, acting and learning |
| The way I study here is really different the way I study in Argentina.<br>　In an MBA course, you have a set reading and you just need to read about that, that's it.<br>　And we have more classes, like lecturer sitting there and giving the class to the rest, giving knowledge and not much participation.<br>　I didn't use to write even in Spanish, I was terrible in that. | Referencing the new academic context through his previous experience in Argentina |

## Learning the system

Javier emphasises in Turn 1 of the transcript that his learning in the Issues course is primarily **the way** of learning rather than **what** he is learning: 'I think I'm learning more on the way of studying than on what I'm studying'. The nature of the interaction with the lecturer enables him to negotiate his own choice of assessment topics. This negotiated, self-directed approach enables him to pursue issues that he is 'really interested in'. As shown in Table 7.1, he constructs his new learning in terms of new skills such as 'learning a lot to write' and learning 'to get into new books and new groups' and a new approach that is more independent and driven by 'your ideas, your interests, your skills'.

He reiterates this position four months later at the end of the Issues course and his MEd programme. Rather than facts about leadership, he refers to becoming wiser and knowing more:

> It's hard to tell exactly what I've learned because it's not, you know, facts. I'm so used to learning facts that I can't see, I can remember facts that I've learned. It's more that I've become, this is probably not the right word, wiser, would that be a word? It's more a context thing. I can't recall one thing that I've learned but I think I know more. I don't know how to put it. (Javier: Interview 2)

The difficulties in explaining abstract concepts like learning and personal change in words are evident in Javier's account; the markers of difficulty are 'this is probably not the right word' and 'I don't know how to put it'. Javier elaborates on his point about the Issues course teaching him 'how to think':

> I think that the main thing that comes through is not just make you learn about leadership in this case but rather, teach you how to think. And I think I've learned how to think and research and how to look for things, and I've learned how to learn, rather than learning about leadership. (Javier: Interview 2)

He names the lecturer's approach as a major contributor to his learning. To communicate her approach, Javier resorts to metaphor, specifically the music metaphor of jazz. Jazz is the music genre that famously accommodates improvisation, and he uses jazz to conceptualise freedom of assignment topics that the lecturer allows while always within the boundaries of the discipline and the assessment task: 'She sets the main theme, but going back to the musical metaphor, you could do a jazz theme, you would have a main theme, but you can play the way you like'.

For her part, the lecturer noted that negotiation of assignment topics was not a licence for the students to 'go off and do what they like' (Lecturer: Interview 2). Rather, students needed to negotiate their topic with her and she penalised those who did not adhere to these conditions:

> To do a good assignment it has to relate to the course. So it doesn't mean that [the students] go and off do what they like. I'm strict about referring to the readings and I don't give good marks to students who are just out there doing their own thing. I want them to do their own thing with this material. (Lecturer: Interview 2)

By the end of the Issues course and his MEd programme, Javier maintained that his writing had improved and he attributed this to 'learning the system': 'I suppose it's not very nice to say this but I kind of think that I've learned the system, I worked it out' (Javier: Interview 2). His comment points to an assumption that academic practice, notably constructing argument in scientific writing, should be something nobler than simply 'learning the system'. He is rather irreverent in his appraisal of the approach:

> I learned the system to pick books, found bits and pieces, put them altogether. If you need 3000 words get 6000 words and just chop them and put them altogether and put my bits and pieces and that's it. [laughs] I don't know how it works out but it works out well. (Javier: Interview 2)

## Metaphor as discursive strategy

The prevalence of metaphor in Javier's, and indeed the other students', accounts warrants closer investigation of metaphor and its use. Metaphor is not just a way with language; rather, it is a powerful means by which a social subject constructs meaning in the context of a social interaction. In instances when the meaning is abstract or unfamiliar and the means of articulation is difficult and elusive, the speaker may turn to metaphor, utilising existing domains to construct meaning about the new context for the listener. This socially oriented, discourse perspective on metaphor production and processing draws on the work of Wee (2005) which builds on earlier psycholinguistic models of metaphor oriented to the relationship between thought and metaphor.

Foundational work by Lakoff and Johnson (1980) claimed that our ordinary conceptual system is fundamentally metaphorical and structures what we perceive, how we get around in the world and how we relate to people. Metaphor provides conceptualisations for words as we use them in everyday life and is a primary way of defining our experiences. Metaphor is one of our most important tools for 'trying to comprehend partially what cannot be comprehended totally: our feelings, aesthetic experiences, moral practices, and spiritual awareness' (Lakoff & Johnson, 1980: 193). These kinds of experiences are often abstract and not clearly delineated in their own terms. For this reason, they need representation through other objects that have a more delineated internal structure. In English, the abstract experience of 'ideas' is defined in terms of plants, that is, IDEAS ARE PLANTS (the convention for writing metaphor is in capitals):

> The idea has come to *fruition*.
> She has a *fertile* imagination.

The IDEAS ARE PLANTS metaphor is an example of the *correspondence* (Wee, 2005) or *structural* (Lakoff & Johnson, 1980) model of metaphor production and processing. In this model, relations in the source domain are mapped onto relations in the target domain; in other words, words representing one part of the world are extended to represent another. A pervasive example of this metaphor is the 'conduit' metaphor which accounts for about 70% of the expressions used in English to talk about language (Lakoff & Johnson, 1980):

> It's hard to *get* the idea *across* to him.
> Just *put* your ideas *into* words.

The metaphor is constructed primarily through the following complex metaphor:

> IDEAS (or MEANING) ARE OBJECTS.
> LINGUISTIC EXPRESSIONS ARE CONTAINERS.
> COMMUNICATION IS SENDING.

In this model of processing, the properties of the source domain OBJECTS are mapped onto the target IDEAS/MEANING. Similarly, CONTAINERS are mapped onto LINGUISTIC EXPRESSIONS, and SENDING is mapped onto COMMUNICATION. A system of meaning or systematicity is built up through entailment relationships between the various concepts: language entails the speaker putting ideas (objects) into words (containers) and sending them along a conduit to a hearer who receives the containers/words and takes the objects/ideas out of them.

Through the entailment relationships, the concept of communication is structured in a particular way. These conceptual structurings are deeply embedded in culture and linked to ontologies and epistemologies, that is, views of the world and understandings of knowledge. The masking and manipulation of particular entailment relationships means that metaphor can be put to work ideologically (Fairclough, 2003). For example, the conduit metaphor hides aspects of the communication process: by implying that MEANINGS ARE OBJECTS, a proposition is built that meanings exist independently in communication, thus ignoring the importance of context – the people, their social relationships and their resources for making meaning.

Another model of metaphor production and processing is *class-inclusion* (Wee, 2005) which resembles *metonymy* (Lakoff & Johnson, 1980). This type of metaphor use also involves source and target domains but instead of structuring the meaning of one thing in terms of another, the source domain is a prototype of a larger category; one thing stands for another. In this model, the metaphorical discourse is more backgrounded because attention is not drawn to the prototypes as metaphors (Wee, 2005). In the sentence *He is a subject of the Crown,* the crown represents the entire monarchical system. Choices of particular parts to represent the whole can operate ideologically. For example, in English *I'm a bit rusty today* points to the mind as an entity and indeed, the MIND AS MACHINE – one that is brittle and unreliable: *She fell to pieces.*

The social model of metaphor use extends the 'in the head' focus of psychological models to metaphor as a discursive strategy. Metaphor choices are seen as socially contextualised strategies for meaningful interaction. A major part of the strategy is recontextualisation, that is, actively transferring meaning across contexts 'in the service of discursive goals' (Wee, 2005: 224). In the recontextualisation process, the source domain is taken from one context (decontextualised) and imported into the new context (recontextualised). The nature of the recontextualisation depends on which model of metaphor processing is involved, that is, correspondence or class-inclusion. It also depends on the type of activity being conducted. Activities are socially constituted, bounded events characterised by particular settings, participants and discursive goals. The social constraints in particular activities contribute to the different types of metaphor used in the interactions.

For example, in the research interviews in this study, the extensive use of metaphor by the students can be understood as their efforts to meet the discursive goals of the interview questions. The range of questions was extensive: their emotions, decisions, actions and achievements in the unfamiliar academic context. To accurately represent these abstract experiences, the students utilised metaphor as strategy to fulfil the meaning-making requirements of the interview. The students' adept use of metaphor as a discursive strategy aligns with Wee's (2005) findings that texts explaining technical and abstract concepts tend to exhibit the correspondence model of metaphor use, that is, meanings from the source domain are placed in a correspondence relation with the target domain.

Another feature of explanatory texts is foregrounding (Wee, 2005). Foregrounding is a social strategy that signals metaphor use to the listener. The strategy was used extensively by Anna in interviews through the words 'what I mean': 'So before, **what I mean** I'm flying in the air, **I mean** I don't actually catch anything' (Anna: Interview 2). Javier also foregrounded his metaphor use through the words 'but going back to the musical metaphor'. Metaphor use in explanatory texts is also characterised by the optional incidence of metaphor. In our interviews, the students used metaphor when they believed it would benefit conceptualisation of an experience. Because usage was discourse-sensitive, there was a vast array of metaphors used. The metaphors ranged across myriad source domains: for example, Javier's metaphors included playing jazz and making salads; Anna referred to flying in the air and getting down to the ground; Sonny used the concepts of journey and a rough road. The diverse use of metaphor was generated in the context of the research interviews and their wide-ranging questions about the international experience: 'a variety of metaphors are called upon as and when the authors (or students) feel that this will facilitate the reader's (or interviewer's) understanding' (Wee, 2005: 230).

### Javier's experience: Topic selection is jazz

In the transcript of the interview above, Javier's choice of the jazz metaphor represents a strategy to conceptualise the complexity of his experience of the lecturer's approach to assignment topics. In Turn 5, he foregrounds his impending use of metaphor and then proceeds with structuring the metaphor ASSIGNMENT TOPIC SELECTION IS JAZZ through a series of associations and entailments:

> She sets the main theme, **but going back to the musical metaphor**, you could do a jazz theme, you would have a main theme, but you can play the way you like … You have a main theme, but you can jazz around it, which is good. And you're encouraged to do that by Helen.

Jazz is the source domain which he recontextualises for the purpose of articulating his point to the researcher. His usage is appropriate and highly effective in conceptualising his experience of the assessment approach. Other instructive metaphor use is related to his assessment writing practices.

## Actioning writing: Octopus, glue and making a salad

Javier names 'writing' as the most problematic activity in the new study context: 'the only problem I have here was the writing because it was the first time I have to massive writing in English. But I coped with it' (Javier: Interview 1). Unlike students such as Erica, Anna and Grace who expressed concerns about the reading load and the extra effort required to understand the new theoretical concepts, Javier was confident in his ability to read and comprehend English texts. Most of the readings in his MBA programme had been in English and he found reading the Issues course materials and articles in the library relatively unproblematic.

Writing, on the other hand, was a skill he rarely practised in his Argentinean studies and his experience was that 'Writing is very, very difficult for me'. For him, writing extended beyond grammar: 'I'm not saying the grammar thing; it's writing – it's hard work'. The account of his actions to complete written assignment tasks is thick with metaphor. He refers to finding literature sources on the topic of followship in leadership as an 'octopus' because the reference lists in course readings lead to other sources which lead to other sources; it is 'an octopus' because 'it opens more chances, more opportunities' (Javier: Interview 1). Once he has found an article in a journal in the library catalogue, he writes 'it down on paper and then I take the thing that I write in paper into the computer and I type it' (Javier: Interview 1).

His next action involves synthesising the information that he has summarised to create an argument that addresses the assignment topic. In the light of the literature citing academics' complaints that international students have trouble thinking critically (as discussed in Chapter 2), I was particularly interested in Javier's account. To fully encapsulate his meanings, he draws on a plethora of metaphorical concepts including 'a puzzle', 'voice', 'making a salad', 'glue' and 'the system'. These concepts assemble a system of meaning about his understandings and actions, including strategies and skills – in short, his emergent practice of writing at postgraduate level in the discipline of educational leadership.

Javier indicates an element of mystery in the process of taking the respective summaries of articles and chapters, or 'very different voices', and synthesising them into 'one voice', which is his. He defines it as 'like trying to make a puzzle' (Javier: Interview 1). He refers to the summaries as 'a lot of little summaries', 'lots of bits and pieces' and 'very different voices'. He names his task as bringing these disparate pieces together to make 'one voice' – his. My understanding of his metaphor is that the experience is similar to completing a jigsaw puzzle: there are many disparate pieces; there is mystery about how they fit together; there are points of connection; and with time, the pieces are fitted together and the puzzle is resolved.

In a highly effective metaphor choice, Javier conceptualises his process of using the summaries to construct a critical argument as 'making a salad':

> When you put different ingredients on all the salad, you're making a new thing ... So I realise that I'm using other people's voices to make a new voice which is the one I want to say, it's something that I want to say. (Javier: Interview 1)

Javier's metaphor CREATING MY POSITION IS MAKING A SALAD conceptualises clearly the complex process of assembling disparate views from the literature into his own argument on the topic. The entailment relationships structured in the metaphor point to the complexity of the experience: EXISTING ARGUMENTS ARE SALAD INGREDIENTS,

CREATING IS MIXING and A CRITICAL ARGUMENT IS A SALAD. By mixing the ingredients in a particular way, a new salad is created. The outcome of the process is a new position generated through his 'voice' on the topic – where 'voice' is also a metaphor.

The metaphorical concept of making a salad involves Javier in decontextualising 'salad' from its traditional context and transferring it to the new target domain. He calls on metaphor in response to my questions about his processes of doing critical reading and writing. What does 'critical' mean to him? How does he *do* 'the critical'? Metaphor proves to be a useful strategy for explaining his actions and understandings, and for achieving his discursive goals in the research interview. Javier also used the metaphor 'voice' in response to my questions about critical writing and how he ensures that his writing is critical. He defines 'voice' as 'something that I want to say'. Voice is 'the glue for all those papers, all those pieces will be my thoughts. That's where the voice comes in' (Javier: Interview 2).

## Voice as a metaphor in writing

'Voice' is a metaphorical concept which is used by a number of students in the study, although differently. Javier and Hanh use voice to mean 'my opinion, my position' whereas Anna refers to voice more literally as speaking aloud to make a contribution to class discussions: 'a kind of difficult situation … you put yourself in an embarrassing situation virtually like you have to say something in a discussion' (Anna: Interview 2). Voice is a powerful metaphor which is prevalent in writing research in relation to how writers establish their identity and authority in writing (Hirvela & Belcher, 2001). It remains popular in discussions of teaching writing, especially for second language (L2) students. In L2 education research, voice is viewed as an indication of developing learner autonomy; it is often associated with political-critical perspectives and gaining access to cultural and power structures in the L2/culture context (Oxford, 2003).

Cultural issues often arise in relation to voice. Concerns have been raised that voice is an essentially Western notion and relatively inaccessible to students who are not members of the culture (Ramanathan & Kaplan, 1996). Culture is also recognised as deeply embedded in the organisational and rhetorical principles of writing. Contrastive rhetoric is the field of study that investigates the impact of culture on a writer's first language (L1) writing patterns (Kaplan, 1966). Within the at times controversial claims in contrastive rhetoric, traditional Chinese patterns are characterised as centrifugal while Western traditions are linear (Leki *et al.*, 2008).

For students schooled in Western traditions, the focus is on context-reduced arguments with high levels of subordination and elaboration to illuminate relationships within and between entities. Western rhetoric has its bases in Greek and Roman philosophies with emphases on originality, individualism and authentic voice. The writer has the responsibility for logically connecting all the evidence for the reader (Matalene, 1985). In contrast, in Eastern-based rhetoric with its influences in Confucian philosophy, the emphasis is on conventions, poetic images and references to the Classics. Writing in this tradition is considered more inductive with little explicit connecting of evidence. The responsibility for linking the points and making meaning lies with the reader (Kim & Lim, 2013; Matalene, 1985).

New approaches to contrastive rhetoric are rejecting the cultural fixedness implied in the work above (Connor, 2002). Instead, views of culture and writing are recognising that writers can have a plurality of writing repertoires and can operate across multiple epistemological and rhetorical contexts. For writers moving from one cultural context to another, however, the transition to successful writing is complex (Kettle & Ryan, in press). Text-oriented research has documented the trajectory in L2 writing as the writer's language proficiency increases. The changes include progressively sophisticated texts with more complex syntax and morphology; a greater range of vocabulary; and improved command of rhetorical forms and signalling devices for articulating relations within the text and with other texts (Cumming, 2001). In terms of compositional processes, developing writers have better control over planning, revising and editing texts; the increased competence contributes to socialisation in disciplinary discourse communities and greater capacity to take authorial positions and establish their writer identity (Cumming, 2001; Duff, 2010; Leki *et al.*, 2008).

## Javier's Programme of Engagement

Thus far, this chapter has focused on the engagement of one student, Javier, with the writing demands of the Issues course. The rationale for the focus was Javier's success with the demands of the course and his clear articulation of strategies, often conceptualised in metaphor. Engagement as action is the state of sustained individualised attention to a task drawing on all possible resources. Previous work has described this as a psychological state involving affect, cognition and behaviour (Kahu, 2013). The argument here is that engagement can be best seen as the mobilisation of particular actions to deal with the institutional demands. Based on the interview accounts and other data including assignment drafts and classroom interactions, the basis of Javier's actions is a suite of strategies that include cognition and affect, and most importantly, metacognition. Strategies provide the means by which Javier was able to convert understandings of task requirements into action. The following section introduces L2 learning strategies and shows how they were deployed so effectively by Javier.

## Learning strategies: Getting things done

Learning strategies are tools used to improve learning and learning outcomes. Gu (2007) maintains that the ideal strategy involves problem identification and selective attention; analysis of task, situation and self; choices of decisions and planning; execution of plan; monitoring of progress and modifying of plan; and evaluation of results. Learning strategies provide the learner with the ability to become an autonomous and self-regulated learner.

Research on English as a second language (ESL) students undertaking academic studies at a Western university has found that the students reported three categories of strategies to complete tasks: metacognitive, cognitive and social/affective (Chamot & O'Malley, 1994). Metacognitive strategies are higher-order executive processes directed at planning, monitoring and evaluating progress; cognitive strategies enable the manipulation of information for learning purposes and include resourcing, elaboration of prior knowledge, inferencing and summarising; and social and affective strategies involve seeking clarification and cooperation through interactions with other persons and emotional control through tactics such as self-talk (O'Malley & Chamot, 1990).

Metacognition rather than the frequency of strategy use was found to be a major factor in determining the effectiveness of a person's attempt to learn and use another language, notably in an academic context (Chamot & O'Malley, 1994). The strategies that tend to distinguish a 'good learner' are the ability to match strategies to task demands and variety in strategy use. Effective students are able to make explicit their thought processes as they plan, monitor and evaluate tasks. They appear to be aware of the value of their prior language and general knowledge and use this knowledge to assist them in completing tasks. Students with greater metacognitive awareness often understand the similarity between the learning task and previous tasks and are able to recognise which strategies are best deployed for successful problem-solving and learning in a particular task.

Metacognition has been found to benefit learners' writing. It is recognised that metacognitive knowledge pervades all stages of the writing experience, from task recognition and analysis to language choices, self-monitoring and revision (e.g. Hacker et al., 2009; Myhill, 2009; Myhill & Jones, 2007). Metacognition is the link between the cognitive and the social (Atkinson, 2002; Negretti & Kuteeva, 2011). It provides the means by which the writer recognises the task and its institutionally prescribed requirements and mobilises the requisite cognitive and social/affective strategies, skills and knowledge to accomplish the task.

Javier's account reveals a number of strategies that likely contributed to his success in the Issues course. He indicates a metacognitive awareness of his strategies for completing tasks. He recognises the complex demands of an assignment and is able to break down the task into doable parts: for example, the assignment requires taking a topic of interest and giving it a particular theoretical 'treatment'; it involves the synthesis and critique of existing 'voices' in the literature with the goal of constructing a unique personal position; and the text is bound by conventions on organisational structure and word limits. As shown in the metaphor analysis, Javier is a 'good learner' in that he can articulate explicitly his thought processes as he plans, executes and monitors his progress during a writing task. He is also able to reflect evaluatively on the success of his actions, concluding that they worked well.

The cognitive strategies that Javier mobilises in response to task recognition and planning show high levels of information manipulation including summarisation and synthesis. He is conscious of what needs to be learned and recognises the differences and similarities between his new and old learning contexts. He is able to elaborate on prior learning particularly from his postgraduate-level MBA in Argentina and bring across this knowledge for comparative purposes in his MEd course. He is confident in his English capability and indicates that he can 'manage' negotiations with the lecturer in order to craft himself the ideal learning experience. The nature of his social interactions with the lecturer and his confidence in English, together with his multiplicity of strategies contribute to him being a highly engaged learner, one who is resourced to achieve success – an outcome that corresponds with research on other successful ESL students (e.g. Chamot & O'Malley, 1994).

## The social consequences of engagement

Javier's account shows him involved in the complex processes of engaging in course writing practices. What he calls 'writing' is in fact the network of practices which have come to constitute academic literacy in the Issues course. Javier identifies a 'system' in which the student is required to be an independent and an autonomous learner, able to engage in flexible and negotiated learning. This expectation requires a new set of social relations between himself as student and the lecturer. He recognises that as learner, he must occupy a critical position in relation to existing knowledge and must be able to 'voice' that position in his writing. Tasks foreground personal knowledge and experience as a launch pad into engagement with course concepts and theoretical perspectives. Moreover, tasks privilege a particular performativity that demands particular ways of knowing, doing and being. Javier's strategies might be seen as 'technologies of the self' (Foucault, 1988) by which he attempts to fashion his practice to the requirements of the academic discourse and its associated practices in the course.

Javier's account shows an academic subject actively engaged in the processes of discerning, enacting and mastering the practices of the Issues course. His commitment to the academic practices of the Issues course might be seen as an investment (Norton Peirce, 1995) in a new future for himself and by extension, his family. Following insights from Chapter 3, it can be understood that by positioning himself within the discourse, Javier makes available certain speaking positions and statuses for himself. It follows that he is afforded opportunities and legitimacy, and is able to fulfil academic expectations. He achieved a High Distinction (Grade 7) for the Issues course.

## Engagement as Achievement

The final part of this chapter focuses on engagement and achievement, that is, engagement and its association with outcomes. The emphasis is the learning, academic achievements, academic transitions and personal transformation derived from engagement. The section presents the students' stories about the outcomes of their actions in the Issues course: their achievements, sacrifices and transformations.

A number of themes emerged in the students' stories. They can be clustered broadly as follows:

- Life goals and aspirations.
- Personal change.
- MEd programme, Australia and international education as 'conditions of possibility'.
- Being an international student in an English-speaking country.

The details presented differently for each student but the consistency of the themes suggests that they were relevant to all. I have no particular means of ordering the students so have decided to sequence them according to their family situation. Grace and Javier were the only parents in the group; their sense of responsibility to their children impacted significantly on their motivations and actions. Grace's experience was particularly acute because of the separation from her two-year-old son. Grace's and Javier's stories are presented first, followed by Anna, Sonny, Hanh and Erica. To capture the duration of the course, I first provide the students' views from the interview at the beginning of the course followed by those recorded some four or five months later after the course had ended.

### Grace

In our first interview, Grace states that her main goal for accepting the offer of an Australian government-sponsored study position was the opportunity to secure a financial future for her and her son. She indicates that while it is a sacrifice to be separated from him during her 18-month study period, it is worth it (she only went home once during her study programme). She says that it wouldn't have helped her situation to stay in Mozambique to be with her son because she would not have had a good salary: 'Although he needs my presence, but he needs to have enough resources to grow in his society with money' (Grace: Interview 1).

In terms of personal change, Grace identifies that while she has learned new behaviours, they have not meant profound and permanent change:

> I think I have changed. But there are some things I don't know if I really change but I learn new things. I learn to behave differently but I have my way of behaving; when I go back I'll go back to it again. (Grace: Interview 1)

Her new ways of acting include learning 'to listen and speak' in class as opposed to just speaking all the time. In response to the question about advice she would give to a prospective student based on her own experience, she points to analytical thinking skills and underlines their importance for democracy in Mozambique. She stresses the need to read a lot 'because everything I'm experiencing here are new. Everything are new so you have to be prepared for new things'.

Grace's view of the everyday life of an international student is that it appears to be similar to that of domestic students: 'It seems like Australia is an international country so you can't see the difference between so many international students and then Australian students'. Australian students 'have a culture of dealing with international students, accommodating international students'. In her after-hours socialising, however, Grace mixes mainly with Mozambicans: 'But you know you don't socialise with Australians. But they are very open … It's easier to be with people what close to you'. She uses the metaphor of CLOSE IS FAMILIAR AND DISTANT IS UNFAMILIAR to explain her need to socialise with fellow Africans:

> When we are far from home, our feeling is to find someone who's close to us. From Mozambique or from Africa and then we go to another foreigner; it's like gradual. When we don't find another foreigner, we will go to Australian. But first we go to the closest one and the Australians are the far-est.

Her reference to a lack of social contact with Australians recalls the 2015 'Draft National Strategy for International Education (For Consultation)' (Australian Government, 2015a) that prioritises increased opportunities for contact between international students and Australian students and communities. That being said and in line with Grace's experiences, research has found that many international students enjoy lively interactions with co-national students (Green, 2013). It is through these relationships that the culture of origin and values from home are affirmed. Many international students also form alliances as a response to their shared challenges (Lee, 2015).

Grace reiterates her goal to return to Mozambique after her MEd programme to work for the development of education: 'I'd like to go back and get a good position ... work in education and I believe there are many people who foresee a new future in our country and just join them' (Grace: Interview 2). She believes that she has changed little but knows 'more things now'. She refers to Australia as safe and multicultural and says that after six months, apart from longing for family, life in Australia 'feels great'. Australian people are not very expansive but that aside, life is 'exciting'.

## Javier

Javier lists a number of motivations for undertaking the Master's programme. Earlier in Argentina he wanted to change his career but with four children, he figured it was better to pursue a career that 'has to do with something that I'd done before' (Javier: Interview 1). He was interested in education and decided to pursue a career in school counselling. Simultaneously, he and his wife were interested in living with their family in an English-speaking country. They selected Australia and chose their current city because of its weather and cheaper cost of living.

He indicates a touch of cynicism about Australian universities and their recruitment of fee-paying international students. When his application was accepted by a number of universities, he thought it because he was 'very intelligent'. But then he realised 'they [universities] are looking for international students because we pay more than local students'. Despite this, he said he was happy in the city and at the time of the first interview, was applying for Australian permanent residency.

Javier considers the Master's programme not just as an opportunity to change career but as a chance to fulfil his dream of becoming a school counsellor. He is clear that he has not changed during his 10 months in the Master's programme. He said that he has always been very open-minded and interested in other people and countries. To live in Australia, the family had slashed their standard of living which Javier said was more of a problem for the children than for him and his wife. A particularly difficult aspect of moving countries was taking his children away from their grandparents. He names the positive aspects as feeling safe and being removed from the economic difficulties in Argentina.

Despite his international student status, Javier says it is hard to see himself as international. He identifies himself as 'Western' and finds it difficult to relate to being 'international'. As a result, he positions himself 'in the middle'. He says that 'for some people' international students mean money. For him being an international student is unproblematic and, apart from the lack of resources for international student families, his approach is that 'I just fit like another normal student'. His advice to a prospective student from Argentina is to utilise the student support services; start writing as soon as possible; and 'try to meet as much people as you can'.

In our second interview four months later, Javier repeats his point about Australia as the place where new possibilities were opening up for him and his family. The words he chooses to describe his study experience and life more generally in Australia are 'change' and 'growth'. He continues in a comment that is rich with references to 'becomings' and 'dreamings':

> It's been a fantastic experience, one that I've never dreamed of having, and it's allowing me the chance of becoming in the future doing the work that I just dreamed of doing, that I thought it would be best working with kids in a school. And I had the dream. But I'm doing it now. (Javier: Interview 2)

The new possibilities for Javier through his relocation to Australia include a new career and the realisation of a dream, safety for his family and economic security. The move has not been without difficulties but these are offset by the advantages. Like Grace, he represents Australia as 'predictable' and stable, and that this contributes to 'conditions of possibility' not just for an international student like himself, but for the population at large. As a student on campus, he feels 'normal', due in a large part to his confidence in English, and he rejoices in the chance to meet people from all over the world. The 'growth' and 'change' he attributes to his study are linked to the opportunities and new 'becomings' that it has afforded him.

## Anna

Anna is in her second semester at the time of the study. When asked if she has changed during her time in Australia, Anna answers with a definitive: 'Yes of course'. Her first response is language, that her comprehension of English has improved and that she is starting to imitate an Australian accent. Her next point is that she is 'beginning to observe myself and to thinking what my future will be, what kind of person I want to be'. The chance to reflect on life is something she is unable to do in China: 'I never have this kind of thing, this kind of time to think about these issues'. She said she was thinking about her future and contemplating leaving her government job for a new position.

A further insight into Anna's sense of change is her advice to a prospective Chinese student 'to be more optimistic, and to be more open-minded, to be more adapt, to open to all the things'. She links this advice directly to her own experience that she locates 'inside myself': 'I'm changing to be a more flexible person. I have become increasingly confident in myself – confident and comfortable in myself'.

In her advice to the hypothetical student, she uses the metaphor DARKENESS IS PESSIMISM AND BRIGHTNESS IS OPTIMISM:

> If you care how you position yourself, if you position in more inferior position, you tend to feel in a more pessimistic way, in the dark side. If you put yourself to the brighter of the road, everything will be fine. (Anna: Interview 1)

In terms of being an international student on campus at The University, Anna's initial concerns are largely linked to a lack of confidence in her English ability. She was worried that she would be rejected by local students in group work but this had not happened, although her friend in the business faculty had experienced this problem. Anna refers to 'a little bit discrimination' and traces it to people she knew who had been in Australia for some time who had given her the impression that Australian people did not like Asian people 'or especially Chinese because Chinese people seem to be everywhere'. But she has not had any direct experience of discrimination or racism.

In our second interview, Anna indicates that she had developed a sense of belonging with the change occurring over time: 'When I was first arrived here I was a stranger here but now I'm part of it' (Anna: Interview 2). She elaborates that the 'strangeness in your own mind' is related to language and to 'old thinking' which she says made her feel embarrassed: 'Mentally you think that you are strange and you feel it is difficult to go out'. She uses the word 'old' metaphorically to represent her thinking, work and friends from her life in China before she came to Australia. Indeed, she refers to herself as 'an old clock':

> When I talk with my friends back in China, I think I've changed. I mean that's the old stuff ... I mean before I was like an old clock – there's no grease, no oil. I just enjoy my life there. Or I might have stopped working but now I've got oil and keep on. (Anna: Interview 2)

There is a transformative dimension to Anna's account of her experience; she refers to transitions and reinvigoration. Where she was previously 'an old clock' with 'no oil, no grease', the overseas study experience has 'oiled' and renewed her. She has been changed by her new confidence, practices and sense of belonging.

## Sonny

Across the duration of the course, Sonny thinks that while he has not changed 'something changed I think'. He puts this down to the fact that he is alone in Australia and has to work out for himself 'how I can improve myself'. He talks of the need to be strong and to overcome his solitariness in order to manage the new academic experience:

> I had to be strong. So I feel that, it's not true, but I alone have to overcome the problem. So just like whatever will be will be but I have to do it in order to make it better. (Sonny: Interview 1)

His acceptance of 'whatever will be will be' (a translation of the famous Thai saying *mai pen rai*) contrast with his motivation to make the situation better. His immediate goals are the mastery of English/academic practices that he has recognised in the Issues course, in particular, participation in class discussions as presented in Chapter 5.

Sonny's advice to a prospective Thai student is conditional upon that student being from a rural area. He claims marked differences exist between students from urban areas such as Bangkok and those from provinces such as his in northern Thailand. Urban students are familiar with English and the context and 'study system' in Australia while rural students will find the system very different. He recommends that rural-based Thai students bound for study in Australia 'change very much about their vocabulary, change their idea'. His main advice relates to the need for excellent English and being adaptable to change. Based on his experience, he advises: 'You have to be ready for the changes because it's not like in Thailand. You have to study by yourself, you have to read a lot, you have a lot of assignments'. His view is that the experience of studying in Australia will be enriching but full of surprises: 'I think the experience will teach them how to live but they have to prepare themselves. They have to expect anything that they don't know'.

Sonny's capacity to discern and rhetorically identify course practices appears to have not progressed to enactment five months later. After the course, he reflects on an initial feeling of strangeness – with the education system, postgraduate study, English and Australian culture – but indicates his feeling that he actually needs to 'start' if he is to 'get anything from here':

> The first semester I am strange here. And so I know no one. I don't know much about educational system here, how to study, master degree and Australia foreign country, different language, different culture. So from the first semester I learned and I get more familiar. I think I come here to learn to study, so I don't have to be afraid for anything. I should adapt myself into new environment … I'm still afraid so I can't get anything from here so I think, right now I have to start, I have to do anything that is different from the past. (Sonny: Interview 2)

The affective impact of difference seems acute for Sonny and is most evident in his use of the word 'afraid'. He uses the word four times in the second interview. He consistently references Australian academic practices in terms of the Thai education system, and is patriotic about Thailand and Thai ways of life. Part of his anxiety about not contributing in class is the loss of the opportunity to showcase Thailand:

> Everyone in class participates and if we don't participate in class assumption, we are nobody. Nobody knows about my country, my background ... Nobody know how different if I don't explain my own context. So I feel I have to. (Sonny: Interview 2)

Sonny uses the word 'changeable' to describe his time in Australia. For him there is an urgency to his experience because his scholarship-funded study programme is the 'once in my life I have time to study abroad'. He believes that he will not have time to travel overseas again and that 'this chance is the only chance in my life'. For this reason, he plans to combine his study programme with as much travel to different parts of Australia as possible.

## Hanh

Hanh utilises metaphor to explain his goal for the Master's programme. His metaphor LEARNING IS GOING FURTHER DOWN conceptualises his desire to go 'further down into how to get to know the ropes of education, the ropes of teaching' (Hanh: Interview 1). He sees this as a multifaceted goal, catering to both his personal dreams and career development. Hanh says that goal-setting helps him to learn well: 'I set down my own outcome [for each course] and that the lectures and the delivery just meet the outcome'.

In terms of being an international student, Hanh considers himself international to the extent that 'I'm not from here'. But on the other hand, his programme in Australia is similar to his Master's programme in Vietnam. A significant part of his experience in Australia is working as a 'public window cleaner' at the Hilton Hotel: 'I go to the Hilton; I talk to people all in English ... I meet nice persons, although I'm in a not so good position ... but I'm proud of that one'.

Time is important to Hanh: 'I mean time to me is so important ... I value time'. He represents himself as 'a very active person' and a self-starter who sees himself as 'very different' to other Vietnamese students. He considers that he has not changed in the five months since his arrival in Australia: 'I think I have been that guy and I am now that guy and will be that guy ... That's myself and I haven't changed and I will never change'. His advice to a prospective student is to 'dig up the website' for the university for information. But the 'one size fits all' approach of the information does not provide information about 'real life experience over here', for example, tips on ways to save money.

Hanh describes critical analysis as 'my success for first semester'. He thinks of critical thinking as to 'have my own voice' while critical analysis has helped his learning: 'it gave me great pictures, very good pictures' (Hanh: Interview 2). His main goal for the Master's programme is to gain knowledge of the education field; where his previous interests were teaching and learning, they now include finance, resources leadership and marketing. The Master's programme is an important source of new knowledge and learning but Hanh sees it as an ongoing personal project which he is responsible for driving: 'I can do it, I can learn by myself. I can be self-taught ... Self discipline, it's self start, self study'.

Hanh describes his experience in Australia as 'happy' and 'fulfilling' because he is 'free from every problem with life': 'I don't need money to survive because I have a scholarship. The environment is great. I like the atmosphere here. I like the weather. I like the library'. He is excited by the new possibilities being extended to him: 'you know I've never done this sorts of thing before'. His level of drive is perhaps best revealed in his list of must-dos and must-haves in life. The list prioritises family, financial security and marriage, as well as a PhD and career:

> I should be happy because my life is great, I have good friends. I have a younger sister and she's going to move to Japan to work in five years. I have a good career back home probably for life I think if I don't want to change. I have a big house. In the city. I think the only thing I haven't got is a car, a luxurious car; and a swimming pool ... For marriage I think I am gonna get married before 35. So okay before I finish my PhD. I mean I just love I don't have anything to worry about. My life is great now. I have an account in the bank; I have shares; I have stocks; I have everything. I don't even have to worry about my mum and dad because they have got their own business. They also have stocks and shares, money I give to them. (Hanh: Interview 2)

## Erica

For Erica, life is an ongoing quest for challenges and development: 'I like to challenge my way of thinking and ways of doing things' (Erica: Interview 1). Her initial interest in the leadership course stemmed from her own lack of understanding of 'what it means to lead'. She felt that in her home context of Singapore, she 'was doing it by instinct ... by modelling other people' but was not convinced that that was enough: 'there were too many gaps'. Her choice of Australia as a study destination was informed by her desire to experience a 'multicultural perspective' as well as an experience that will challenge her view of education: 'I wanted to immerse myself into this culture, so that would challenge my way of understanding, my way of seeing education. Not from a Singaporean perspective, but from a more international perspective'. Erica seems to revel in the international-ness of the Issues course and the wider university environment: 'this overseas experience here now allows me to get in contact with internationals from all over the world and that's very valuable'. She refers to the university as 'like a global village' (Erica: Interview 1).

A key motivation for Erica to do well is the cost of the Master's programme: 'the fees are just multiples of what I pay back home'. The cost has created a heightened sense of personal accountability and caused her to place greater expectations on herself: 'therefore my learning experience is like a steeper learning curve because I want to learn and I'm making myself learn because I'm looking at the cost of even coming here to learn'. She talks about her studies in Singapore where she spent a lot of time with family and friends; however, because of cost, her study experience in Australia is different: 'all the time my main priority here is really my studies'.

In relation to being an international student, Erica laughs that she can definitely feel that difference because of the fees, but on a more serious note she sees herself as contributing to 'the global village' that is the university: 'It enriches everyone's experience not just mine, but also my classmates and my lecturer's just as they enrich my experiences when I am here'. In the same vein, she says that she hopes that lecturers and domestic students value international students because of 'the experiences and totally different cultures that we come from and the different ways of making meaning in our world'.

In terms of adapting to Australian cultural and academic conditions, Erica is enthusiastic about the compatibility with her personality: 'Here I find that the culture suits my personality'. She represents herself as 'very modernised ... not traditional. I'm not too Chinese in my outlook, in the way I view people'. The conditions of possibility opened up to her during her sojourn in Australia are defined in terms of personal freedom and a feeling of relaxedness: 'I feel that when I'm here I'm less inhibited. I'm the sort of person I like to say "hi" to everyone and anyone ... So I find that over here, I can be in quite a number of ways, more myself and more relaxed'.

Erica's advice to a hypothetical future student is to take 'full advantage of the learning experience here and really be accountable for your own learning'. She stresses that there is a wealth of experience available – classrooms are very multicultural and there is a lot of 'quality interactions between the class mates and the lecturers because all these individuals are so proactive and they're so interested in what they're doing and so focused on learning'. She emphasises the need to have an open mind and to be prepared to discuss issues and ideas, 'which perhaps could be different ... from our Singaporean experience'.

At the end of the Issues course and after five months in Australia, Erica effusively refers to a complete transformation in her world view:

I remember one day after our first assignment … telling Helen [lecturer] that, 'my gosh, my mind had just been blown away'. My thinking has evolved and I had actually moved on to the next stage level of thinking and the way I look at the world, it's just, I will never see the world in the old pattern again. (Erica: Interview 2)

She attributes this epiphany to certain conditions that were available in the Issues course:

you need the setting, the content to stimulate the dialogue and then the questioner, the person that really can probe you with particular questions to really set you thinking and from then on, really grow, I mean mentally. (Erica: Interview 2)

Her reference to 'the questioner' as the person who poses provocative questions which stimulate new thoughts and possibilities is reminiscent of Foucault's point about facilitative individuals who help a person in his/her transformation of herself/himself. In Erica's case, the Issues lecturer and class colleagues can be seen as assisting her transformation to someone with diversely informed views on leadership and the social world more generally. Erica attributes the expansion of her perspectives to her decision at the outset of her study programme to be 'what kind of student I wanted to be' and to the practice of critical analysis which she defines as studying all angles of an issue: 'the limitations of whatever idealised theory, of whatever picture perfect issue there is, to always look for the complete picture, to always look for the dark side of things and to really investigate it thoroughly'.

## Sculpting an Existence

This chapter has focused on the students' representations of themselves as subjects within the context of the Issues in Education and Leadership course: Javier as a detailed mini-case study at the beginning followed by the stories of all the students. The more problematic issues presented by the students include the difficulties and sacrifices of being alone; not being confident or communicative in English; being separated from a child; removing children from their grandparents; overcoming fears and feelings of strangeness; needing to be careful with money; and struggling with coming to know the new forms of academic practice. The positive effects of the study programme include the excitement of learning new ways of thinking and studying; of meeting people from all over the world; of being afforded the freedom to take time out of work and to try new adventures such as working as a window cleaner and a fruit picker; of discovering new perspectives on knowledge and one's rights to a 'voice'; of developing new academic capabilities; and ultimately, of building the potential to make a contribution to social change at home.

Some common themes are discernible in the students' accounts: first, a commitment to taking up course practices; second, a belief in their ability to mobilise the necessary resources to enact English-medium academic practices; third, a belief in the value and benefits of the Issues course; fourth, an acknowledgement of English as a significant element in course practices; fifth, a recognition of differences between home and Australian academic practices; sixth, identification of personal changes in ways of knowing, doing and being; and finally, personal transformation to a greater or lesser degree. The new social space that is the Issues course and life more generally in Australia appears to have afforded the students new intellectual, social, cultural and personal opportunities. The outcomes of their engagement include new skills and knowledge, new world views, new accomplishments, new friendships, new job prospects, new challenges realised and, of course, the successful completion of a postgraduate-level course at a university in an overseas context.

To explain these findings I draw together considerations on subjectivity, social and discursive constraints, austerity and agency. Specifically, I am interested in the ways the students engage with the Issues course in order to achieve successful personal and academic outcomes. My analysis reveals that the students while subjected to myriad constraints are engaged in what Foucault (1987) calls 'the practices of self' to craft a 'mode of being' in the new Australian context. In so doing, they reveal a certain understanding of their own agency and a desire to shape their lives both within and in response to the conditions of the academic situation. The students' crafting of new situated subjectivities can be seen as a particular care and concern for the self and a corresponding commitment to the 'art of existence' (Foucault, 1996b), where 'existence' may refer to the immediate context of the study programme and to the greater project of their lives.

The students' representations of their engagement with the practices of the Issues course indicate an 'active fashioning' of the self. Much of their crafting points to strategies aimed at facilitating their uptake of course practices. The students are also active in fashioning lives that contain resonances of aesthetic and moral values. They describe a moral stance that values sacrifice as a means to personal transformation. Their 'technologies of the self' resemble those identified by Foucault – they are marked by a sense of austerity and sacrifice in the pursuit of a particular form of life. Foucault (1986) talks of the ancient Greeks and Romans training themselves through abstinences, examinations of conscience and listening to others; similarly, the students engage myriad 'practices of the self' in an effort to adapt to and enact the discourses, practices and texts of the Issues course. Their efforts point to agency and a belief in their capacities as agents to effect change in their lives.

The complex picture of the subject work undertaken by the students in their study experiences raises questions about the formation of new subjectivities. Following Foucault's notions of an 'aesthetics of existence' and 'life as art', I have referred to the students' efforts as 'crafting' and 'sculpting'. I suggest, based on their consistent references to time and the acculturation process over time, that the students are engaged in the protracted formation of a new subjectivity for their Australian experience, a 'becoming' for the particular time and place (Grosz, 2004). The students indicate that they expect the experience to have residual effects on their subsequent lives when they return home; furthermore, it has contributed to their personal transformation in many and varied ways. As Erica noted, thanks to the course, her own strategic efforts and the facilitation of the lecturer and colleagues, her thinking has been transformed: 'I will never see the world in the old pattern again' (Erica: Interview 2).

# 8 International Student Engagement in Higher Education

## Introduction

The aim of this book has been to conceptualise international student *engagement* in higher education. As noted above, the term *engagement* is ubiquitous in university policy documents and discussions, from aspirational mission statements to classroom-based teaching and learning initiatives. Engagement in all forms – engagement, engaging, engaged – is currently pervasive in the language of educators across all levels of education, none more so than in higher education. The danger of such prevalence is that the concept comes to mean different things to different people; it is in danger of becoming washed out conceptually and losing its potency in practice. The book is an attempt to rescue engagement and to reassert its value through explication. To this end, the complex elements constituting engagement are revealed and explained; the argument is that engagement comprises multiple dimensions that policymakers and teachers need to know. Exemplars of engagement in action, that is, the act of engaging, are also provided. The conceptualisation and examples of practice can inform and deepen the understandings of university stakeholders tasked with promoting student engagement across their institutions.

The book focuses on engagement by international students at a Western-orientated, English-speaking university. This is especially relevant within the current context of heightened efforts by universities around the world to increase international student numbers. The previous chapters have documented these recruitment efforts in detail. In countries such as Australia, where education as aid morphed into education as trade decades ago, the parlous state of government funding to universities, coupled with domestic programmes of massification, is causing universities to turn their attention – again – to international student recruitment as a solution to funding problems. The increasing diversification of students' linguistic, cultural and educational profiles is creating a need for university policymakers, administrators and teachers to understand pedagogies of engagement. The argument in this book is that university personnel have a key role and responsibility in knowing what engagement is and how it can be promoted for students within the care of the institution. Following the conceptualisation provided here, this means pedagogies that generate learning, participation and legitimacy within class, course and institutional communities.

The role of this chapter is to draw together the foundational principles of international student engagement argued and explained in the book. The principles derive from student practice. Through a study of six international students' actions to make sense of postgraduate studies at an Australian university, the dimensions to engagement have emerged. They extend previous work on engagement and attend notably to the experiences of international students. The approach adopted in the study and presented here is innovative in that it foregrounds the students as the agents and arbiters of engagement; their experiences evidenced in interview data, class observations and assessment documents provided the phenomena on which the thinking about engagement was based. Guiding the conceptualisation were questions such as: What is engagement? What part do institutional conditions play in international student engagement? How does teaching relate to engagement? What is the act of engaging? Why is engagement pervasive as a construct; what are its perceived benefits? What achievements do international students derive from engagement?

The function of this book is to address these questions for the purposes of advocacy and critical awareness raising. In terms of advocacy, the book is dedicated to disrupting the discourses and practices of deficiency that have circulated around international students in the Western academy for decades. As pointed out in earlier chapters, the discourses of deficiency have largely emanated from a fear of difference and the difficulties of the university as a traditional instrument of nation building to reconcile domestic agendas of unity with global objectives foregrounding diversity. The critical awareness raising function is related to reimagining the university as a learning institution, not just an institution of learning (Ryan, 2011). Awareness raising is a necessary first step in providing key university stakeholders with the understandings of engagement that they need to discharge their duties effectively with international students. In the current higher education context featuring confluences of discourses on accountability, rationalisation, digitalisation and standardisation, university decision makers have a responsibility to speak from informed positions about engagement. Their decisions and practices have implications for 'renorming' the university to more transformational approaches of teaching that enable international students to learn, participate and flourish within the institutional conditions.

## The Complexity of Engagement: Antecedents, Actions and Achievements

International student engagement is a response to the practices of an unfamiliar academic context. Engagement as it is proposed here is a multidimensional construct incorporating antecedents and actions with subsequent achievements and outcomes. Engagement cannot be understood without recognition of its antecedents. These antecedents are the institutional and personal conditions that influence and shape the actions of engaging; the conditions that precede action. Within a practice-based model, the institutional conditions materialise for students in the social practices of a course. Each social practice is a configuration of elements such as tasks, people, values and language related dialectically to produce institutional ways of knowing, doing and being. For many international students including those in the study, language – in the Australian case, English – is an overdetermined element because of its powerful and overriding influence on other elements. It is a powerful antecedent to engagement.

The study found that teaching operates as a powerful mediator of student engagement. It is an external force that provides conditions of possibility within the institution for international students to participate in the practices of a course. Thus, teaching can work as an intervention to scaffold opportunities for enactment. It inducts students into the ways of favoured practices. Antecedents pave the way for action; engaging is the students' behavioural, cognitive and emotional response to the demands of the practices constituting their courses. The study found that strategies (metacognitive, cognitive and social/affective) underpin the act of engaging. Metacognitive strategies are a powerful means of converting academically contextualised task demands into cognitive processes and behavioural skills.

The final dimension which must be considered in understanding engagement is the achievements, that is, the outcomes that derive from the actions of engaging. For example, learning and academic success are achievements; they are the outcomes of mobilising strategies, skills and certain emotions within a task. Engagement inherently indexes the outcomes of people's efforts. For most of the students in this book, their processes of engagement led to successful academic outcomes. Of the six students, four achieved a High Distinction (Grade 7) for the Issues course; one was awarded a Pass (Grade 4); and one failed (Grade 3) but successfully completed the course with a Pass in the following semester.

## Social Practice: How Academic Life Gets Done

International students' engagement with their new course demands can be best understood as social practice. This perspective ensures not only recognition of social life as a complex process of doing, knowing and being but also allows examination of how social life is *done*. Practice foregrounds discernible elements interrelated in particular configurations that are the products of and simultaneously contribute to the production of the social order. As noted above, elements in social practice include activities, people in roles and relationships, values and identities, spatial and temporal organisation and semiotic resources such as language. In education, language is overdetermined; the prominence of language is assisting the special status of English in higher education around the world. For students engaging in academic practices in English as their second or additional language, the influence of English on other elements is a source of emotional and social stress.

Interestingly, the students identified that the impact of English reduced and assumed a more proportionate relationship with other elements over time. The change was generated by personal strategies and actions, mediation by the lecturer and informal support from course colleagues. As elements move closer to academic expectations, the dialectical relations between elements mean that the students' overall practice changes, resembling more those practices valued by the institution. Social practice affords the insight that while student practices are subjected to change so are the entities of practices themselves. The reflexive relations between social elements and practices within the order of the institution mean that the insertion of change into the norms of practice – for example the presence of international students and the diversification of linguistic, cultural and educational repertoires – cause the practice itself to be irrevocably changed. Social practice is an effective means of explaining complexity, change and the contestation that often accompanies change.

## The Engaged International Student

This book has focused on international students as the authoritative voices on engagement in the foreign university. The approach enables insights into the students' 'readings' of favoured academic practices and their actions in response. In play as well are the students' aspirations and their personal ambitions for the overseas study programme. The students in the study were from Argentina, China, Mozambique, Singapore, Thailand and Vietnam; they represent some of the biggest source countries in international education and reflect to a degree the ratio of students from Asian countries in Australian universities. The focus on the students in this book was not remedialisation but rather re-mediation (Gutiérrez *et al.*, 2009), that is, the emphasis was on the students' agency and intent as they reshaped existing resources for the new context.

The students in the study were committed to engaging in the practices of the Issues course. They identified a gradual 'coming to know' what was expected and how it could be achieved. They recognised the favoured ways of doing academic work and being an academic subject, and were able to articulate a number of strategies dedicated to achieving these outcomes. This is not to suggest that the students were slavishly capitulating to the pursuit of all things Western. Nor were they being co-opted by forces beyond their control.

Rather, the students' accounts point to conscious uptake of the Issues practices and their attendant discourses, speaking positions, subjectivities and so on. As agents, they were investing time and effort in their studies as part of a broader project of personal change. The new ways of knowing, doing and being accrued during their study programme abroad constituted key parts of their transformation. They were seeking to use these new-found proficiencies and practices as leverage into improved new jobs and migration. For some, there was a communal goal to apply what they had learned to their communities once they arrived home.

As well as academic and professional outcomes, the students were invested in a greater, more superordinate project of personal transformation, fashioning themselves a life in the 'conditions of possibility' offered by international higher education. They willingly exercised 'technologies of the self' involving austerity and sacrifice in order to create opportunities that would enrich their lives. The students all indicated that their international sojourn was more than an academic endeavour; it was also an aesthetic experience offering unique cross-cultural encounters and the pursuit of a cosmopolitan consciousness. For some of the students, their Master of Education (MEd) course in Australia was probably the only opportunity in their lives to travel overseas so they were intent on crafting an existence that was rich in adventure and challenge.

## The Power of Pedagogy

As noted above, diversity is now mainstream in higher education; minority groups are combining to become a majority presence. The question for universities is how to teach for diversity. The argument presented here is that diversity can be used to provide an illusion of pluralistic harmony (Bhabha, 1994). This pluralism is tolerated only so long as it does not threaten dominant discourses and practices. As societies diversify through mobility, migration and dislocation, 'diversity in unity' has become the favoured trope (Cameron, 2002). In practice, the concept of diversity can be used to mask the ethnocentric norms that characterise social groups (Bhabha, 1990). Difference, on the other hand, does not assume consensus and directs the focus onto the norms that differentiate people and practices. For the lecturer in the Issues course, the differentiation in international students' backgrounds and experiences was a resource. She utilised it to extend all students' exposure to a range of perspectives on educational leadership. The international students valued the array of cultural and educational experiences available in the class.

That being said, the lecturer and students were aware that the course was far from the genuinely internationalised curriculum advocated by numerous scholars introduced above. Both the lecturer and students noted that the focus was primarily Western without the necessary materials and literature to accommodate wide-ranging international perspectives. For universities contemplating ways to reconcile national priorities and international goals associated with global entrepreneurship, some of the conundrums are as follows:

| National | International |
|---|---|
| Domestic or home students | International students and curricula |
| Nation-building priorities | Global goals and foci |
| Monocultural | Multicultural |
| Homogeneity, solidarity | Heterogeneity, pluralism |
| Preservation | Change |

The question is how to resolve these conundrums in ways that preserve highly valued quality and standards within the university while genuinely embracing difference and equity of opportunity for all students.

The lecturer in the Issues course provides exemplars of teaching that address some of these conundrums through the reconfiguration of binaries. Rather than being juxtaposed against each other, the oppositions are placed in productive partnerships with each other. For example, in class interactions, the lecturer choreographs turns between international and domestic students through the use of techniques such as namings. She nests non-Western knowledge within the expectations of the Western academy, and makes it explicit to students that while the latter is only one way of doing knowledge, it is, however, the prevailing 'game'. Playing this game brings its rewards that she acknowledges are localised but nonetheless highly relevant to the students' academic success in the Issues course. It is a pragmatic approach of 'working through the middle' of the oppositions.

Many of the lecturer's teaching methods and techniques are reminiscent of English as a second language (ESL) teaching. She concedes that she is not a language specialist but her teaching approach is, nonetheless, one that generates knowledge, participation and legitimation for second language students. She is culturally and linguistically aware and exhibits the 'international consciousness' advocated by Lee (2015). From a language point of view, international students have met the threshold language requirements imposed by universities through gatekeeping tests such as English as an International Testing System (IELTS). These students might have partial competence in multiple languages although none might be as complete as their first or native language (Canagarajah, 2014). Their studies require a plurilingual competence in which they pull together their accumulated language experiences to negotiate communication and cultural interaction skills in the new context (Council of Europe, 2001). Rather than a bilingualism experience in which separate languages are foregrounded (Auger, 2014), second language higher education is an exercise in linguistic mobilisation and negotiation. The lecturer worked proactively with international students in full recognition of the impact of second language use on knowledge construction, social participation and self-representation.

The implication of this work is that teachers in university matter; they can make the difference between students floundering or flourishing. The lessons provided in this book demonstrate approaches, methods and techniques that academics can use when teaching students from diverse linguistic, cultural and educational backgrounds. They derive from the practices of the lecturer in the study who the international students recognised as offering them 'the gift of teaching' (Biesta, 2013); she extended their thinking in directions that were new and revelatory.

## Transformation in the University

Internationalisation is changing universities, simultaneously presenting possibilities and conundrums that need to be recognised in order to exploit the potential in the changes. The empirically based arguments in this book provide a means of addressing international student engagement within the current higher education context. To summarise, key principles include:

- engagement is a multidimensional construct comprising antecedents, actions and achievements/outcomes;
- social practice is the basis of academic life; practice mediates institutional structures and individual agency; practice is an external entity as well as something that people *do*;
- English is an overdetermined element for second language students impacting overall practice;
- pedagogical practices are key mediators of international student engagement; they are powerful in generating opportunities for learning and participation;
- 'making visible' exemplars of lessons is deemed highly effective by students; in this book, lessons are augmented with the language and science of teaching;
- the international student is reconceptualised as authoritative, engaged and agentive;
- the university is a learning institution that needs to be informed about international student engagement and how it can be accomplished.

The book is designed for university policymakers and teachers who are interested in understanding how language, academic practices, pedagogies and participation intersect and influence each other. By showing the dialectical relationships between all elements of the academic experience, the book highlights the importance of teaching to key ways of knowing, doing and being. It has provided comprehensive explanations of international student engagement and the implications for university teaching and learning.

To conclude, the powerful concept of unknowing from the Walpiri language in the Lajamanu area of the Northern Territory in Australia is invoked. Unknowing is the joy of people from different cultural backgrounds, languages and experiences committing to unknowing in order to learn from each other. The book borrows the concept to underscore the possibilities in international higher education of unsettling the familiar and relearning together.

# References

Aglietta, M. (1979) *A Theory of Capitalist Regulation: The US Experience*. London: New Left Books.

Alexander, D. and Rizvi, F. (1993) Education, markets and the contradictions of Asia-Australia relations. *The Australian Universities' Review* 36 (2), 16–20.

Alexander, R. (2005) Culture, Dialogue and Learning: Notes on an Emerging Pedagogy. Education, Culture and Cognition: Intervening for Growth, International Association for Cognitive Education and Psychology (IACEP), 10th International conference, University of Durham, UK, 10–14 July 2005.

Alexander, R. (2008) *Essays on Pedagogy*. London: Routledge.

Altbach, P.G. (2004) Globalization and the university: Myths and realities in an unequal world. In National Education Association (ed.) *The NEA 2005 Almanac of Higher Education* (pp. 63–74). Washington, DC: National Education Association.

Altbach, P.G. and Knight, J. (2007) The internalization of higher education: Motivations and realities. *Journal of Studies in Higher Education* 11 (3–4), 290–305.

Al-Youssef, J. (2013) An international approach to teaching and learning from a UK university management perspective: Implications for international students' experience on campus. In S. Sovic and M. Blythman (eds) *International Students Negotiating Higher Education: Critical Perspectives* (pp. 54–66). Abingdon: Routledge.

Ammon, U. (2000) Towards more fairness in International English: Linguistic rights of non-native speakers? In R. Phillipson (ed.) *Rights to Language: Equity, Power and Education* (pp. 111–116). Mahwah, NJ: Lawrence Erlbaum.

Ammon, U. (2001) Editor's preface. In U. Ammon (ed.) *The Dominance of English as a Language of Science: Effects on Other Languages and Language Communities* (pp. v–x). Berlin: Mouton de Gruyter.

Ang, I. (2000) Introduction: Alter/Asian cultural interventions for 21st century Australia. In I. Ang, S. Chalmers, L. Law and M. Thomas (eds) *Alter/Asians: Asian-Australian Identities in Art, Media and Popular Culture* (pp. xiii–xxx). Annandale: Pluto Press.

Arkoudis, S., Baik, C., Marginson, S. and Cassidy, E. (2012) *Internationalising the Student Experience in Australian Tertiary Education: Developing Criteria and Indicators*. Melbourne: AEI/Centre for the Study of Higher Education.

Atkinson, D. (2002) Toward a sociocognitive approach to second language acquisition. *Modern Language Journal* 86, 525–545.

Auditor-General (2002) International students in Victorian Universities. See www.audit.vic.gov.au/reports_par/agp7601.html (last accessed 2 May 2003).

Auger, N. (2014) Exploring the use of migrant languages to support learning in mainstream classrooms in France. In D. Little, C. Leung and P. Van Avermaet (eds) *Managing Diversity in Education: Languages, Policies, Pedagogies* (pp. 223–242). Bristol: Multilingual Matters.

AEI (2013) End of Year Summary of International Student Enrolment Data – Australia – 2012. See https://aei.gov.au/research/International-Student-Data/Documents/Monthly%20summaries%20of%20international%20student%20enrolment%20data%202012/12_December_2012_MonthlySummary.pdf (last accessed 24 January 2014).

AEI (2014a) *Export* Income to Australia from International Education Activity in 2013. See https://www.aei.gov.au/research/Research-Snapshots/Documents/Export%20Income%20CY2013.pdf (accessed 1 June 2014).

AEI (2014b) Research Snapshot: International Student Enrolments by Nationality in 2013. See https://www.aei.gov.au/research/Research-Snapshots/Documents/Enrolments%20by%20Nationality%202013.pdf (last accessed 5 May 2014).

AEI (2015a) Research Snapshot: Export Income to Australia from International Education Activity in 2014. See https://internationaleducation.gov.au/research/Research-Snapshots/Documents/Export%20Income%20CY2014.pdf (accessed 14 September 2015).

AEI (2015b) Research Snapshot: International Student Enrolments by Nationality in 2014. See https://internationaleducation.gov.au/research/Research-Snapshots/Documents/Enrolments%20by%20Nationality%202014.pdf (accessed 14 September 2015).

AEI (2015c) Research Snapshot: International Students in Australia up to 2014. See https://internationaleducation.gov.au/research/Research-Snapshots/Documents/International%20students%20in%20Australian%20Uni_2014.pdf (accessed 14 September 2015).

AEI (2015d) Research Snapshot: Onshore Higher Education International Students as a Proportion of all Onshore Students, by University, 2014. See https://internationaleducation.gov.au/research/Research-Snapshots/Documents/International%20students%20in%20Australian%20Uni_2014.pdf (accessed 14 September 2015).

ABS (2013a) Australian Social Trends, April 2013: The 'Average' Australian. See http://www.abs.gov.au/AUSSTATS/abs@.nsf/Lookup/4102.0Main+Features30April+2013 (accessed 1 September 2013).

ABS (2013b) Australian Social Trends, July 2013. See http://www.abs.gov.au/AUSSTATS/abs@.nsf/Lookup/4102.0Main+Features20July+2013 (accessed 1 November 2013).

ACER (2010) *Doing More for Learning: Enhancing Engagement and Outcomes: Australasian Survey of Student Engagement Australasian Student Engagement Report.* Camberwell: ACER.

Australian Government (2015a) Draft National Strategy for International Education (For Consultation) April 2015. See https://www.google.com.au/url?sa=t&rct=j&q=&esrc=s&source=web&cd=1&cad=rja&uact=8&ved=0CBwQFjAAahUKEwjlvIvH2IzIAhUFNqYKHTENBwo&url=https%3A%2F%2Finternationaleducation.gov.au%2Fnational-strategy-international-education&usg=AFQjCNH5WkQWF3MmmadgIv1IW35c-h55sw (accessed 20 September 2015).

Australian Government (2015b) Monthly Summary of International Student Enrolment Data – Australia – YTD July 2015. See https://internationaleducation.gov.au/research/International-Student-Data/Documents/Monthly%20summaries%20of%20international%20student%20enrolment%20data%202015/07_July_2015_MonthlySummary.pdf (accessed 14 September 2015).

Australian Government (2016) Driving Innovation, Fairness and Excellence in Australian Higher Education. See https://docs.education.gov.au/documents/driving-innovation-fairness-and-excellence-australian-education (accessed 26 August 2016).

AITSL (2013) Engagement in Australian schools. See http://www.aitsl.edu.au/docs/default-source/default-document-library/engagement_in_australian_schools__grattan (accessed 15 August 2016).

AVCC (2005) *Key statistics: Internationalisation Data 2003.* See http://www.avcc.edu.au/documents/publications/stats/international.xls (last accessed 9 May 2006).

Back, K., Davis, D. and Olsen, A. (1996) *Internationalisation and Higher Education: Goals and Strategies.* Canberra: Australian Government Publishing Service.

Bailey, C. (2013) Negotiating writing: Challenges of the first written assignment at a UK university. In S. Sovic and M. Blythman (eds) *International Students Negotiating Higher Education: Critical Perspectives* (pp. 173–189). Abingdon: Routledge.

Baldauf, R.B. and Kaplan, R.B. (2014) Understanding Sources of Institutional Power: The Key to Social-Structural and Public Sphere Agency in Language Planning. Paper presented at the AILA Conference, Brisbane, Australia.

Ballard, B. (1987) Academic adjustment: The other side of the export dollar. *Higher Education Research and Development* 6 (2), 109–119.

Ballard, B. and Clanchy, J. (1984) *Study Abroad: A Manual for Asian Students*. Kuala Lumpur: Longman.

Ballard, B. and Clanchy, J. (1991) *Teaching Students from Overseas*. Melbourne: Longman Cheshire.

Bamgboṣe, A. (2009) A recurring decimal: English in language policy and planning. In B. Kachru, Y. Kachru and C.L. Nelson (eds) *The Handbook of World Englishes* (pp. 645–660). Oxford: Blackwell.

Barker, M., Child, C., Gallois, C., Jones, E. and Callan, V.J. (1991) Difficulties of overseas students in social and academic situations. *Australian Journal of Psychology* 43 (2), 79–84.

Baron, P. and Corbin, L. (2012) Student engagement: Rhetoric and reality. *Higher Education Research & Development* 31 (6), 759–772.

Bassett, J. (1994) *The Concise Oxford Dictionary of Australian History*. Melbourne: Oxford University Press.

Beelen, J. (2011) Internationalisation at home in a global perspective: A critical survey of the 3rd global survey report of IAU. *Revista de Universidad y Sociedad del Conocimiento* 8 (2), 249–264. See http://rusc.uoc.edu/ojs/index.php/rusc/article/view/v8n2-beelen/v8n2-beelen-eng (accessed 25 November 2013).

Benhabib, S. (1991) Feminism and postmodernism: An uneasy alliance. *Praxis International* 11 (2), 135–149.

Bhabha, H. (1990) DissemiNation: Time, narrative, and the margins of the modern nation. In H. Bhabha (ed.) *Nation and Narration* (pp. 291–322). London: Routledge.

Bhabha, H.K. (1994) *The Location of Culture*. London: Routledge.

Biesta, G.J.J. (2013) Receiving the gift of teaching: From 'learning from' to 'being taught by'. *Studies in Philosophy and Education* 32, 449–461.

Biesta, G.J.J. (2014) *The Beautiful Risk of Education*. London: Paradigm Publishers.

Biggs, J. (2003) *Teaching for Quality Learning at University: What the Student Does* (2nd edn). Maidenhead: Open University Press.

Borrello, E. (2015) Student teachers will need to pass literacy and numeracy test before being allowed to graduate. *ABC News*, 13 February. See http://www.abc.net.au/news/2015-02-13/teaching-students-to-sit-literacy-and-numeracy-test-to-graduate/6090062 (accessed 22 June 2016).

Bourdieu, P. (1993) *Sociology in Question*. London: Sage.

Boyle, J. (2015) Around 1 in 10 Teaching Students Fail Numeracy, Literacy Exam. *ABC News*, 1 December. See http://www.abc.net.au/news/2015-12-01/around-one-in-ten-teaching-students-fail-literacy-and-numeracy-/6988168 (accessed 4 December 2015).

Bradley, D. and Bradley, M. (1984) *Problems of Asian Students in Australia: Language, Culture and Education*. Canberra: Australian Government Publishing Service.

Bradley, D., Noonan, P., Nugent, H. and Scales, B. (2008) *Review of Australian Higher Education: Final Report*. Canberra: Department of Education, Employment and Workplace Relations.

Brandenburg, U. and de Wit, H. (2012) Higher education is losing sight of what higher education is all about. *The Guardian*, 2 April. See http://www.theguardian.com/higher-education-network/blog/2012/apr/02/internationalisation-labeling-learning-outcomes (accessed 24 February 2014).

Brew, A. (2007) Integrating research and teaching: Understanding excellence. In A. Skelton (ed.) *International Perspectives on Teaching Excellence in Higher Education* (pp. 74–88). London: Routledge.

Bruch, T. and Barty, A. (1998) Internationalizing British higher education: Students and institutions. In P. Scott (ed.) *The Globalization of Higher Education* (pp. 18–31). Buckingham: The Society for Research into Higher Education and Open University Press.

Bryson, C., Hardy, C. and Hand, L. (2009) An In-Depth Investigation of Students' Engagement throughout their First Year in University. Paper presented at the UK National Transitions Conference, London, 22–24 May.

Bullen, E. and Kenway, J. (2003) Real or imagined women? Staff representations of international women postgraduate students. *Discourse: Studies in the Cultural Politics of Education* 24 (1), 35–50.

Burns, R.B. (1991) Study and stress among first year overseas students in an Australian university. *Higher Education Research and Development* 10 (1), 61–77.

Butler, J. (1991) Contingent foundations: Feminism and the question of postmodernism. *Praxis International* 11 (2), 150–165.

Butler, J. (1997) *The Psychic Life of Power: Theories in Subjection*. Stanford, CA: Stanford University Press.

Cameron, D. (2002) Globalization and the teaching of 'communication skills'. In D. Block and D. Cameron (eds) *Globalization and Language Teaching* (pp. 67–82). London: Routledge.

Canagarajah, A.S. (1997) *Safe Houses in the Contact Zone: Coping Strategies of African-American Students in the Academy*. See http://proquest.umi.com/pqdlink?index=20&sid=1&srchmode=3&vinst=PROD&fmt=4 (last accessed 13 January 2004).

Canagarajah, S. (2014) Theorizing a competence for translingual practice at the contact zone. In S. May (ed.) *The Multilingual Turn: Implications for SLA, TESOL and Bilingual Education*. (pp. 78–102). New York: Routledge.

Cazden, C. (2001) *Classroom Discourse: The Language of Teaching and Learning* (2nd edn). Portsmouth, NH: Heinemann.

Chalmers, D. and Volet, S. (1997) Common misconceptions about students from South-East Asia studying in Australia. *Higher Education Research & Development* 16 (1), 87–98.

Chamot, A. and O'Malley, M. (1994) Language learner and learning strategies. In N.C. Ellis (ed.) *Implicit and Explicit Learning of Languages* (pp. 371–392). San Diego, CA: Academic Press.

Chouliaraki, L. and Fairclough, N. (1999) *Discourse in Late Modernity: Rethinking Critical Discourse Analysis*. Edinburgh: Edinburgh University Press.

Chowdhury, R. and Phan, L.H. (2014) *Desiring TESOL and International Education: Market Abuse and Exploitation*. Bristol: Multilingual Matters.

Clark, C. (2013) *Talk at Mealtimes*. A research report for the National Literacy Trust 2013. See http://www.literacytrust.org.uk/assets/0001/7937/Mealtimes_2013.pdf

Clark, N. (2012) Understanding transnational education, its growth and implications. *World Education News and Reviews*, August 1. See http://wenr.wes.org/2012/08/wenr-august-2012-understanding-transnational-education-its-growth-and-implications/ (accessed June 17, 2015).

Clegg, S. (2009) Forms of knowing and academic development practice. *Studies in Higher Education* 34 (4), 403–416.

Coaldrake, P. and Stedman, L. (2013) *Raising the Stakes: Gambling with the Future of Universities*. St. Lucia: University of Queensland Press.

Colbeck, R. (2016) Record numbers of international students choose Australia, The Department of Education and Training. See https://ministers.education.gov.au/colbeck/record-numbers-international-students-choose-australia (accessed 6 October 2016).

Committee of Review of Private Overseas Student Policy (1984) *Mutual Advantage*. Canberra: Australian Government Printing Service.

Commonwealth of Australia (n.d.) *Higher Education and Research Reform Amendment Bill 2014.* See http://www.aph.gov.au/Parliamentary_Business/Bills_LEGislation/Bills_Search_Results/Result?bId=r5325 (accessed 10 September 2015).

Commonwealth of Australia (2013a) *StudentsFirst.* Teacher Education Ministerial Advisory Group (TEMAG). Canberra: Department of Education and Training. See http://www.studentsfirst.gov.au/teacher-education-ministerial-advisory-group (accessed 15 December 2014).

Commonwealth of Australia (2013b) Why study in Australia? Future Unlimited. See http://www.studyinaustralia.gov.au/global/why-australia (accessed 24 February 2014).

Commonwealth of Australia (2016) The G20 – Department of Foreign Affairs and Trade. https://www.google.com.au/url?sa=t&rct=j&q=&esrc=s&source=web&cd=&cad=rja&uact=8&ved=0ahUKEwiDnYSXo93RAhUKjpQKHeMsAjUQFggZMAA&url=http%3A%2F%2Fdfat.gov.au%2Finternational-relations%2Finternational-organisations%2Fg20%2Fpages%2Fthe-g20.aspx&usg=AFQjCNELeZLPDFQkN5C_rPFa30u0A8JREw (accessed 25 January 2017).

Connor, U. (2002) New directions in contrastive rhetoric. *TESOL Quarterly* 36 (4), 493–510.

COAG (2010) *International Students Strategy for Australia: 2010–2014.* See http://www.coag.gov.au/sites/default/files/International%20Students%20Strategy%20-%20PDF.pdf (last accessed 29 May 2014).

Council of Europe (2001) *Common European Framework of Reference for Languages: Learning, Teaching, Assessment.* Cambridge: Cambridge University Press.

Cumming, A. (2001) Learning to write in a second language: Two decades of research. *International Journal of English Studies* 1 (2), 1–23.

Davies, B. (1990) Agency as a form of discursive practice: A classroom scene observed. *British Journal of Sociology of Education* 11 (3), 341–361.

Delpit, L. (1988) The silenced dialogue: Power and pedagogy in educating other people's children. *Harvard Educational Review* 58 (3), 280–298.

Delpit, L. (1995) *Other People's Children: Cultural Conflict in the Classroom.* New York: The New Press.

Delpit, L. (1998) The politics of teaching literate text. In V. Zamel and R. Spack (eds) *Negotiating Academic Literacies across Languages and Cultures* (pp. 207–218). Mahwah, NJ: Lawrence Erlbaum.

DEST (2005) *Students 2003 Tables: Selected Higher Education Statistics.* See http://www.dest.gov.au-Students2003Tables:Selected-HigherEducationStatistics (last accessed 2 May 2006).

Devlin, M. and Samarawickrema, G. (2010) The criteria of effective teaching in a changing higher education context. *Higher Education Research & Development* 29 (2), 111–124.

Doherty, C. and Singh, P. (2003) How the West is done: Simulating Western pedagogy in a curriculum for Asian international students. In P. Ninnes and M. Hellsten (eds) *Internationalizing Higher Education: Critical Explorations of Pedagogy and Policy* (pp. 53–73). Hong Kong: Comparative Education Research Centre, The University of Hong Kong.

Doherty, C., Kettle, M., May, L. and Caukill, E. (2011) Talking the talk: Oracy demands in first year university group assessment tasks. *Assessment in Education* 18 (1), 27–39.

Dreyfus, H.L. and Rabinow, P. (1982) *Michel Foucault: Beyond Structuralism and Hermeneutics.* Chicago, IL: University of Chicago.

Duff, P.A. (2010) Language socialization into academic discourse communities. *Annual Review of Applied Linguistics* 30, 169–192.

Edwards, A.D. and Westgate, D.P.G. (1994) *Investigating Classroom Talk* (2nd edn). London: RoutledgeFalmer.

Eldridge, M. (2011) Democracy – Practice as needed. In J.M. Green, S. Neubert and K. Reich (eds) *Pragmatism and Diversity: Dewey in the Context of Late Twentieth Century Debates* (pp. 85–98). New York: Palgrave Macmillan.

Ellsworth, E. (1989) Why doesn't this feel empowering? Working through the repressive myths of critical pedagogy. *Harvard Educational Review* 59 (3), 297–325.

Fairclough, N. (1992) *Discourse and Social Change*. Cambridge: Polity Press.

Fairclough, N. (1993) Critical discourse analysis and the marketisation of public discourse: The universities. *Discourse and Society* 4, 133–168.

Fairclough, N. (2001a) *Language and Power* (2nd edn). Harlow: Pearson Education Limited.

Fairclough, N. (2001b) The discourse of new labour: Critical discourse analysis. In M. Wetherell, S. Taylor and S.J. Yates (eds) *Discourse as Data: A Guide for Analysis* (pp. 229–266). London: Sage.

Fairclough, N. (2003) *Analysing Discourse: Textual Analysis for Social Research*. London: Routledge.

Felix, U. (1993) Support strategies for international postgraduate students. *HERDSA* 15 (1), 6–8.

Ferguson, N. (2011) *Civilization: The West and the Rest*. London: Penguin Books.

Ferris, D. (2011) *Treatment of Error in Second Language Student Writing*. Ann Arbor, MI: University of Michigan Press.

Ferris, D. and Roberts, B. (2001) Error feedback in L2 writing classes: How explicit does it need to be? *Journal of Second Language Writing* 10 (3), 161–184.

Fishman, J.A. (1981) Language policy: Past, present and future. In C. Ferguson and S.B. Heath (eds) *Language in the USA* (pp. 516–526). Cambridge: Cambridge University Press.

Foster, G. (2012) The impact of international students on measured learning and standards in Australian Higher Education. *Economics of Education Review* 31 (5), 587–600.

Foucault, M. (1972) *The Archaeology of Knowledge and the Discourse on Language* (1969, trans.). London: Tavistock.

Foucault, M. (1977) *Discipline and Punish: The Birth of the Prison* (1975, trans.). London: Allen Lane.

Foucault, M. (1978) *The History of Sexuality. Volume 1: An Introduction* (R. Hurley, trans.). New York: Random House.

Foucault, M. (1980) Two lectures. In C. Gordon (ed.) *Power/Knowledge: Selected Interviews and Other Writings 1972–1977* (pp. 78–108). New York: Pantheon Books.

Foucault, M. (1982) The subject and power. In H.L. Dreyfus and P. Rabinow (eds) *Michel Foucault: Beyond Structuralism and Hermeneutics* (pp. 208–226). Chicago, IL: University of Chicago Press.

Foucault, M. (1984) The order of discourse. In M.J. Shapiro (ed.) *Language and Politics* (pp. 108–138). Oxford: Basil Blackwell.

Foucault, M. (1986) On the genealogy of ethics: An overview of work in progress. In P. Rabinow (ed.) *The Foucault Reader* (pp. 340–372). New York: Pantheon Books.

Foucault, M. (1987) The ethic of care for the self as a practice of freedom: An interview with Michel Foucault on January 20, 1984 (J.D. Gauthier, trans.). In J. Bernauer and D. Rasmussen (eds) *The Final Foucault* (pp. 1–20). Cambridge, MA: The MIT Press.

Foucault, M. (1988) Technologies of the self. In L.H. Martin, H. Gutman and P.H. Hutton (eds) *Technologies of the Self: A Seminar with Michel Foucault* (pp. 16–49). Amherst, MA: University of Massachusetts Press.

Foucault, M. (1996a) An aesthetics of existence. In S. Lotringer (ed.) *Foucault Live: Collected Interviews 1961–1984* (pp. 450–454). New York: Semiotext (e).

Foucault, M. (1996b) The concern for truth. In S. Lotringer (ed.) *Foucault Live: Collected Interviews 1961–1984* (pp. 455–464). New York: Semiotext(e).

Foucault, M. (1996c) The discourse of history. In S. Lotringer (ed.) *Foucault Live: Collected Interviews 1961–1984* (pp. 19–32). New York: Semiotext(e).

Foucault, M. (1996d) The ethics of the concern for self as a practice of freedom. In S. Lotringer (ed.) *Foucault Live: Collected Interviews 1961–1984* (pp. 432–449). New York: Semiotext(e).

Foucault, M. (1996e) The order of things. In S. Lotringer (ed.) *Foucault Live: Collected Interviews 1961–1984* (pp. 13–18). New York: Semiotext(e).

Foucault, M. (1996f) What our present is. In S. Lotringer (ed.) *Foucault Live: Collected Interviews 1961–1984* (pp. 407–415). New York: Semiotext(e).

Foucault, M. (2000) Truth and juridical forms. In J.D. Faubian (ed.) *Power* (Vol. 3; pp. 1–89). New York: The New Press.

Fraser, N. (1991) False antitheses: A response to Seyla Benhabib and Judith Butler. *Praxis International* 11 (2), 167–177.

Fredricks, J.A. and McColskey, W. (2012) The measurement of student engagement: A comparative analysis of various methods and student self-report instruments. In S. Christenson, A.L. Reschly and C. Wylie (eds) *Handbook of Research on Student Engagement* (pp. 763–782). New York: Springer.

Fredricks, J.A., Blumenfeld, P. and Paris, A. (2004) School engagement: Potential of the concepts, state of the evidence. *Review of Educational Research* 74, 59–109.

Freebody, P. (2003). *Qualitative Research in Education: Interaction and Practice.* London/Thousand Oaks, CA/New Delhi: Sage.

Frijters, P. (2011) Are we going easy on foreign students in order to get more revenue? *Club Troppo*, March 16. See http://clubtroppo.com.au/2011/03/16/are-we-going-easy-on-foreign-students-in-order-to-get-more-revenue/ (accessed August 20, 2015).

Gale, T. and Tranter, D. (2011) Social justice in Australian higher education policy: An historical and conceptual account of student participation. *Critical Studies in Education* 52 (1), 29–46.

Garrison, J. (2011) Dewey, Levinas on pluralism, the Other, and democracy. In J.M. Green, S. Neubert and K. Reich (eds) *Pragmatism and Diversity: Dewey in the Context of Late Twentieth Century Debates* (pp. 99–126). New York: Palgrave Macmillan.

Gassin, J. (1982) The learning difficulties of the foreign student and what we can do about them. *HERDSA* 4 (3), 13, 16.

Gibbons, P. (2002) *Scaffolding Language, Scaffolding Learning: Teaching Second Language Learners in the Mainstream Classroom.* Portsmouth, NH: Heinemann.

Gibbons, P. (2007) Mediating academic language learning through classroom discourse. In J. Cummins and C. Davison (eds) *International Handbook of English Language Teaching Volume 15* (pp. 701–718). New York: Springer.

Gillard, J. (2008) *Equity in the Education Revolution.* See http://www.aacs.net.au/imagesDB/news/TheHonJuliaGillardMP-EquityintheEduca...pdf (last accessed 11 March 2009).

Giroux, H. (1992) *Border Crossings: Cultural Workers and the Politics of Education.* New York: Routledge.

Green, W. (2013) Great expectation: The impact of friendship groups on the intercultural learning of Australian students abroad. In S. Sovic and M. Blythman (eds) *International Students Negotiating Higher Education: Critical Perspectives.* London: Routledge.

Green, J.M., Neubert, S. and Reich, K. (2011) *Pragmatism and Diversity: Dewey in the Context of Late Twentieth Century Debates* (pp. 211–225). New York: Palgrave Macmillan.

Grin, F. (2001) English as economic value: Facts and fallacies. *World Englishes* 20 (1), 65–78.

Grosz, E. (2004) *The Nick of Time: Politics, Evolution, and the Untimely.* Crows Nest: Allen & Unwin.

Gu, Y. (2007) Strategy-based instruction. In T. Yashima and T. Nabei (eds) *Proceedings of the International Symposium on English Education in Japan: Exploring New Frontiers* (pp. 21–38). Osaka: Yubunsha.

Gubrium, J.F. and Holstein, J.A. (2000) Analyzing interpretive practice. In N.K. Denzin and Y.S. Lincoln (eds) *Handbook of Qualitative Research* (2nd edn; pp. 487–508). Thousand Oaks, CA: Sage Publications.

Gutiérrez, K., Hunter, J.D. and Arzubiga, A. (2009) Re-mediating the university: Learning through sociocritical literacies. *Pedagogies: An International Journal* 4, 1–23.

Hacker, D.J., Keener, M.C. and Kircher, J.C. (2009) Writing is applied metacognition. In D.J. Hacker, J. Dunlosky and A.-C. Graesser (eds) *Handbook of Metacognition in Education* (pp. 154–172). New York: Routledge.

Hale, G., Taylor, C., Bridgeman, B., Carson, J., Kroll, B. and Kantor, R. (1996) *A Study of Writing Tasks Assigned in Academic Degree Programs* (TOEFL Research Report No. 54). Princeton, NJ: Educational Testing Service.

Halliday, M. (1978) *Language as Social Semiotic*. London: Edward Arnold.

Halliday, M.A.K. (1985) *Spoken and Written Language*. Victoria: Deakin University.

Halliday, M. (1994) *An Introduction to Functional Grammar* (2nd edn). London: Edward Arnold.

Halliday, M.A.K. and Hasan, R. (1985) *Language, Context, and Text: Aspects of Language in a Social-Semiotic Perspective*. Melbourne: Deakin University.

Hammond, J. and Macken-Horarik, M. (1999) Critical literacy: Challenges and questions for the ESL classroom. *TESOL Quarterly* 33 (3), 528–544.

Hammond, J. and Gibbons, P. (2005) Putting scaffolding to work: The contribution of scaffolding in articulating ESL education. *Prospect* 20 (1), 6–30.

Hanson, P. (1996) Maiden Speech to Parliament. See http://www.nswonenation.com.au-PAULINE_HANSON'S_MAIDEN_SPEECH (accessed 20 August 2002).

Hare, J. (2013) Indifferent Outcomes for Chinese Graduates. *The Australian*, 3 July. See http://www.theaustralian.com.au/higher-education/indifferent-outcomes-for-chinese-graduates/story-e6frgcjx-1226673358109 (accessed 26 July 2015).

Harper, S.R. and Quaye, S.J. (2015) Making engagement equitable for students in US higher education. In S.J. Quaye and S.R. Harper (eds) *Student Engagement in Higher Education: Theoretical Perspectives and Practical Approaches for Diverse Populations* (2nd edn; pp. 1–14). New York: Routledge.

Harris, G.T. and Jarrett, F.G. (1990) *Educating Overseas Students in Australia: Who Benefits?* Sydney: Allen & Unwin.

Harvey, D. (1996) *Justice, Nature and the Geography of Difference*. London: Blackwell.

Havergal, C. (2015) Academic values 'at risk' in internationalisation, says report. *Times Higher Education*, August 15. See https://www.timeshighereducation.co.uk/news/academic-values-%E2%80%98-risk%E2%80%99-internationalisation-says-report (accessed 22 August 2015).

Hewings, A. (2012) Learning English, learning through English. In A. Hewings and C. Tagg (eds) *The Politics of English: Conflict, Competition, Co-existence* (pp. 93–120). Abingdon: Routledge.

Hirvela, A. and Belcher, D. (2001) Coming back to voice: The multiple voices and identities of mature multilingual writers. *Journal of Second Language Writing* 10, 83–106.

Holliday, A. (1994) *Appropriate Methodology and Social Context*. Cambridge: Cambridge University Press.

Holliday, A. (2006) Native-speakerism. *ELT Journal* 60 (4), 385–387.

Horwitz, E.K. (2001) Language anxiety and achievement. *Annual Review of Applied Linguistics* 21, 112–126.

Horwitz, E.K. (2012) *Becoming a Language Teacher: A Practical Guide to Second Language Learning and Teaching* (2nd edn). Old Tappan: Pearson Education.

House, C. (2003) English as a lingua franca: A threat to multilingualism? *Journal of Sociolinguistics* 7 (4), 556–578.

Hyland, K. and Hyland, F. (2006) Feedback on second language students' writing. *Language Teaching* 39 (2), 83–101.

Ichimoto, T. (2005) *Recrafting 'Selves': Identity Transformation among Japanese Women Students Studying in Australian Universities.* Brisbane: The University of Queensland.

IIE (2011) *Student Mobility and the Internationalization of Higher Education: National Policies and Strategies from Six World Regions.* New York: Institute of International Education.

IIE (2013) *Open doors report on international educational exchange.* See http://www.iie.org/ research-and-publications/open-doors/data#.WAq6ieB96Un (accessed 6 October 2016).

IELTS (2003) *IELTS – International English Language Testing System Handbook.* See http:// www.ielts.org/pdf/ielts_hb_2003.pdf (last accessed 11 March 2004).

Ivanič, R. (2004) Discourses of writing and learning to write. *Language and Education* 18 (3), 220–245.

Iyer, R., Kettle, M., Luke, A. and Mills, K. (2014) Critical applied linguistics as a social field. In C. Leung and B. Street (eds) *Handbook of English Language Studies* (pp. 317–332). London: Routledge.

Jenkins, J. (2003) *World Englishes: A Resource Book for Students.* London: Routledge.

Jericho, G. (2014) Government's low blow on higher education. *ABC: The Drum,* 4 June. See http://www.abc.net.au/news/2014-06-04/jericho-governments-low-blow-on-higher-education/5496386 (accessed 5 June 2014).

Joint Committee on Foreign Affairs and Defence (1985) *The Jackson Report on Australia's Overseas Aid Program.* Canberra: AGPS.

Kachru, B. (1992) Teaching world Englishes. In B. Kachru (ed.) *The Other Tongue: English Across Cultures* (2nd edn; pp. 355–365). Urbana, IL: University of Illinois Press.

Kahn, P.E. (2014) Theorising student engagement in higher education. *British Educational Research Journal* 40 (6), 1005–1018.

Kahu, E.R. (2013) Framing student engagement in higher education. *Studies in Higher Education* 38 (5), 758–773.

Kaplan, R.B. (1966) Cultural thought patterns in inter-cultural education. *Language Learning* 16, 1–20.

Kaplan, R.B. (2001) English – the accidental language of science? In U. Ammon (ed.) *The Dominance of English as a Language of Science: Effects on Other Languages and Language Communities* (pp. 3–26). Berlin: Mouton de Gruyter.

Kennett, B. (2003) *Resourcing Identities: Biographies of Australians Learning Japanese.* Brisbane: The University of Queensland.

Kettle, M. (2005) Agency as discursive practice: From 'nobody' to 'somebody' as an international student in Australia. *Asia Pacific Journal of Education* 25 (1), 45–60.

Kettle, M. (2011) Academic practice as explanatory framework: Reconceptualising international student academic engagement and university teaching. *Discourse: Studies in the Cultural Politics of Education* 32 (1), 1–14.

Kettle, M. (2013) The Right to a Voice and the Fight to be Heard: The Experience of Being an ESL User. Paper presented at the 13th International Pragmatics Association (IPrA) Congress, Symposium on Implicit Discrimination in Public Discourse, New Delhi, 8–13 September.

Kettle, M. and May, L. (2012) The ascendancy of oracy in university courses: Implications for teachers and second language users. In C. Gitsaki and R. Baldauf (eds) *The Future of Applied Linguistics: Local and Global Perspectives* (pp. 49–66). Newcastle upon Tyne: Cambridge Scholars.

Kettle, M. and Luke, A. (2013) The critical meets the cultural: International students' responses to critical, dialogic postgraduate education in a western university.

In S. Sovic and M. Blythman (eds) *International Students Negotiating Higher Education* (pp. 104–123). London: Routledge.

Kettle, M. and Ryan, M. (in press) Using reflexivity to explain transitions in second language writing: Implications for international postgraduate students' academic success. In K. Spelman Miller and M. Stevenson (eds) *Transitions in Writing*. Leiden: Brill.

Kim, L.C. and Lim, M-H. (2013) Metadiscourse in English and Chinese research article introductions. *Discourse Studies* 15 (2), 129–146.

Kirkpatrick, A. (2012) English in ASEAN: Implications for regional multilingualism. *Journal of Multilingual and Multicultural Development* 33 (4), 331–344.

Knight, J. (2006) *Higher Education Crossing Borders: A Guide to the Implications of the General Agreement on Trade in Services (GATS) for Cross-Border Education. A Report Prepared for the Commonwealth of Learning and UNESCO.* Paris: COL/UNESCO.

Knight, J. (2008) *Higher Education in Turmoil: The Changing World of Internationalization.* Rotterdam: Sense.

Knight, J. (2011) Is internationalisation having an identity crisis? Programme on institutional management in higher education. *IMHE Info* (OECD) August 2011. See http://www.oecd.org/edu/imhe/48506334.pdf (accessed 24 February 2014).

Kristeva, J. (1986) The system and the speaking subject. In T. Moi (ed.) *The Kristeva Reader* (pp. 24–33). Oxford: Basil Blackwell.

Kubota, R. (2001) Discursive construction of the images of US classrooms. *TESOL Quarterly* 35 (1), 9–38.

Kuh, G.D. (2001) *The National Survey of Student Engagement: Conceptual Framework and Overview of Psychometric Properties.* Bloomington, IN: Indiana University Center for Postsecondary Research & Planning.

Laclau, E. and Mouffe, C. (1985) *Hegemony and Socialist Strategy.* London: Verso.

Lakoff, G. and Johnson, M. (1980) *Metaphors We Live By.* Chicago, IL: The University of Chicago Press.

Lee, J. (2015) Engaging international students. In S.J. Quaye and S.R. Harper (eds) *Student Engagement in Higher Education: Theoretical Perspectives and Practical Approaches for Diverse Populations.* (2nd edn; pp. 105–120). New York: Routledge.

Lee, J. and Rice, C. (2007) Welcome to America? International student perceptions of discrimination. *Higher Education* 53 (3), 381–409.

Leki, I. (2001) 'A narrow thinking system': Nonnative-English-speaking students in group projects across the curriculum. *TESOL Quarterly* 35 (1), 39–68.

Leki, I., Cumming, A. and Silva, T. (2008) *A Synthesis of Research on Second Language Writing in English.* New York: Routledge.

Leung, C. and Street, B.V. (eds) (2014) *The Routledge Companion to English Studies.* London/New York: Routledge.

Liddicoat, A.J. (2011) Language teaching and learning from an intercultural perspective. In E. Hinkel (ed.) *Handbook of Research in Second Language Teaching and Learning* (pp. 837–855). London: Routledge.

Lippi-Green, R. (2012) *English with an Accent: Language, Ideology, and Discrimination in the United States* (2nd edn). London: Routledge.

Livingstone, T. (2004a) Foreign students fail on their own terms. *The Courier-Mail,* 19 February, p. 9.

Livingstone, T. (2004b) Universities face tests on cash and credibility. *The Courier-Mail,* 14 February, p. 12.

Luke, A. (1996) Genres of power? Literacy education and the production of capital. In R. Hasan and G. Williams (eds) *Literacy in Society* (pp. 308–338). London: Longman.

Luke, A. (2002) Beyond science and ideology critique: Developments in critical discourse analysis. *Annual Review of Applied Linguistics* 22, 96–110.

Luke, A. (2004) Notes on the future of critical discourse studies. *Critical Discourse Studies* 1 (1), 149–157.

Luke, C. (2001) *Globalization and Women in Academia: North/West-South/East*. Mahwah, NJ: Lawrence Erlbaum.

Macaro, E. (2003) *Teaching and Learning a Second Language*. London: Continuum.

Macken-Horarik, M. (2005) Tackling multimodal news: Some implications of critical analytical research on the 'children overboard' affair. *Melbourne Studies in Education* 46 (2), 45–66.

Mackie, J. (1997) The politics of Asian immigration. In J.E. Coughlan and D.J. McNamara (eds) *Asians in Australia: Patterns of Migration and Settlement* (pp. 10–48). South Melbourne: Macmillan Education Australia.

Malmö University (n.d.) IaH – Internationalisation at home website. See http://www.mah.se/english/About-Malmo-University/International/IaH---Internationalisation-at-Home/ (last accessed 24 February 2014).

Mann, S. (2001) Alternative perspectives on the student experience: Alienation and engagement. *Studies in Higher Education* 26, 7–19.

Marginson, S. (2002) Nation-building universities in a global environment: The case of Australia. *Higher Education* 43, 409–428.

Marginson, S. (2006) Dynamics of national and global competition in higher education. *Higher Education* 52, 1–39.

Marginson, S. (2014) Higher education: The age of Pyne the destroyer begins. *The Conversation*, 16 May. See http://theconversation.com/higher-education-the-age-of-pyne-the-destroyer-begins-26483 (accessed 25 May 2014).

Marginson, S., Nyland, C., Sawir, E. and Forbes-Mewett, H. (2010) *International Student Security*. Melbourne: Cambridge University Press.

Matalene, C. (1985) Contrastive rhetoric: An American writing teacher in China. *College English* 47 (8), 789–808.

May, S. (2014) *The Multilingual Turn: Implications for SLA, TESOL and Bilingual Education*. New York/London: Routledge.

McGeown, K. (2012) The Philippines: The world's budget English teacher. *BBC Business*, 12 November. See http://www.bbc.com/news/business-20066890 (accessed 24 January 2014).

McHoul, A. and Grace, W. (1993) *A Foucault Primer: Discourse, Power and the Subject*. Carlton: Melbourne University Press.

McNamara, D.J. and Coughlan, J.E. (1997) *Asians in Australia: Patterns of Migration and Settlement*. South Melbourne: Macmillan Education Australia.

Mehan, H. (1979) *Learning Lessons*. Cambridge: Harvard Press.

Mercer, N. (1995) *The Guided Construction of Knowledge: Talk Amongst Teachers and Learners*. Clevedon: Multilingual Matters.

Miller, J. (2000) Language use, identity and social interaction: Migrant students in Australia. *Research on Language and Social Interaction* 33 (1), 69–100.

Miller, J. (2003) *Audible Difference: ESL and Social Identity in Schools*. Clevedon: Multilingual Matters.

Moll, L.C., Amanti, C., Neff, D. and Gonzalez, N. (1992) Funds of knowledge for teaching: Using a qualitative approach to link homes and classrooms. *Theory into Practice* 31, 132–141.

Murray, D.E. and Christison, M. (2011) *What English Language Teachers Need to Know Volume II: Facilitating Learning*. New York: Routledge.

Myhill, D. (2009) Children's patterns of composition and their reflections on their composing processes. *British Educational Research Journal* 35 (1), 47–64.

Myhill, D. and Jones, S. (2007) More than just error correction: Students' perspectives on their revision processes during writing. *Written Communication* 24, 323–343.

Neff-van Aertselaer, J. (2013) Contextualising EFL argumentation writing practices within the Common European Framework descriptors. *Journal of Second Language Writing* 22, 198–209.

Negretti, R. and Kuteeva, M. (2011) Fostering metacognitive genre awareness in L2 academic reading and writing: A case study of pre-service English teachers. *Journal of Second Language Writing* 20, 95–110.

Neumann, R. (1985) English language problems and university students from non-English speaking backgrounds. *Higher Education Research and Development* 4 (2), 193–202.

Nichols, S. (2003) 'They just won't critique anything': The 'problem' of international students in the Western academy. In J. Satterthwaite, E. Atkinson and K. Gale (eds) *Discourse, Power and Resistance: Challenging the Rhetoric of Contemporary Education* (pp. 135–148). Stoke on Trent: Trentham Books.

Ninnes, P. (1999) Acculturation of international students in higher education: Australia. *Education and Society* 17 (1), 73–101.

Nixon, U. (1993) Coping in Australia: Problems faced by overseas students. *Prospect* 8 (3), 42–49.

Norman, J. (2016) Pauline Hanson calls for Muslim immigration ban in maiden speech to Senate. See http://www.abc.net.au/news/2016-09-14/one-nation-senator-pauline-hanson-makes-first-speech-to-senate/7845150 (accessed 1 October 2016).

Norton, B. and Toohey, K. (eds) (2004) *Critical Pedagogies and Language Teaching.* Cambridge: Cambridge University Press.

Norton Peirce, B. (1995) Social identity, investment and language learning. *TESOL Quarterly* 29 (1), 9–31.

O'Malley, J.M. and Chamot, A.U. (1990) *Learning Strategies in Second Language Acquisition.* Cambridge: Cambridge University Press.

OECD (2006) Cross-border education: An overview. *Internationalisation and Trade in Higher Education: Opportunities and Challenges.* See http://www.keepeek.com/Digital-Asset-Management/oecd/education/internationalisation-and-trade-in-higher-education/cross-border-education_9789264015067-3-en#page1 (accessed 24 February 2014).

OECD (2008) *Education at a Glance 2008: OECD Indicators.* See http://www.oecd.org/dataoecd/23/46/41284038.pdf (accessed 20 September 2009).

OECD (2013a) *Education at a Glance 2013: OECD Indicators.* See http://www.oecd.org/edu/eag2013%20(eng)--FINAL%2020%20June%202013.pdf

OECD (2013b) Education at a glance 2013: Country Note: Australia. See http://www.oecd.org/edu/Australia_EAG2013%20Country%20Note.pdf (accessed April 7 2014).

OECD (2014) *Education at a Glance 2014: OECD Indicators.* See http://dx.doi.org/10.1787/eag-2014-en

OECD (2015) *OECD Education Policy Outlook 2015: Making Reforms Happen.* See www.oecd.org/edu/EPO%202015_Highlights.pdf (accessed 16 October 2015).

OECD (2016). Members and partners. http://www.oecd.org/about/membersand partners/ (accessed 25 January 2017).

Oxford, R. (2003) Toward a more systematic model of L2 learner autonomy. In D. Palfreyman and R.C. Smith (eds) *Learner Autonomy Across Cultures: Language Education Perspectives* (pp. 75–91). Basingstoke: Palgrave Macmillan.

Ozolins, U. (1993) *The Politics of Language in Australia.* Cambridge: Cambridge University Press.

Pavlenko, A. and Lantolf, J.P. (2000) Second language learning as participation and the (re)construction of selves. In J.P. Lantolf (ed.) *Sociocultural Theory and Second Language Learning* (pp. 155–177). Oxford: Oxford University Press.

Pennycook, A. (2001) *Critical Applied Linguistics: A Critical Introduction.* Mahwah, NJ: Lawrence Erlbaum Associates.

Peters, M.A. (2004) Educational research: 'Games of truth' and the ethics of subjectivity. *Journal of Educational Enquiry* 5 (2), 50–63.

Phillipson, R. (1992) *Linguistic Imperialism*. Oxford: Oxford University Press.

Piketty, T. (2014) *Capital in the Twenty-First Century* (A. Goldhammer, trans.). Cambridge, MA: Belknap Press of Harvard University Press.

QUT (2016) *Blueprint 5: September 2016*. Brisbane: Queensland University of Technology. See https://cms.qut.edu.au/__data/assets/pdf_file/0013/71113/qut-blueprint.pdf (accessed 25 September 2016).

Ramanathan, V. and Kaplan, R.B. (1996) Audience and voice in current L1 composition texts: Some implications for ESL student writers. *Journal of Second Language Writing* 5, 21–34.

Ramsden, P. (2003) *Learning to Teach in Higher Education* (2nd edn). London: RoutledgeFalmer.

Rao, S. (2015) Pauline Hanson calls for calm at Reclaim Australia rallies in Sydney, Queensland, Perth and Hobart. 19 July. *News Limited*. See http://www.news.com.au/national/politics/pauline-hanson-calls-for-calm-at-reclaim-australia-rallies-in-sydney-queensland-perth-and-hobart/story-fns0jze1-1227447659928 (accessed 23 September 2015).

Reclaim Australia (2015) Reclaim Australia: Australia wide: Will you help protect the Australian way of life? See http://www.reclaim-australia.com/ (accessed 23 September 2015).

Reich, K. (2011) Diverse communities – Dewey's theory of democracy as a challenge for Foucault, Bourdieu, and Rorty. In J.M. Green, S. Neubert and K. Reich (eds) *Pragmatism and Diversity: Dewey in the Context of Late Twentieth Century Debates* (pp. 165–194). New York: Palgrave Macmillan.

Renshaw, P.D. and Volet, S.E. (1995) South-East Asian students at Australian universities: A reappraisal of their tutorial participation and approaches to study. *Australian Higher Educational Researcher* 22 (2), 85–106.

Rice, J. (2014) The death of evidence in education policy? *The Conversation*, 10 June. See http://theconversation.com/the-death-of-evidence-in-education-policy-27505?utm_medium=email&utm_campaign=Latest+from+The+Conversation+for+10+June+2014+-+1708&utm_content=Latest+from+The+Conversation+for+10+June+2014+-+1708+CID_9f161bd450e8059a83ed576ba10098c6&utm_source=campaign_monitor&utm_term=The%20death%20of%20evidence%20in%20education%20policy (accessed 10 June 2014).

Rigg, P. (2013) English as the lingua franca of higher education? *University World News*, November 22. See www.universityworldnews.com/article.php?story=20131121152245865 (accessed 12 June 2015).

Rizvi, F. (2000) International education and the production of global imagination. In N. Burbules and C. Torres (eds) *Globalization and Education: Critical Perspectives* (pp. 205–225). London: Routledge.

Rizvi, F. (2011) Experiences of cultural diversity in the context of an emergent transnationalism. *European Educational Research Journal* 10 (2), 180–188.

Rizvi, F. and Walsh, L. (1998) Difference, globalisation and the internationalisation of curriculum. *Australian Universities' Review* 2, 7–11.

Robertson, M., Line, M., Jones, S. and Thomas, S. (2000) International students, learning environments and perceptions: A case study using the Delphi technique. *Higher Education Research and Development* 19 (1), 89–102.

Rose, D., Lui-Chivizhe, L., McKnight, A. and Smith, A. (2003) Scaffolding academic reading and writing at the Koori centre. *Australian Journal of Indigenous Education* 32, 41–49.

Rowbottom, P.D. (2011) Kuhn vs. Popper on criticism and dogmatism in science: A resolution at group level. *Studies in History and Philosophy of Science Part A* 22 (1), 117–124.

Ryan, J. (2000) *A Guide to Teaching International Students*. Oxford: Oxford Centre for Staff and Learning Development.

Ryan, J. (2005) Improving teaching and learning practices for international students: Implications for curriculum, pedagogy and assessment. In J. Carroll and J. Ryan (eds) *Teaching International Students: Improving Learning for All* (pp. 92–100). London: Routledge.

Ryan, J. (2011) Teaching and learning for international students: Towards a transcultural approach. *Teachers and Teaching* 17 (6), 631–648.

Ryan, J. (2013) Introduction. In J. Ryan (ed.) *Cross-Cultural Teaching and Learning for Home and International Students* (pp. 1–12). London: Routledge.

Ryan, J. and Viete, R. (2009) Respectful interactions: Learning with international students in the English-speaking academy. *Teaching in Higher Education* 14 (3), 303–314.

Samuelowicz, K. (1987) Learning problems of overseas students: Two sides of a story. *Higher Education Research and Development* 6 (2), 121–133.

Schmidt, R. (2001) Attention. In P. Robinson (ed.) *Cognition and Second Language Instruction* (pp. 3–32). Cambridge: Cambridge University Press.

Scott, P. (1998) Massification, internationalization, globalization. In P. Scott (ed.) *The Globalization of Higher Education* (pp. 108–129). Buckingham, PA: Society for Research into Higher Education and Open University Press.

Seargeant, P. (2012) The politics and policies of global English. In A. Hewings and C. Tagg (eds) *The Politics of English: Conflict, Competition, Co-existence* (pp. 5–45). Abingdon: Routledge.

Shanghai Ranking (2015) *Academic Ranking of World Universities 2015*. See http://www.shanghairanking.com/aboutarwu.html (accessed 22 August 2015).

Sheen, Y. and Ellis, R. (2011) Corrective feedback in language teaching. In E. Hinkel (ed.) *Handbook of Research in Second Language Teaching and Learning* (pp. 593–610). New York: Taylor & Francis.

Sidhu, R.K. (2006) *Universities and Globalization: To Market, to Market*. Mahwah, NJ: Lawrence Erlbaum.

Singh, M. (2009) Using Chinese knowledge in internationalising research education: Jacques Rancière, an ignorant supervisor and doctoral students from China. *Globalisation, Societies and Education* 7 (2), 185–201.

Skelton, A. (2007) Introduction. In A. Skelton (ed.) *International Perspectives on Teaching Excellence in Higher Education* (pp. 1–12). London: Routledge.

Smart, D. and Ang, G. (1996) The internationalisation of higher education. *International Higher Education* 6, 4–5.

Smart, D., Volet, S. and Ang, G. (2000) *Fostering Social Cohesion in Universities: Bridging the Cultural Divide*. Canberra: Department of Education, Training and Youth Affairs.

Smith, G., Morey, A. and Teece, M. (2002) *How International Students View their Australian Experience: A Survey of International Students Who Finished a Course of Study in 1999*. Canberra: Commonwealth of Australia.

Smolicz, J.J. (1995) Australia's language policies and minority rights: A core value perspective. In T. Skutnabb-Kangas, R. Phillipson and M. Rannut (eds) *Linguistic Human Rights: Overcoming Linguistic Discrimination* (pp. 235–252). Berlin: Mouton de Gruyter.

Sonntag, S. (2003) *The Local Politics of Global English: Case Studies in Linguistic Globalization*. Lanham, MD: Lexington Books.

Sovic, S. (2013) Classroom encounters: International students' perceptions of tutors in the creative arts. In S. Sovic and M. Blythman (eds) *International Students Negotiating Higher Education: Critical Perspectives* (pp. 87–103). London: Routledge.

Storch, N. (2010) Critical feedback on written corrective feedback research. *International Journal of English Studies* 10 (2), 29–46.

Summers, A. (2014) Tony Abbott's Team Australia entrenches inequality. *The Sydney MorningHerald.*Seehttp://www.smh.com.au/comment/tony-abbotts-team-australia-entrenches-inequality-20140822-106sdk.html (accessed 16 December 2014).

Swan, M. (1995) *Practical English Usage* (2nd edn). Oxford: Oxford University Press.

Taylor, S. (2001). Locating and conducting discourse analytic research. In M. Wetherell, S. Taylor and S.J. Yates (eds) *Discourse as Data: A Guide for Analysis* (pp. 5–48). Milton Keynes/London: The Open University and Sage.

Teichler, U. (2004) The changing debate on internationalisation of higher education. *Higher Education* 48, 5–26.

TEQSA (2015a) *National register of higher education providers.* See http://www.teqsa.gov.au/national-register (accessed 14 September 2015).

TEQSA (2015b) *Statistics report on TEQSA registered higher education providers. Australian Government.* See http://www.teqsa.gov.au/news-publications/statistics-report-teqsa-registered-higher-education-providers-2015 (accessed 14 September 2015).

TES Global (2016) *Times Higher Education World University Rankings 2016–2017.* See https://www.timeshighereducation.com/world-university-rankings/2017/worldranking#!/page/1/length/25/sort_by/rank_label/sort_order/asc/cols/rank_only (accessed 25 October 2016).

The Age (2010) Australia says some attacks on Indian students race-based. See http://www.theage.com.au/world/australia-says-some-attacks-on-indian-students-racebased-20100107-lv88.html (accessed 7 January 2013).

Threadgold, T. (2000) Poststructuralism and discourse analysis. In A. Lee and C. Poynton (eds) *Culture & Text: Discourse and Methodology in Social Research and Cultural Studies* (pp. 40–58). Lanham, MD: Rowman & Littlefield Publishers.

Tootell, K. (1999) *International students in Australia: What do we know of the quality of their education.* See www.aare.edu.au/99pap/too99642.htm (accessed 9 October 2001).

Trounson, A. (2011) Free ride past the language barrier. *The Australian.* See http://www.theaustralian.com.au/higher-education/free-ride-past-language-barrier/story-e6frgcjx-1226022052413 (accessed 17 March 2015).

Tsui, A.B.M. (1996) Reticence and anxiety in second language learning. In K. Bailey and D. Nunan (eds) *Voices From the Language Classroom* (pp. 145–167). Cambridge: Cambridge University Press.

Tupas, T.R.F. (2006) Standard Englishes, pedagogical paradigms and their conditions of (im)possibility. In R. Rubdy and M. Saraceni (eds) *English in the World* (pp. 169–185). London: Continuum.

United Nations Educational, Scientific and Cultural Organization (UNESCO) (2012) *The impact of economic crisis on higher education.* Bangkok: UNESCO. See www.lhmartininstitute.edu.au (accessed 21 September 2015).

UA (2013) Global Engagement. See https://www.universitiesaustralia.edu.au/global-engagement (accessed 30 May 2014).

UA (2014) Keep it Clever: Let's Not Get Left Behind Australia. See http://keepitclever.com.au/ (accessed 6 June 2014).

UA (2015a) Key Facts & Data: Data snapshot 2015. See https://www.universitiesaustralia.edu.au/australias-universities/key-facts-and-data#.VfkLYtEcSUk (accessed 16 September 2015).

UA (2015b) *Universities Australia Submission to the Senate Committee Inquiry into the Higher Education and Research Reform Bill 2014,* February 2015. See https://www.universitiesaustralia.edu.au/ArticleDocuments/728/UA%20Submission%20to%20Senate%20Inquiry%20into%20Higher%20Education%20and%20Research%20Reform%20Bill%202014.pdf (last accessed 22 September 2015).

Uysal, H.H. (2008) Tracing the culture behind writing: Rhetorical patterns and bidirectional transfer in L1 and L2 essays of Turkish writers in relation to educational contexts. *Journal of Second Language Writing* 17, 103–207.

Visentin, L. (2014) Students buying assignments online could be charged with fraud. *The Sydney Morning Herald*, 12 November. See http://www.smh.com.au/national/education/students-buying-assignments-online-could-be-charged-with-fraud-20141111-11kfjt.html (accessed 26 July 2015).

Volet, S.E., Renshaw, P.D. and Tietzel, K. (1994) A short-term longitudinal investigation of cross-cultural differences in study approaches using Biggs' SPQ questionnaire. *British Journal of Educational Psychology* 64, 301–318.

Walqui, A. (2000) *Access and Engagement: Program Design and Instructional Approaches for Immigrant Students in Secondary School*. McHenry, IL: Delata Systems for Center for Applied Linguistics.

Wardhaugh, R. (2010) *An Introduction to Sociolinguistics* (6th edn). Malden, MA/Oxford: Wiley-Blackwell.

Wee, L. (2005) Class-inclusion and correspondence models as discourse types: A framework for approaching metaphorical discourse. *Language in Society* 34 (2), 219–238.

Wicks, R. (1996) Effects of English language proficiency on the academic performance of international students: A USQ study. *Distance Education* 17 (1), 196–204.

Widdowson, H. (1993) The ownership of English. In J. Jenkins (ed.) *World Englishes: A Resource Book for Students* (pp. 162–168). London: Routledge.

Zepke, N. and Leach, L. (2010) Beyond hard outcomes: 'Soft' outcomes and engagement as student success. *Teaching in Higher Education* 15 (6), 661–673.

# Index

Abbott, Tony 70
Aboriginal English 92
academic English 88–91, 94 *see also*
    written English
academic literacy practices 27, 88 *see also*
    written English
Academic Ranking of World Universities
    (ARWU) Shanghai Jiao Tong 5–6, 7
accent 20
accommodation, student 76–7, 78
achievement 48, 156–65, 170
active subject, the 56–9, 60
adaptive, international students as 33–5
admission policies, and English 96
aesthetics of existence 56, 60, 166,
    167, 172
affect 46–7, 66, 153, 154, 161–2, 170
affirmative discourses 85
affordances versus affordability 26
African universities 2
agency
    –and engagement xv, 166, 171–2
    –Foucault on 57–8
    –teacher agency 121
Aglietta, M. 98
Alexander, D. 20, 21
Alexander, R. 119, 120
alienation 47
Altbach, P.G. 8, 9
Al-Youssef, J. 8, 10
ambiguities 101–2, 119–20, 142
Ammon, U. 88, 93
Ang, G. 21
Ang, I. 17, 18
anglicisation of names 77, 81, 94
Anna
    –classroom participation 131
    –on critical thinking 135
    –engagement as achievement 159–61
    –English 80–1, 94–5, 108–10, 131, 137,
        150, 160
    –profile 73, 80–1
    –on teaching genre 134
    –use of metaphor 110, 150, 160
    –use of 'voice' 152

antecedents of engagement 47, 48, 110,
    142, 170
anti-Islamism 19
anxiety, language 112
apartheid 83–4
Arkoudis, S. 22
art of existence 56
ASEAN (Association of Southeast Asian
    Nations) 92
Asia, and Australia 17–19
Asian crisis (1997) 15
Asian students
    –Asian learning styles 31–2, 35, 36
    –in Australia 18–20, 21–2, 24
    –class participation 138
Asianisation 18–19
assessment 97–8, 113
assignment presentation guidelines
    98–102
assimilation policies 18, 70, 96
asylum seekers 19
Atkinson, D. 154
Atlantic Philanthropies 78
attendance 44, 77
attribution 138–9
attrition 44
Auger, N. 174
AusAid scholarships 25, 76, 77, 80, 81,
    82, 95
AUSSE (Australasian Survey of Student
    Engagement) 46
Australia
    –Asian students in 18–20, 21–2, 24
    –commercially-driven higher
        education 7, 10
    –deficiency-based views of
        international students 29–33
    –as destination for overseas students
        2, 23–5
    –and the GFC 15
    –higher education 12–25
    –internationalisation of education 3,
        11–12, 20
    –key international education statistics
        23–5